D0436879

Dining with the Famous and Infamous

Dining with Destiny Series
as part of the Rowman & Littlefield Studies in Food and Gastronomy

The volumes in the Dining with Destiny series explore food biography, examining the private eating lives of icons from across the span of literature, art, music, politics, and revolution. If you've ever wondered what Lenin lunched on, whether George Orwell really swigged Victory Gin, or if there's such a thing as a Freudian supper, then the Dining with Destiny series is for you. Behind every great man and woman is a great meal. Their peccadilloes are explored anecdotally against the backdrops of history and culture, with accompanying recipes. Taste the disconsolate marriage of Marilyn Monroe to Arthur Miller, make red gravy and pasta Sinatra-style, or shake up the kind of chocolate malted that Woody Allen likes. How about a banana sandwich with Queen Elizabeth? Or a road trip picnic with Hemingway and F. Scott Fitzgerald?

Dining with Destiny is not just for all the "foodies" out there—the night-time cocoa will lie forgotten as you realize that Malcolm X entered the civil rights movement by rejecting anything piggy on his plate and as the Swinging Sixties are revealed through the hedonism and hashish cookies of Mick Jagger and Bob Dylan. The reader will dream of sitting at the table prepared by Hitchcock, Nelson Mandela, or Picasso. But beware: Dalí's lobster in chocolate sauce means that he has a desire to sleep with you rather than paint.

Each of these figures took part in landmark historical and cultural events that have shaped and defined our way of life—but they also had to eat. Now it is time to reveal the real man by looking in his fridge to discover what makes him a revolutionary, a hero, a rogue! Dining with Destiny lets you taste what's on Darwin's fork.

Dining with the Famous and Infamous

Fiona Ross

ROWMAN & LITTLEFIELD
Lanham • Boulder • New York • London

Published by Rowman & Littlefield
A wholly owned subsidiary of The Rowman & Littlefield Publishing Group, Inc.
4501 Forbes Boulevard, Suite 200, Lanham, Maryland 20706
www.rowman.com

Unit A, Whitacre Mews, 26-34 Stannary Street, London SE11 4AB

British Library Cataloguing in Publication Information Available

Library of Congress Cataloging-in-Publication Data
Ross, Fiona, 1966–
Dining with the famous and infamous / Fiona Ross.
pages cm. — (Rowman & Littlefield studies in food and gastronomy. Dining with destiny)
Includes bibliographical references and index.
ISBN 978-1-4422-5225-7 (cloth : alk. paper) — ISBN 978-1-4422-5226-4 (electronic)
1. Cooking. 2. Celebrities—Miscellanea. 3. Antiheroes—Miscellanea. 4. Food habits—History—Miscellanea. 5. Food in popular culture—History—Miscellanea. I. Title.
TX714.R6745 2016
641.5—dc23 2015024476

™ The paper used in this publication meets the minimum requirements of American National Standard for Information Sciences—Permanence of Paper for Printed Library Materials, ANSI/NISO Z39.48-1992.

Printed in the United States of America

I would like to dedicate this book to these special people, lost and found, and their food:

Olive Bucket's Heart Pie
Elsie Turner's Stovies
Alastair Ross's Pizza
Jimmy Turner's Hogmanay Shandy
Rachel McWalter's mugs of *Mellow Birds* (plus toast and raspberry jam)
Moira Ross's Kenyan Beef Curry
Angeline Levy's Sole-in-a-Drawer
Glenys Sanger's Welsh Cakes
Agnes Kasule's Matoke (plus a glass or two of Waragi)
Sarah Parry's Plum and Brandy Tart . . .

Here’s tae us; wha’s like us?
Damn few, and they’re a’ deid!

—Robbie Burns

Contents

Acknowledgments

Like all books, this one is indebted to many people. I want to thank my kindly and talented editor, Ken Albala, for his advice and support. The library staff in the hot and dusty Upper Reading Room of the Bodleian Library has been wonderful, carting endless volumes of peculiar books from deep down in the stacks. Thank you to my dear friend Gillian Harrison for introducing me to the Bodleian and for all her fine companionship there in the golden hours. Thanks to Moira and Alastair Ross for their huge delight in undertaking ancillary research on food. I'd also like to thank Margaret and Ken Conway for letting me curry a goat in their kitchen; Shelley Cooper for helping me cook a suckling pig on a makeshift spit in her back garden; and the Allen and Harris property-letting agency for allowing me to marinade the aforementioned pig in the bath of the flat they rented to me. To Mary Birtill and Irene Tominey, I owe a debt for inspiring me with the Going Foot, as I do to all my Camino friends for walking the way with me. Jane Ganly has been a great help with ICT advice and her intimate knowledge of chocolate; also to Nathan Shelton of Bread and Butter Creative, I owe eternal thanks for all his wonderful design work on my website and blog. To Yorick, Roberta, and Louise, I would like to express gratitude for all those mad dining experiments in the Allam Street kitchen, and I must also thank Jean and Richard Haigh for advice on the vast subject of vegetables. Thank you, Emily Gray, for letting me camp in your attic. Thanks to Titch Hughes for showing me how to zip up! I'd like to send a kiss to Roisin Ross for teaching me how to love, swim, and be a mum, and also for being my best girl forever. May you always have a bubble bath with the dog.

Finally, I'd like to express deep-hearted thankfulness to my dear husband and best friend, Gareth Sanger, for all the immense generosity, love, and belief he has shown in giving me a room of my own and £500.

Introduction

A book about food begins with the writer's taste buds; close up, they look like something you'd find waving in a rock pool, but taste buds are, in fact, little rocket launchpads of delight. So, without forgetting my nose and its wonderful olfactory abilities, let this book begin with my taste buds!

Being brought up in North East Scotland in the 1960s and 1970s, a world where middle-class women still cooked and their side-burned husbands worked, it was in my mother's and grandmother's kitchens that I first discovered food. Like lots of women who were manacled to the kitchen sink in the 1960s, my mother, Moira, poured every ounce of the opera singer–lawyer–artist–writer–scientist–burlesque dancer she might have been into crayfish bisques, duck ballotines, and Peasant-Girl-in-a-Veil plum puddings. “Try this,” she would say, holding out a whisk clouded with sherried, whipped cream. And I knew it not only tasted delicious but also was the stuff of dreams. She seemed the very opposite of my staunchly religious Brethren grandmother, Olive Bucket, who wore thick, tan tights and a variety of ladies' wigs, and who decorated the inside of her house in shades of peach. But from Olive's kitchen, too, came moist coconut towers, rhubarb crumbles, and miracles of pies, with buttery, crumbling crusts and steaming, savory cores. If these pies reflected her inner life, Olive Bucket was the Mata Hari. When Olive passed away, quietly and respectably, her food vanished with her; she had never written down a single recipe. It was up to me to try to rediscover the lost tastes and smells of Olive Bucket's kitchen.

My taste buds, then, are driven by nostalgia.

A hankering for the past, a longing to be *there*, wherever it was. And people, in the pasts I longed and long for, were not just Olive and Moira, but all the movers, the shakers, the crooners who sang some moonshine for us, the actors and actresses who walked across our black-and-white television screens, the artists through whose eyes we see the days gone by, the writers and poets who show us we are not alone. I wanted, right from the start, to know intimately what life was like for them. I wanted to know what Marilyn did after a long day filming on the set. Did she light a cigarette? Drink a Manhattan? Eat pasta? Did C. S. Lewis bite into buttered toast and drink tea like Mr. Tumnus in Narnia?

My first hunt for such a ghost was when, about thirty years ago, I trundled down to London to march on a Campaign for Nuclear Disarmament demonstration. Yep, I was a bit of a hippie in my youth. After all, the Berlin Wall was still up and the UK government was all set to hand out "What to Do in the Event of a Nuclear Disaster" self-help sheets, full of useful advice about stashing baked beans and long-life milk, and then lying under your front door holding your breath while your housecoat melted. But I was also a food-obsessed rebel and got distracted in London. It just so happened I had just read somewhere of a restaurant that one of my personal heroes, Oscar Wilde, used to go to in London's Soho: I decided to try to find it.

After wandering around the labyrinth of Soho in the rain, I found Wilde's restaurant down a darkened street; it was small and crooked, with discolored lace curtains in the window. That didn't matter, though. This was the closest I'd ever got to Wilde. I could almost see Oscar's coattails before me, and I imagined his heavy cheeks bright with the cold and a little too much of his yellow wine.

I followed him into the restaurant. The poor, old place was a shadow of its former self, dusty and a little fly blown, with a broad, Greek waitress dressed in frumpy folds of black and white. I wondered what it would have been like to have shared a table here with Wilde, watched the way he held his knife and fork, smelled the grilled lamb fin-de-siècle aroma of the London chophouses, listened to the splash of the coach wheels. I sat at my own white-clothed table, ate scallops and oysters, and imagined Wilde was my companion. Even though I couldn't share my oysters with him, I could still savor his existence. It was on my fork.

Finding Wilde was really the beginning of *Dining with the Famous and Infamous*. It has been a bid to meet old friends whom I've never encountered, to break bread with them. My research into the food lives of the key icons of the twentieth century has led me on a fascinating food history journey; many, many hours were spent in the Bodleian Library in Oxford poring through crooked stacks of books connected with icons as diverse as Einstein, Laurel and Hardy, Freud, Steinbeck, Lewis, Churchill, Christie, Stalin, Allen, and Lennon, looking simply for the word *sausages* or *eggs*. Sometimes, my leads went cold; some icons seem to have not eaten so much as a cracker in the course of their lives—but nothing beats the discovery of a meal, a favorite dish, an unforgettable food moment that encapsulates character. And the further I went with my food detection, the more I realized one simple, fundamental lesson: what we are is revealed in what we eat. Of course, Agatha Christie or Humphrey Bogart had other things to do with their time than write down recipes, so, when I got wind of a dish and cooking story for my icons, I went on to develop a relatively authentic, of-the-age, and tasty version of their food experience. The recipes in *Dining with the Famous and Infamous* are, then, entirely my own. Hopefully, they are tasty, close to life, and aromatic with nostalgia. Just because Van Gogh might have cooked, that doesn't mean he cooked well. I didn't want to poison you, my reader. Some things I thought you'd prefer not to eat, so I haven't given a recipe, for instance, for the semen cakes enjoyed by Aleister Crowley, the notorious wizard. Nor did I want to produce a book packed with recipes without any background or anecdotes. If there can be no resurrection of a moment, there can be no food nostalgia.

Unexpected insights into the course of the history of art, literature, music, and film are exposed on dinner dates. Van Gogh and Gauguin's tangled, heated, artistic relationship is expressed through their insane eating life together in Arles, and it was no accident that one of the most damning pieces of evidence offered up at Oscar Wilde's trial for sodomy was that he was witnessed feeding another man—and a lower-class one at that—candied cherries. It took supper in the Seagram Building to persuade the artist Mark Rothko that he couldn't beat the establishment, and would you ever have imagined a romantic date with Cary Grant or the writer of *Catcher in the Rye*, the reclusive J. D. Salinger, would have involved TV dinner trays? Both Salvador Dalí and Alfred Hitchcock's perverse sense of humor and frustrated passions are evident in their food foibles; Dalí was sure that his lobster in chocolate sauce would have you heading for the bedroom with him. Dorothy Parker becomes even more endearing when you find out that she didn't know (like W. H. Auden) what to do with bacon in the kitchen: Did it *really* need to be cooked? George Orwell, by contrast, could make a fine blackberry jelly, and John Steinbeck liked to make hotcakes for his dog, Charley. Salinger tried to smoke a whole salmon in a basket on top of his chimney. Shake up a mint julep, and you are sitting across from F. Scott Fitzgerald, looking rumpled and endearing in his suit, with his boyish side-parting. Taste Ian Fleming's Jamaican cocktail Poor Man's Thing, which reveals much more about the real 007 than a Bond martini. Like Marilyn Monroe with Arthur Miller, Sylvia Plath tried to bake her way into Ted Hughes's heart; Liz Taylor's vast appetite for husbands is mirrored in her food passions. Frank Sinatra's and Richard Burton's eating lives were shaped by their fidelity to their food origins. In Frank's case, it was by delicious Sicilian dishes and his mother, Dolly's, kitchen—she would stir up her red sauces with knuckle-headed mafia types dipping bread crusts and offering advice on the seasoning.

Dining with the Famous and Infamous offers up the lives of the famous and infamous on a plate. Come, pull up a seat at history's table.

1

❖ ❖

Dining with Famous and Infamous Artists

Study the art of eating with the greats. In the frame and painting the town red are: Salvador Dalí, Mark Rothko, Paul Gauguin and Vincent Van Gogh, Andy Warhol, Auguste Renoir, Diego Rivera and Frida Kahlo, and Pablo Picasso.

SALVADOR DALÍ

Some artists impress through their near indifference to food—their pure and holy dedication to art means they don't even think about biscuits or cakes or cheese. Good old Michelangelo was so obsessed with his work on the Sistine Chapel that he forgot all about lunch, clinging to the scaffolding for hours while his servant scurried up and down the rigging, juggling soup and bread to tempt his master's appetite. Van Gogh barely remembered to eat so much as a crust and was always shocking people with his wild, almost feral, skinniness, popping up like John the Baptist every couple of months to cough over some garlic soup or wipe up a smidgen of wine, bread, and cheese before vanishing again to be tortured, prophetic, and visionary in some awful, distant corner of Arles. In contrast, Claude Monet floated around like an early sort of River Cottage–style guru. The Monets insisted on only dishing up what was seasonal at their table in Giverny, picked from their walled garden in the lovely, steamy, early morning sunlight, and (a little like that later horror, Stalin) Monet always made a point of carving his meat at the table—though not, in Monet's case, to spook his guest. Beware turning up late, though; Monet's lunch table was set for 11.30 a.m. so that he could make the most of the daylight for painting. Leonardo da Vinci is up there with food saints of vegetarianism. He'd buy caged birds not for dinner but to release them like winged angels into the blue Florentine air. Da Vinci was the father of the meat-is-murder movement, cheerfully reflecting that your common human carnivore lives "by the death of others; we are burial places"—a sentiment that would either teach the world to sing "Heaven Knows I'm Miserable Now" or leave you toying with your bacon sandwich.

For Salvador Dalí, da Vinci's carnal, charnel-like references only served to pique his appetite. Anything weird foodwise turned Dalí on, and his dietary habits were full of contradictions and bodily quirks. Toast and art went together when our nine-year-old Surrealist's gaze fixed on an Impressionist painting in a neighbor's house. Dalí bit slowly into the buttered, honeyed toast steeped in café au lait; what with the honey, the yellow butter, and the iridescent light on the painting, Dalí literally tasted art for the first time.

Pubescent Dalí was forbidden to visit the family kitchen, and no wonder—he prowled at its doors, hoping to catch the aroma of kidneys wafting from the kitchen as they mingled with the suggestive smells of kitchen maids "in heat." Indeed, Dalí's first erotically charged encounter came while watching his father swallow sea urchin eggs. Dalí's formative family years are food charged, then, and the arousing properties of food may well have been genetic: the only thing guaranteed to rouse his grandmother from senility was the prospect of meringues.

A seat should have been reserved for Dalí at one of Alfred Hitchcock's dinner parties; they were possessed by a very similar food imagination. Dalí's verdict on cherries would have had Hitchcock casting him in *Frenzy*—they have to be like virgins in their ripeness, juicy with blood and unplucked. Not only do they make men give incest a second thought, but they are also highly aphrodisiacal. They make cannibals of us. When Mia Farrow, aged nineteen and allegedly unplucked, caught Dalí's eye, he decided to show up at the apartment she shared with her mother, sisters, and brothers. Without so much as a hello, Dalí placed a bottle in their hallway. "Violence in a bottle," he said enigmatically, turned on his heel, and left. The Farrows gathered giggling around the brightly colored jug, peering through its wet paint to see what delight it might hold. A chocolate heart? A single red rose? Something living was inside. . . . Suddenly, a sister shrieked: a rat was devouring a lizard inside the bottle in a grim supper ritual. Mia's mother wailed, "Get it out of here. *Out!*" and the brothers charged out of the apartment to throw the bottle over a nearby wall and into Central Park. It was only later that it dawned on them all that they'd just thrown away a Dalí original.

Dalí's appetite was piqued by the bodily and physical aspects of what he was eating. Sardines he ate whole, Catalan style, with obstinately tough bread dipped in olive oil. A great posturer, he loved the idea of "Dalí the revolutionary," and his sardine passion came about when he was imprisoned for twenty-one days as a Catalan

Spanish Meringues (with the promise of maids . . .)

INGREDIENTS

¼ lb. raspberries
½ cup hot water
1 cup granulated vanilla sugar
4 egg whites
1 tsp. fresh lemon juice
2 tbsp. powdered sugar
¼ lb. extra raspberries

METHOD

Preheat the oven to 250°C. Prepare a baking tray lined with baking paper (or you can bake your meringues in paper baking cups on a baking tray). Blend the raspberries into a gloop. Add the hot water and blend. Next, strain the raspberry gloop into a smallish saucepan. Add the vanilla sugar, stir, and bring to boil. Turn down the heat to a gentle simmer and, stirring occasionally, allow the mixture to reduce; it will become more and more syrupy. Test drops of it in a cup of ice cold water. When a droplet of the syrup lands in the cup and maintains a continuous, threadlike structure that bends but does not break against your fingertip, then your syrup is ready to use. Patience is necessary, as the syrup can take about 30 minutes to reach this soft-crack stage.

When you feel the syrup is nearing completion (it will have reduced by about two-thirds), start whisking the egg whites and the teaspoon of lemon juice. An electric whisk is best! The egg white will begin to stiffen, and at this point you should add 2 tablespoons of powdered sugar. The egg white mix should become stiff but not dry. Gradually add your hot syrup, whisking all the time. When the syrup is almost ready, beat the egg whites with the lemon juice. When the egg starts to stiffen, add the 2 tablespoons of powdered sugar and continue beating until stiff but not dry. Very gradually, pour the hot syrup into the egg whites, whisking continuously. Continue to whisk the raspberry meringue mix for a further 10 minutes.

If you'd like your meringues to have little explosions of raspberry inside them, then, using a metal spoon, fold in some extra whole raspberries now. Alternatively, you can retain all the raspberries and serve them alongside the meringues. Now, using a metal spoon, drop your meringues, allowing about 2 tablespoons per meringue.

Bake at 250°C for 60 to 90 seconds. Remove immediately, let them stand for 5 minutes, and then serve them warm with raspberries and a dollop of cream.

separatist agitator in 1924. He claimed that he was thrown only a tin of sardines to eat daily and, when telling the story, he often stretched out his sentence to a more respectable three months. Sardines and political independence went hand in hand; they tasted of martyrdom, and Dalí claimed nobly that he'd be happy to eat nothing but sardines for the rest of his life. As if. This infuriated George Orwell, who spat with rage at the very mention of Dalí! He claimed that as World War II approached, all Dalí wanted to do was to find a bolthole away from danger, near a good restaurant!

Given the liberty of a life beyond sardines, Dalí was very partial to crispy, flavorsome chops, chuletas, and snails. Snails, he said, left a lovely trail behind them like a wake of semen and were also very nice cooked in garlic. Now there's a recommendation for you. Tummy rumbling yet? Like the rest of us, sporadically, Dalí worried about his health. He'd sup on date juice (a favorite) and try to opt for fruit salad, but he could never resist a dollop of cream: the cherries and raspberries wallowed in beds of cream. He must have been awful to eat with. If he wasn't popping off to masturbate because of the way you ate sea urchins, then he couldn't resist making crass remarks, often about bottoms. "The French live to eat," he opined. "I eat to fart." Never one to miss an anal moment, Dalí said of Rodin's *The Thinker*, "He is not thinking. He is taking a long and fantastic shit."

If you think this is a bit rich, imagine what his sidekick Violetera thought when one morning Dalí offered him invitingly to "pass me my trousers. You can sniff the crotch. The fragrance is sublime." Yes, Violetera is a "he"—Dalí could never resist renaming fascinating individuals (he was obsessed with Violetera's belly button and loved popping his finger into it) or groups of people. If you were gorgeous, like Violetera, also known as Carlos, a young Colombian with waist-length hair, red hipsters, and heavily kohled eyes, or particularly dull or had an unpronounceable name, then you were simply renamed. So anyone Asian became the "Red Guard" and any aristocratic bore was called "Fillet of Sole."

Dalí's various prejudices were great fun: no one with *z* in their name or who came from England were ever to be trusted. Dalí's cook, Paquita, understood Dalí's eating world, the buried symbolism of the food he loved. If you were a new friend of Dalí's and had been invited round for dinner, beware the arrival of lobster in chocolate sauce at the table. It often meant that Dalí wanted to have sex with you. Amanda Lear attracted Dalí not so much because she was a model but because, he observed, she had a beautiful skull. An adoring protégée of Dalí's, Lear dined with him on cold fruit soup, followed by doves killed by Paquita, no doubt using a bow and arrow, and accompanied, ludicrously and prosaically, by chips. The Christian symbolism of the doves made the meal all the more piquant. The odd pet went that way as well. When Dalí's wife and muse, Gala, decided to pop back to Paris for Christmas, she quickly sorted out what would happen to her beloved pet rabbit; it would be killed and stewed by Paquita.

True to form, Dalí loved androgyny: he manufactured all sorts of rumors about the gender of the model, muse, and friend Amanda Lear, which proved so convincing that a substantial portion of the 1960s public swore with conviction that the model had been born a male named Alain Tapp, who remodeled himself as Lear. Lear or "Alain" then got excellent coverage of her sizeable breasts in *Playboy* photo shoots, perhaps to make a point! Violetera also seemed like an androgynous gift from the gods. Dalí liked to murmur to him/her, "Angels are androgynes . . . I will inspect your back. You will have scars where they cut off your wings." Both were incredibly vain, and Violetera recalls in his memoirs their arrival for lunch at the posh Parisian restaurant Lasserre. Apparently, the lunchtime clientele fell silent as Dalí and Violetera entered, with Dalí whispering, very stagily, "Is it Hermes and Aphrodite? Is Dalí a pederast or a dirty old man? Let their tongues wag, Violetera." They then sat at a table together that was raised on a minipodium with the other diners arranged (not by design) in a semicircle around them.

Dalí caught a buxom Parisian lady in a décolleté green dress staring in awe at the lovers. Loudly, he began to share his thoughts on the subject of breasts, which went like this: "Aphrodite had a *very* small bust. She came out of the sea shivering, her teeth chattering, and intuitively she put her arms up to hide her breasts. Women always hide their breasts first and leave the black triangle of curly hair on display like a battle flag. Women with small breasts are goddesses who bring pleasure to sex. I am a tit man. I revere, esteem and worship *small* breasts." The waiter appeared. At last, the woman must have thought, the menu would take Dalí's attention. Dalí waved him away, the food unordered. "Big breasts are the base element of the bovine principle; women with big breasts are cows and cows are bred to eat and procreate." The woman blushed furiously. The waiter reappeared and, while Violetera read the menu, Dalí impatiently muttered, "Yes, yes, yes?" Violetera ordered caviar, and Dalí, as ever odd, pronounced, "Fried eggs."

On to the main course, but Violetera hemmed and hawed so much that Dalí took over and ordered lobster for himself and—to Violetera's horror—a pigeon, deboned, stuffed with liver, and served with white mushrooms for Violetera. Dalí ordered it on the grounds that an attractive man sitting by the window ordered it every day. Well, that's all right then, isn't it? Later Violetera found it "primeval and delicious," of course! Dalí loved to order food for other people. He ordered ortolans for Amanda Lear in Lasserre, and when she exclaimed over how delicious they were, he broke in to make sure she didn't miss the point that ortolans were strangled to keep their flesh tender.

As Dalí waited for his fried eggs, he declaimed, "Leda, in the body of a swan, worked on the sewing machine with Zeus and from her egg emerged Dalí and Gala, the Divine Twins." Then he changed tack: "The embryo grows from bodily waste and putrescence. You are not going to have embryos," he said with such fervor that Violetera shuddered in horror at the very prospect. Dalí got eggs and bread all over the table and spilled water down his front. Egg yolk on his chin, he whipped around to the woman with the large breasts and said, "What is the difference between capitalism and communism?" he barked. "Capitalism is the exploitation of man by man. Communism is the reverse."

When they finished he told Violetera, "You are not having coffee." Then he sprung nimbly to his feet and advanced on the woman in the green dress. "I adore green," he told her. In truth, he loathed it.

Dalí-esque Lobster and Chocolate Sauce (prepare to be seduced . . .)

INGREDIENTS

1 live ½ lb. lobster
2 oz. butter
1 glass brandy
1 tsp. crushed, dried chilies

FOR THE CHOCOLATE SAUCE . . .

The finely grated zest of 2 oranges, plus the orange juice
1 measure cognac
5 oz. very dark chocolate, grated

METHOD

Make the lobster nice and sleepy by leaving it in the fridge for two hours. Kill it with a knife, stabbing quickly and decisively through the cross marking between its eyes in the center of its head. Split in half and discard the intestine. In a large frying pan, heat the butter until it foams, and then sauté the lobster, flesh side down, for 10 minutes. Pour the brandy over the lobster and have a match ready to strike so that you can immediately flame the lobster. Add the crushed chilies. Cover and cook the lobster for a further 10 minutes.

Meanwhile, prepare the chocolate sauce. In a pan, heat up the orange zest, juice, and the cognac. Add the grated chocolate and stir until the chocolate melts and a sauce forms.

Remove the lobster from the heat and serve with a delicious slick of chocolate sauce alongside.

MARK ROTHKO

Although it personally hurt Mark Rothko to spend more than $5 on a meal, his wounding marriages and the negligible glories of fame had left Rothko with two certainties in life: pleasure would always be found in calories and booze. But not *expensive* calories. Although not miserly, Rothko was deeply suspicious of fine dining. After an impoverished childhood chewing on Dvinsk bean soup in Russia and an impoverished early adulthood in the Great Depression—yes, bean soup was on the gas ring then, too—Rothko knew in his bones that food was political and, famously, Rothko's art led him to have his Manhattan-shaking gunfight with the dining world in the Seagram Murals Incident in 1958.

Rothko rubbed his hands in glee when he was commissioned to produce a series of paintings (six hundred feet's worth) for the mezzanine floor of the famous Four Seasons Restaurant in its swanky Seagram Building on 99 East 52nd Street in Manhattan; this was the first restaurant to serve customers American wine *and* introduce its diners to the revolutionary notion of a *seasonal* menu.

Nor was Rothko's glee simply confined to the $35,000 commission. No, his joy was cunningly subversive: the diners at the Seagram Building represented the high point of 1950s consumerism—the *New York Times* picked up on the capitalist self-confidence of the building, ringing out, "Four Seasons Termed Spectacular Both in Décor and Menu." And this, Rothko confided in John Fischer, an editor of *Harper's Magazine* whom Rothko bumped into over drinks, was his chance to make the American dining rich "feel that they are trapped in a room where all the doors and windows are bricked up." He was going to lock them in with some explosive art.

This was a plum opportunity for Rothko to cause some trouble and shake up those fancy rich diners at the Four Seasons, being served by people whom they considered underlings with, as the restaurant boasted, full training to serve at the table. Rothko reasoned he could produce the type of art that would spoil the appetites of each and every posh rotter ever to dine in the restaurant. He got to work on the Seagram series, including the claustrophobic, closed portals of pieces such as *Black on Maroon*. Death to capitalism, each of them secretly spelled.

Or so he thought. His work well under way, he whimsically decided to visit the Seagram Building for dinner in the summer of 1959, booking a table for him and his wife, Mell. Inside the cool womb of the Seagram Building, Rothko and Mell passed the three Miro tapestries that hung in the entrance lobby. There in the mezzanine hung Jackson Pollock's *Blue Poles*, simply in a holding position until Rothko's work was ready. It was already too late for Pollock to object to the fate of *Blue Poles*, as Pollock had died in a drunkenly suicidal car crash in 1956. Incidentally, suicide was also Rothko's preferred route out of life—but that was still to come, far off in 1970.

Rothko and Mell were shown elegantly to their seats in the Four Seasons's Pool Dining Room, and Rothko sat toying with the menu by the edge of the twenty-feet-square marble pool that dominated the center of the restaurant, fringed by four fig trees. Gradually, throughout the course of the meal, it must have slowly dawned on Rothko that his act of art terrorism was bound to be a damp squib. As Rothko sat in the place he had described scathingly as the ultimate venue for the wealthiest rats in New York to eat and boast, in a space with hand-loomed carpets and walls set with French walnut, all paid for from a budget of over $4 million, Rothko realized his art would be dwarfed and absorbed by the space.

Baffled by the menu, baffled by wealth, he had realized what a writer for *Evergreen* magazine had already surmised: "It will be a surprise if he [Rothko] transcends décor." Part of the statement Rothko made for the Museum of Modern Art's *15 Americans* exhibition in 1952 was that a picture is created by the art it is exhibited alongside, and this creative companionship makes art live; it can as easily die in a similar way. Holding these sentiments, Rothko had always been cautious in his choice of spots in which to exhibit.

It would take this one dinner to shake Rothko to the core. He gasped in mute amazement at the prices on the menu, and gone was his $5 rule. Never, since emerging from his sickly childhood, when calcium deficiency compelled him to eat the plaster off the walls at home, did a meal so stick in his throat.

For $1.65, you could get a *starter* of Small Clams with Green Onions and Truffle or Beef Marrow in Bouillon and Cream; for ten cents more, you could opt for a Bouquet of Crudités with Hot Anchovy Dressing; another ten cents and on your plate would be Crisped Shrimp with Mustard Fruits. The mains came in at $13 for two to share a Rack of Lamb Persillé with Herbs. Rothko would probably have calculated that he and Mell would be better off sticking to the individual mains, and he certainly wasn't feeling romantic. Between $4 and $5 was Stuffed Breast of Chicken with Tarragon, Demi-Deuil, and Avocado with Sliced White Radish. There were no less than six kinds of coffee, but iced would cost Rothko an extra twenty-five cents.

As Rothko choked down his dinner, he knew his art could never detonate such opulence. "Anybody," he spluttered, "who will eat that kind of food for those kind of prices will never look at a painting of mine." He sent the $35,000 back and refused to hand over *Black on Maroon*. The Seagram series would have to find another home, nine of them arriving at the Tate in London the day after Rothko's own suicide in 1970.

Dvinsk Bean Soup (much better than wallpaper plaster . . .)

INGREDIENTS

1 lb. white beans (soaked overnight)
3 tbsp. oil
3 small onions, finely diced
3 garlic cloves, crushed
1 smoked ham bone
2 liters water
3 large carrots, chopped
2 celery ribs, sliced
3 medium potatoes, peeled and quartered
1 tomato, chopped
3 fresh bay leaves
6 peppercorns
2 tbsp. parsley, chopped
2 tbsp. dill, chopped
4 tbsp. double cream (optional)

METHOD

Heat 3 tablespoons of olive oil in a thick-bottomed stockpot, add the chopped onion and crushed garlic, and cook gently until soft. Add the smoked ham bone, and let it fry gently for a minute or two. Drain the beans and place them in the pot. Cover with water; add the black peppercorns and the bay leaves. Bring to boil, turn down the heat, and simmer for an hour.

Chop the potatoes, carrots, celery, and tomato, and, after the beans have been simmering for an hour, add the vegetables.

Cook for a further hour. Remove the meat from the ham bone and return the pieces of ham to the pot. Add the parsley and dill, and, if you feel like taking Dvinsk to another level, add a slosh of rich cream. Serve in deep bowls with black bread.

Or, to taste how the other half lives, try this:

Crisped Shrimp with Mustard Fruits

Mustard fruit, or mostarda di frutta, is less a sauce and more a way of preserving fruit in piquant honey syrup. Prepare this first, as you'll want to serve the shrimp as soon as it's ready.

Mostarda di Frutta

INGREDIENTS

1 lb. mixed fruit: apricots, peaches, pears, oranges
1½ cups dark, strong honey
Juice and finely grated rind of half a lemon
1 bay leaf
¼ cup brown mustard seeds
½ cup dry white wine

Crisped Shrimp with Mustard Fruits (*continued*)

METHOD

Prepare the fruit by cleaning it and chopping it into 1-inch pieces. You can peel the orange entirely, but leaving a few pieces with their rind attached adds a delicious bitterness to the mostarda, which counterbalances the honeyed sweetness. Place the fruit in a saucepan, barely cover with water, and add ½ cup of honey and the juice and finely grated rind of half a lemon. Over a medium heat, allow this to cook for 20 minutes.

While this is cooking, in a second saucepan and over medium heat, combine the remaining honey and the white wine. Allow this to reduce by a third and then add the brown mustard seeds. Remove from the heat and allow the syrup to cool.

Finally, combine the contents of the two saucepans and keep chilled until it is time to serve.

Crisped Shrimp

INGREDIENTS

Olive oil
1½ lb. fresh shrimp, shelled and deveined
⅓ cup all-purpose flour
Sea salt
Freshly ground black pepper
Pinch of cayenne pepper
Pinch of dried oregano
Pinch of dried chili flakes
1 lemon

METHOD

Heat 3 tablespoons of olive oil in a shallow frying pan. Mix the all-purpose flour with the cayenne pepper, salt, and ground black pepper. Dip the shrimp in the lightly spiced flour and then fry quickly in the hot olive oil, until the shrimp become opaque. Sprinkle with the dried chili flakes and oregano.

Serve the crisped shrimp immediately with a drizzle of freshly squeezed lemon and a dollop of mostarda di frutta on the side.

PAUL GAUGUIN AND VINCENT VAN GOGH

"Life with only bread for breakfast, lunch, and dinner didn't hold many laughs," Paul Gauguin wrote to his long-suffering wife, Mette, in 1886. Gauguin was on his way to Martinique with fellow painter Charles Laval, having renounced his former existence as a father and stockbroker: "I am not getting any fatter as a result of my work. I weigh 138 pounds—less than you. I am becoming as desiccated as a kipper." Somerset Maugham's novel *The Moon and Sixpence* presents Gauguin as a dangerous but rather noble figure, cutting a dash against conservatism by pursuing art irrespective of the claims of wife, children, or a comfy job in the city. But Gauguin's exit from "normal" life as a father and provider was rather more slippery. He shrugged off his responsibilities slowly. First of all, with things like the kipper reference, he was always trying to impress upon Mette how very much he was suffering. He couldn't resist telling her that swinging a pickaxe all day when he worked on the construction of the Panama Canal was very likely to kill him. He made futile attempts to hold down a job (for instance, during a brief stint selling tarpaulin in Copenhagen that proved to be a bit of a disaster, as he knew no Danish). But all the time he was, quietly and perhaps deliberately, moving further and further away from Mette's clutches, which seems in hindsight to have been a good thing for all of us. She thought his art was a pleasant hobby, for goodness' sake!

Things went from bad to worse in Martinique, and he didn't hesitate to let Mette know about it. First, there was a bad attack of dysentery, which laid him very low in his hut at the edge of a plantation. His companion, Laval, soon couldn't even hold a paintbrush. He became so ill, awash with diarrhea, that he tried to kill himself, the first of a line of cheerless, suicidal companions for Gauguin. Then, when the chance of a square meal came along, it was snatched away. A pretty, sixteen-year-old black girl offered Gauguin a guava fruit, which she had split and squeezed for him, but, in the same moment, a short, yellow-skinned, European lawyer grabbed the guava from Gauguin and dashed it to the ground. Gauguin looked down, open mouthed, at the one decent bit of food he'd had the chance of in a long time. "You must never eat a fruit without knowing where it comes from," hissed the lawyer. "This fruit possesses a charm; the negress rubbed it on her stomach, and afterwards you will be at her command." Oh, *really*? And what, I wonder—along with Gauguin, I suspect—would have been so very awful about that?

Finally having ducked his marital responsibilities to pursue art, there were the lean years of the late 1880s sharing digs with Van Gogh in Arles. They tried to establish an artists' community in the house Van Gogh had rented—the Yellow House, latterly a ghastly version of student accommodation. In an attempt to economize, they kept a money box split into four sections to cover eating expenses. No more meals out. Instead, they'd huddle around their gas stove, with Gauguin doing the cooking and Van Gogh the shopping, like a very miserable, neurotic version of *The Odd Couple.* Van Gogh had some particularly bad ideas when it came to making soup. Occasionally, he was visited by a terrible hankering for soup and took over the kitchen. Van Gogh held a deep-seated, private conviction that he was wasting away as a result of not having any "strong broth." Gauguin would manfully try to eat it, but he couldn't bring himself to do so—neither of them could. Gauguin's only bleak comment was "I have no idea what mixtures he used—they seemed like those of the colours on his canvases."

Meanwhile, Van Gogh wrote to his brother bemoaning the fact that neither he nor Gauguin spoke the local dialect, or they'd be able to accustom themselves to bouillabaisse and aïoli to cut their costs. Exactly how dialect and ordering bouillabaisse conflicted is your guess as well as mine. In the meantime, Van Gogh bemoaned the Arles population's inability to do simple things like boil a decent potato or make rice and macaroni without ruining either with fat. In fact, he suspected that they might be deliberately cheating him of macaroni.

All this bold talk of macaroni was pretty deceptive as, throughout his food history, one hardly ever hears Van Gogh's tummy rumble even though he's permanently hungry. He's the least hedonistic of the artists—only in his descriptions of color is he a sensualist. He'd often just simply forget about food. Anton Kerssemakers remembered just how parsimonious Van Gogh really was: "In those days he was starving like a true Bohemian, and more than once it happened that he did not see meat (for the purpose of eating, not painting!) for six weeks on end, always just dry bread with a chunk of cheese. . . . Once in Nuenen, when we were about to set out on a ramble—it was in the afternoon at the height of summer—I said, 'To begin with we'll have a pot of coffee made in that inn over there, and eat a lot of bread and butter with trimmings, then we shall be able to keep going until late in the evening . . . No sooner said than done, for he invariably consented to whatever you proposed.'"

There, inside the inn, lay the table before them, heavy with various local, ripe cheeses and plates of thick slices of ham. But when Kerssemakers looked across at Van Gogh, there he was, chewing a dry piece of bread with a modest smidgen of cheese! "Come on, Vincent," he scolded, "take some ham, and butter your bread, and put some sugar in your coffee; after all, it has to be paid for whether you eat it or not."

"No," replied Van Gogh primly, "that would be coddling myself too much: bread and cheese is what I'm used to." So much for that. In the course of his life, Van Gogh viewed bread as a symbol of biblical righteousness, and he wasn't going to let up on that conviction. When he was a preacher to the Belgian miners, he subsisted on bread and chestnuts or potatoes.

Both Gauguin and Van Gogh did like the fish in Arles, lying as it did close to the Mediterranean. Van Gogh noticed the Mediterranean changed color every day, like a mackerel. The catch of fish for sale in the Arles market was fresh, briny, and infinitely more appetizing than frying the muddy contents of the Seine or the "filthy, greasy steaks" of Paris that made Van Gogh shudder.

Gauguin may have had more than an inkling that things were beginning to sour between them when Van Gogh hurled a glass of absinthe at his head and charged at him with a razor on Christmas Eve, leading to the infamous ear-cutting incident (Van Gogh's rumored partiality to a glass of turpentine may account for his lunacy, too—and on one occasion his brother wrote to him suggesting it might be best if he didn't nibble on his paints). By 1890, Van Gogh was dead. He had, it seems, forgotten to follow the regime he liked to call Dickens's prescription against suicide: whenever melancholy came too close, Van Gogh took Dickens's advice and had a glass of wine, a piece of bread and cheese, and a pipe of tobacco.

By 1891, following the suicide of Van Gogh, Gauguin made his way to Tahiti. Sailing from Marseille, it was there, in April 1891, at the popular Café Voltaire, home to the new wave of Symbolist artists and writers, that Gauguin's friends gathered together to see him off. It was good for Symbolists and Impressionists to dine together. He remembered how different it was when staying at Pension Gloanec in Pont-Aven, where Gauguin and his fellow painters had been forced to dine separately from the "academic" painters who scoffed at them as "Impressionists!" Now Stéphane Mallarmé, the French poet (and impoverished bon viveur), raised his glass at the table to propose a toast: "To cut short the preliminaries, let us drink a toast and wish Paul Gauguin a welcome return, while declaring our admiration for the superb dedication with which, at the zenith of his powers, he looks for renewal in distant lands and deep down into his own soul!" They dined on delicious hors d'oeuvres, soup, fresh brill, and a rich pheasant ragoût, topped off with tasty brie and snug, delicate petit fours.

Gauguin would be glad of that supper when he found himself starving in Tahiti. By 1892 he was on a dry bread and water diet, and each time he gnawed the bread he desperately imagined it was a beefsteak. Things took a turn for the better when he began to eat indigenous Tahitian food—at one wedding Gauguin enjoyed roast suckling pig, cooked whole on hot stones, as well as fish, breadfruit, wild bananas, and taro. Fortunately, the Martinique lawyer was nowhere to be seen. Whether he truly enjoyed Polynesian food, though, is another matter. In his last years in Hiva Oa, another French Polynesian island, he had returned to a rigidly European diet, as is revealed in his shopping list for December 1901: ninety-eight liters of Bordeaux (it had to last him some time!), thirty kilos of potatoes, six tins of tripe, thirteen tins of asparagus, two tins of beans and two of anchovies, one bottle of tomato sauce, two packets of tea. . . . The dullness of this inventory belies the high time Gauguin was having in Hiva Oa, with a native teenage bride in tow. His final heart attack seems more explicable. It wasn't all tripe and potatoes.

Symbolists' Pheasant Ragoût

INGREDIENTS

2 pheasants (remove the legs and breasts of the pheasants for the ragoût and use the carcasses for making pheasant stock the night before you make this dish)
2 tbsp. all-purpose flour
3 tbsp. olive oil
3 tbsp. butter
6 shallots, finely chopped
4 garlic cloves, crushed
1 small bunch fresh thyme
1 tbsp. tomato puree
3 stalks celery, sliced into ½-inch pieces
4 rashers bacon, chopped
1 glass red wine
2 pints pheasant or chicken stock
1 tbsp. redcurrant jelly
1 tbsp. mushroom ketchup
1 tbsp. brandy
Sea salt
Freshly ground black pepper

METHOD

Preheat the oven to 180°C. Salt and pepper the all-purpose flour and dip the legs and breast of pheasant in the flour. Heat 3 tablespoons of olive oil and 1 tablespoon of butter in a deep casserole dish and brown the pieces of pheasant. Remove and set aside.

Next, melt a further 2 tablespoons of butter in the casserole, add the shallots, and cook gently for 5 minutes. Add the bacon and celery. Cover this with a layer of greaseproof paper and sweat gently for 5 minutes. Now add the garlic, thyme, and tomato puree. Place the browned pheasant pieces on top and add the red wine. Pour the pheasant stock over this and place in the oven for an hour.

After the hour is up, take the casserole out of the oven, remove the pheasant sections, and keep them warm. Place the casserole on the stove on medium heat and bring to boil. When the gravy juices are reduced by a third, add the mushroom ketchup and the tablespoon of redcurrant jelly. Stir this vigorously; the gravy will thicken. Finally, season to taste and return the pheasant to its sauce. Sprinkle with the tablespoon of brandy and serve.

For dessert, have guava rubbed on the belly of a loved one.

ANDY WARHOL

While it's easy to imagine Andy Warhol forever opening tins of Campbell's soup, he did take more than a passing interest in other foods. Indeed, in his diaries, even as he records the social whirl of the 1970s, he finds time to regularly comment on food in a comic, slightly subversive, quiet tone that is distinctively Warholian. After a fuzzy-edged evening at Mick Jagger's house, he gently notes that Mick and Bianca forgot to bring out the dessert. Or he leaves us with sage advice, wisdom acquired from New York socializing: "The last place you want to eat meat from is a discotheque."

Warhol is always reassuringly human despite all the pretensions of the New York art scene. An "impromptu" dinner for Bob Dylan, hosted by Yoko Ono, was anything but casual: the guests, on turning up, were asked to take their shoes off, and Warhol was painfully aware of the hole in his sock. He spotted David Bowie there, but Bowie was dressed, disappointingly, in a modern suit. Then, to top it off, everyone had to sit in an awful King Arthur–style circle to eat, but without any gusto; the focus was on heavy-duty conversations. Champagne was poured, but people just pretended to drink it. Worst of all, the food was artificial, blow dried, rubbery, and bought in a store, right down to the precut chicken.

Gate crashing a barbecue at Cher's in August 1985 was much more fun. Warhol dialed her number and heard an automated recording announcing that anyone calling her private line was invited to her barbecue that day. *Whoopee!* thought Warhol. So he and a friend cruised up to Cher's and rang the doorbell, but they didn't fail to notice the shock (and perhaps a flicker of dismay) fleetingly pass over the faces of Cher and her boyfriend when they were admitted. But at least Cher, unlike Yoko Ono, served her own food: very tasty pork and beans. Her secret ingredient? A lot of hot sauce and, almost too good to be true, a can of Campbell's soup.

Visiting a friend's house on Christmas Day in 1976, he tells us that an ancient creature by the name of Kitty Miller was there—Kitty was the eccentric widow of a rich theater impresario, and she liked to disguise any gray hair she had by anointing her head with blue shoe polish. He follows this with "The pies were great—apple, mince, and plum. The turkey had been cut up like a magazine would tell you to before it got to the table, so it was like a Turkey Puzzle. Kitty was drunk and when the Spanish ambassador said a few words she screamed, 'I can't speak Spanish.'" Cecil Beaton recalls Kitty in his diaries as having the posture of a giant turtle when seated at the table.

The clever visual dexterity that lets Warhol see the turkey as a puzzle is also at work when he thinks about the type of fast food he would invent and comes up with the absurdist Waffle Thing, which he explains—and you can almost hear it painting itself—would be a sort of waffle TV tray, with soda pop on one side and ham on the other. Eating and drinking could suddenly become simultaneous. A sense of the iconic nature of food is also present in his account of going to meet Rock Hudson—who never shows, as his plane is delayed—at his friend Marguerite Littman's house in 1978. For dessert, Marguerite invents an amazing dessert of chocolate soup, which is a deeply satisfying concoction of hot, melted chocolate, freshly squeezed orange juice, and a splash of Grand Marnier.

Warholian Chocolate Soup

INGREDIENTS

300 ml. freshly squeezed orange juice
1 tbsp. Grand Marnier
100 g. bittersweet dark chocolate, broken into chunks
½ tsp. dried chili flakes

METHOD

Pour the orange juice into a medium-sized deep pan. Over a low heat, bring the orange juice to boil. Meanwhile, put the chocolate chunks and chili flakes into a heatproof bowl and place over a pan of boiling water. Stir the chocolate until it melts. Next, add the hot orange juice slowly to the chocolate, whisking until the orange and chocolate are one. Add the splash of Grand Marnier and serve immediately, pouring the chocolate soup into bowls. Serve with shards of ripe orange mango, strips of pineapple, and skinned orange segments on the side.

Making regular appearances in his diary is his wonderful eating and drinking friendship with Truman Capote. Their friendship is warm and comic. In 1978 they get gassed on one of Warhol's favorite booze concoctions, fresh grapefruit juice and vodka, which is pretty devastating. When Capote tries to leave he weaves across the room so wildly that he almost knocks Warhol over. But with booze comes confessions and wild boasts, and Truman's is that he gave John Huston forty blow jobs and narrowly avoided sleeping with Humphrey Bogart. (No one, of course, could ever verify this.) Truman shifts over to drinking Jack Daniels and milk in the months to come, but when he goes teetotal Warhol realizes that he's pretty boring. Truman promises that if he smokes dope, he'll become more interesting again—they do, and he doesn't! They eat pizza together—over several nights—and Warhol notices that Truman is getting to look more and more like his bulldog, a bulldog that has gnawed all the fringes and buttons off Truman's furniture. Warhol tries to tape record Truman peeing in the bathroom, but Truman shuts the door.

Then there is the lunch that Truman cooked, or didn't cook, on Sunday, October 15, 1978. Truman was in the kitchen and dramatically claimed to be cooking. It was hot in the kitchen—sunlight poured in—and the oven was on, but it was empty. A few tomatoes sat on the work surface, as if they had nothing better to do. Truman was chugging back large wine glasses of Stolichnaya, clear, strong, and viscous from the refrigerator. He pushed one on Warhol, filled two-thirds with the vodka, with just a smear of orange juice in it. Warhol decided just to hold it, not drink it. Suspicious, Warhol kept an eye on Truman in the kitchen, who kept talking up how great a cook he was and who, exasperated, showed Andy the pie he had baked, letting Warhol photograph him holding it. None of this did anything to allay Warhol's suspicions, though, as he spotted that the "homemade pie" had apparently been baked with a disc of cardboard under it.

Too conveniently, Truman had made veal stew the night before. After stealing Warhol's wine glass of vodka, Capote served his guests black bean soup—except that it was gray. And it was pretty cold. The diners tucked in, pronouncing it great, but Warhol was having none of it. He strolled around the apartment toying with his bowl of soup until he reached the bathroom, and then, quick as a wink, he shot in and poured the soup down the toilet.

Happily, by this time Capote was loaded, and Andy could even get on with taping all afternoon.

"Get Gassed" Vodka and Grapefruit Juice

INGREDIENTS

1 large measure Stolichnaya
3 pink grapefruit, squeezed
Crushed ice
3 mint leaves, shredded
3 drops orange flower water
1 splash of grenadine
1 cocktail shaker
1 large wine glass

METHOD

Two hours in advance of making this cocktail, put a bottle of Stolichnaya in the fridge to chill. You want it to cool to a syrupy, wicked consistency without freezing. An hour before, put a large wine glass in the fridge to chill—if you are pushed for time, then put it in the freezer. When the hour is up, put on all the ovens in the kitchen so that you will want that drink as much as Truman Capote did. Hopefully, lots of sunshine will stream in, too, and you will already have a hangover.

Crush the ice; if you're unsure of how to do this, wrap the ice in a tea towel, grab a rolling pin, and hit the tea towel. Empty a handful of crushed ice into the cocktail shaker and pour in a generous measure of Stolichnaya. Add the sugar-pink freshly squeezed grapefruit juice, the shredded mint, and 3 drops of orange flower water. Shake. Strain the contents of the cocktail shaker into your wine glass. Add a trickle of grenadine; it will sink to the bottom and lie like a lick of ruby at the bottom of your glass.

Pretender's Black Bean Soup

INGREDIENTS

6 tbsp. olive oil
250 g. black beans, soaked overnight in water
3 garlic cloves, crushed
2 chorizo sausages, diced
2 ancho or chipotle chilies, dried and finely chopped or crushed
2 onions, finely chopped
½ tbsp. smoked paprika
1 tsp. crushed cumin seeds (just grind them lightly with some salt in a mortar and pestle)
1 small bunch thyme
1 small bunch cilantro, finely chopped
1 pint chicken stock
¼ pint soured cream
Sea salt
Freshly ground black pepper

FOR THE GARNISHES . . .

1 red onion
1 pack tortilla chips
1 bunch cilantro
3 limes
Monterey Jack cheese
A cluster of ripe tomatoes
1 avocado

METHOD

Warm the olive oil in a large, deep-bottomed stockpot. Add the onion and garlic and sauté gently for 5 minutes. Next, add the chorizo and allow it to brown—it will begin to release some of its rich, spiced, and complex pork fats. Next, add the cumin seeds and fry for 1 minute. Follow this with the ancho or chipotle chilies, paprika, thyme, and cilantro. Drain the beans and add them to the soup base. Add the pint of chicken stock plus a pint of water. Simmer gently, with the lid on the pan, for 1½ hours. After this, blend the soup, season with sea salt and black pepper, and serve it with a small dollop of soured cream on top of each helping. Each diner will be able to garnish their soup with the contents of the little bowls. Don't let any of them go to the toilet.

Serve with small bowls, each containing:

Bowl 1: 1 finely chopped red onion, with the juice of 2 limes squeezed over
Bowl 2: broken-up plain tortilla chips
Bowl 3: grated Monterey Jack cheese
Bowl 4: diced ripe avocado, marinated in lime juice, and finely chopped cilantro
Bowl 5: finely chopped tomatoes

AUGUSTE RENOIR

Renoir grew up in the grimy neighborhood of Rue d'Argenteuil in Paris. From the warren of apartment windows drifted the aroma of all the meals being prepared, and each aroma suggested different origins: garlic suggested a worker from Provençal; the delectable aroma of bacon being casseroled with kidney beans signaled the presence of Burgundians. Six-year-old Renoir weaved his way through the streets on his way to school, carrying a plain sandwich with bacon fat smeared on the bread. By the time he was thirteen, we would have found him standing spellbound in front of the *Fountain of the Innocents* by Jean Goujon, eating a sausage and forgetting to visit the nearby wine shop where he customarily bought fried food and beef. He longed with all his heart to learn to produce something as good and beautiful as Goujon's *Fountain*, but M. Lévy, his boss and the manufacturer of glazed ware, wanted him to earn his eight sous through dedicating himself to producing mawkish profiles of blowsy Marie Antoinette. M. Lévy and Renoir were always at loggerheads about the correct length of her nose—"You have made it too short again; she was no snub-nosed queen," was M. Lévy's constant complaint. M. Lévy was also dead set on teaching his pupil how to drink: "You must drink—but take wine with water in it. If you don't drink," he warned Renoir, "the heat from the furnace will dry you up. I knew one fellow who got so dried up he had no flesh left on him." Meanwhile, back in Renoir's family apartment on Rue d'Argenteuil, Renoir's mother was trying to teach him how to make the perfect coffee, and she fed the family, every Sunday, an enormous, good-hearted pot-au-feu for anyone who cared to drop in, complete with homemade pickles that Mme. Renoir had made with her children. If no one showed up to share Sunday lunch, then the family had to eat cold, boiled beef for the rest of the week—which suited young Renoir perfectly, as he was very keen on pickles.

As a young artist, Renoir survived in part on haricot beans in the studio he shared with Claude Monet, and he loved the liberty of being possessionless, with only, as he liked to say, "My two hands in my pockets." He took to eating across the road from his studio in a local crémerie in Rue Saint-Georges, which sold rich cream and newly laid, feather-warm eggs, but it also advertised a toothsome plat du jour to passersby. The proprietor, a widow, used the single stove that glowed in the corner of the crémerie to make veal or mutton stew. She had also determined that Renoir was going to marry one or the other of her daughters, and she would save a special slice of brie for Renoir—the bachelor was too thin, she claimed. Obviously, not an inch was added to Renoir's waistline by his weakness for brie, which he saluted as the "king of all cheese," advising all who would listen, "You can only eat it in Paris. Once it goes beyond the city limits, it's no good." Although he allowed the widow's daughters to sew his hankies, that didn't stop him from casting glances at a small table across the room from him in the crémerie, where sat his future wife, the lovely, blithe Aline Charigot—she even had a snub nose, like the boy Renoir's idealized version of Marie Antoinette. Once a week the widow invited those she knew well to eat her special bean stew of Dijon haricot beans, grown on vines, and stewed with bacon, and Renoir noted with admiration how his love interest, Aline, tackled her stew: "It was a pleasure," he later told their son, "to see your mother eat. Different from society women, who give themselves stomach pains trying to remain thin and pale." People to be trusted and loved were hearty eaters. Diets were a load of old tosh!

The same love of earthy food appears in Renoir's travels by train. In the first-class compartments he felt like an intruder. In second class, the bourgeoisie were too nosy and always bobbing and nodding at each other, alert to social distinctions. Renoir squatted in third class, where others fed him continuously. Women's pity for his thin, light frame gave him the chance to taste the specialities of each region he traveled through, as carried in the baskets of heavy-skirted matrons boarding the train. He drank mouthfuls of grassy, young wines from the Côte d'Or; sampled springy, cheesy gougère from Burgundy; sipped complex rosé from the Rhône, which lingered in his mouth; or ate plates of Provençal daube, beef simmered in red wine, all the time gossiping with the stout ladies in third class, matriarchal and irrepressible. He probably picked up more information about wearing corsets than had ever been heard by a great painter. One giantess apologized, begged another woman to unlace her corsets, and then, her rolls of fat released from their prison, leaned forward to tuck into her hare pâté, at liberty at last.

Matriarchs were not always as kind to Renoir as this, though—as was the case with his mother-in-law, Madame Charigot, who was at odds with Renoir right from the start when she briefly kept house in their studio in Rue Saint-Georges. All seemed to go swimmingly at first: Mme. Charigot rolled out caramel custards and blanquettes of veal for Renoir, and no soufflé was too much trouble.

Renoir, in truth, preferred simpler food of the third-class compartment type, but he indulged the refinements of Mme. Charigot. Imagine his surprise, then, when she started dishing up sarcasm with his supper: "So, you don't want any more veal? Perhaps you would like a little more pâté de foie gras?" she'd sneer and follow this, insultingly, with references to his money troubles, muttering that he was "dying of hunger" but still "he wants foie gras!" Aline tried to keep the peace by supplying her mother with her favorite sweet, marrons glacés. Mme. Charigot was all too aware of the psychological hold she had over her daughter, claiming in later years, "If I had really been unscrupulous, I could have had marrons glacés every day."

After the hurried, cross departure of Mme. Charigot, Renoir's kitchen must have been a very jolly place, despite the presence of their cook, the "Grand Louise," who liked to weep frequently, a family wisecrack being that this was the cause of excess salt in their soup (though, in truth, fellow artists raved about the wonderful bouillabaisse one could enjoy there).

Caramel Custard

CARAMEL
4 oz. vanilla sugar
3 tbsp. water
Pinch of cream of tartar

CUSTARD
¾ pint milk
Seeds from 1 vanilla pod
1½ oz. sugar
3 eggs, plus 2 egg yolks

METHOD
Place a two-pint ovenproof glass of metal mold on top of a tea towel, folded lengthways (you will use this tea towel to keep your hands from burning when you distribute the hot caramel around the dish). In a small, thick-based saucepan, place the water and the sugar. Bring to boil, stirring until the sugar dissolves. Now add the pinch of cream of tartar. Continue to boil this sugar solution over moderate heat, tipping the pan about to redistribute the sugar syrup as it begins to caramelize. It takes 5 to 10 minutes for the sugar syrup to caramelize, turning a glorious, strong, tea-colored brown. As soon as you reach this color, remove the pan from the heat and pour the caramel into the mold. Using the tea towel, swirl the caramel around the mold, aiming to coat the bottom and sides evenly. The caramel begins to cool immediately—as soon as it stops moving, turn the mold upside down on a plate to cool. When you look next time, stray threads of caramel will have formed beautiful, twisted stalactites.

Preheat the oven to 170°C. In a bowl, whisk together the sugar, eggs, extra egg yolks, and vanilla seeds scooped from the pod. In a small saucepan, bring milk near to boil. When the milk is steaming and hot, remove it from the heat and begin to pour it in a thin stream into the beaten egg mixture, stirring all the time to prevent the eggs from scrambling.

Turn your mold the right way up, and, through a sieve, pour the custard mix into the mold. Place the mold in a large, deep pan in the center of the oven. Pour boiling water into the deep pan so that it reaches halfway up the custard. Now bake the custard for about 1 hour—if the water in your makeshift bain-marie begins to simmer, lower the temperature. Test if the crème caramel is ready by inserting a knife in it. When the knife comes out clean, the custard should be taken out of the oven, cooled, and then chilled for about three hours. Turn it out by turning the custard upside down onto a plate and tapping the mold. The liquid caramel will pool around the island of caramel and can be spooned over as you serve.

"Grand Louise" Bouillabaisse, without the tears

INGREDIENTS

7 lb. mixed, regional fish; this may be langoustes, turbot, eel, mullet (red and gray), gurnard, and so on . . .
6 tbsp. olive oil
3 onions, chopped
3 leeks, finely chopped—discard the green section
5 large, plump, and very ripe tomatoes, chopped, with the skin and seeds removed
3 potatoes, quartered
5 garlic cloves, crushed
½ fennel, finely sliced, or 5 stalks of Florence fennel
3 bay leaves
3 stalks thyme
1 small bunch of parsley, finely chopped
1 strip of orange zest
½ tsp. saffron threads
2 pints fish stock
Sea salt (or Grand Louise's tears) and black pepper
1 French baguette, sliced into twenty pieces
1 garlic clove

METHOD

Slice the fish; leave the shellfish whole. In a big, roomy pan, add the olive oil, warm, and then sweat the onions and leeks gently under a piece of buttered, greaseproof paper. Don't let them brown. Now add the tomatoes, potatoes, garlic, fennel, bay leaves, thyme, parsley, orange zest, saffron, and the fish (not the shellfish). Pour on enough stock to cover the fish, and bring to boil. Boil for 10 minutes—the lid should not be on the pan. Now add the shellfish and cook for a further 5 minutes. Taste and season with sea salt and black pepper.

Now grill the baguette slices and then rub them with the clove of garlic. Line a large soup tureen with the toasted bread and pour the hot soup over this. Serve, perhaps accompanied by aïoli.

Meals and the eating of them clearly made Renoir feel at home wherever he went. In later life, wheelchair bound, Renoir turned up for supper, even though he had little appetite; he was devoted to the ceremony of meals. Aline was proudest, however, not of the pot-au-feu that they continued to have every Sunday in keeping with Renoir's family traditions, but of her chicken sauté, which she considered her finest dish and one for which she kindly left us the recipe.

Renoir-esque Chicken Sauté

INGREDIENTS

1 chicken—ask your butcher to cut it into sections and to keep the chicken's liver for you to use when you add the mushrooms
1 tbsp. olive oil
½ tbsp. butter
3 onions, finely chopped
3 peeled, medium-sized tomatoes
1 bunch of parsley, chopped
4 sprigs of thyme
2 bay leaves
3 garlic cloves, chopped
6 mushrooms, quartered
1 handful black olives
1 glass brandy

GARNISH

1 tbsp. chopped parsley and 1 tsp. chopped garlic
Sea salt
Freshly ground black pepper

METHOD

Warm the olive oil in a heavy casserole and brown the chicken pieces in this. As each chicken piece is browned, remove it from the casserole and keep it warm. After all the chicken is browned, add ½ tablespoon of butter. Return all the chicken to the casserole, along with the onions, tomatoes, parsley, thyme, bay leaves, garlic, salt, and pepper and a little hot water. Cover and allow this to simmer over a low heat for 1½ hours, stirring occasionally to avoid burning.

Chop the mushrooms, stone the olives, and finely chop the chicken liver. Next, add the mushrooms, olives, and chopped liver. Cook for a further half hour. Just before serving, add the glass of brandy, leaving the lid off the casserole to allow the heady fumes of the brandy to evaporate. After 3 minutes, you are ready to serve. Finally, sprinkle each helping with parsley and garlic.

DIEGO RIVERA AND FRIDA KAHLO

Diego Rivera couldn't drink just normal old cow's milk in childhood like the rest of us—oh no, he had to be different. Earlier, his twin had died and his parents worried about him being pallid and weak. So they shipped him off to the countryside—the mountains of the Sierra nonetheless—to the care of his tall, Indian nurse, Antonia. So what was Antonia's solution? Well, she decided Diego needed something stronger than run-of-the mill sustenance and fetched up no less than a very large female goat, gleamingly clean and beautiful, and fed Diego pure, creamy milk straight from the goat's udder. Given this sort of start in life, it's really no surprise that Rivera continued as he meant to go on—eccentrically. Aged four and clearly deranged by the goat's milk, Antonia returned him to his parents, and his mother, now pregnant, told the equally expectant Diego that the baby would soon arrive in a box by train. Diego waited and waited, and then, finally furious that no baby or box had arrived, went and caught a pregnant mouse, cut her belly open with a pair of scissors, dug out the mouse fetuses, and . . . yes, it gets worse . . . flung them at his mother. Wonderfully macabre, or just plain fictitious?

Another tall tale emerges in 1904 when our quirky Mexican just so happened to read an account of a French fur dealer who managed to improve the quality and texture of his cats' fur by feeding them the meat of other cats. Now, while most of us might say, "How perverse!" on hearing such a tale and shudder, or worry about cat welfare in Paris, Diego was keen to open up the experiment and claimed that he persuaded his fellow students of anatomy to pool their money for a little financial venture: to buy fresh corpses from the city morgue—the emphasis was on fresh, mind you, not diseased or senile (cannibalism has to have standards, after all). And it worked a dream. For eight weeks they feasted on human flesh, and their complexions were much improved. No more spots. Diego discovered that he particularly liked women's breasts and legs—as with other animals, these cuts had a delicacy all of their own. He also recommended women's brains in vinaigrette and young women's breaded ribs. Female flesh, wrapped in a tortilla, tasted divine, like the tenderest of young pigs. Eventually, though, he gave up eating other humans because of social pressure. It would be hard to make and keep friends.

By 1911, Diego had his sights fixed on a protracted visit to Europe and had worked out that Spain was the easiest point of entry for those with questionable papers. Sailing on the *Alfonso Trece*, an elderly Spanish steamboat, the journey lasted several weeks. From Havana to Spain the seas made the cabins shift and sway, threw passengers about, and were so nauseating that Diego watched in bleak satisfaction as his fellow passengers dropped off the diners' list. Eventually only three people remained who could still stomach food—Diego and two sea captains. Victorious, all spoils were theirs. The dining room steward swayed toward them with his tray held high, his pants rolled up high above his knees, as the sea washed its way through every door.

The ship's cook, freed from the constraints of mass production, exercised his art. Breakfast was endless, long, and languorous, with only time for a cigar or two before lunch began, the water lapping at heels. Soup was off the menu; it would simply have spilled over the sides of its bowl and joined the tidal sway. Instead, dishes with more gravity were called for: muscular red snappers, succulent beef-steak, and large, sweet-meated, coral-pink crabs. Every dish brought to the table was laid before the captain first. Solemnly, he crossed himself and cut the dish into three equal portions. Placing portions on plates, he'd intone, "In the name of the Father," and the central section of the crab meat would go on his own plate; "in the name of the Son," and the next portion would land on the junior captain's plate; and, with "in the name of the Holy Ghost," the third portion would appear on Diego's plate.

From the point at which Antonia climbed into the Sierra mountains to fetch him a goat, our lovable heel Diego seemed to elicit the most passionate reactions in women. One sliced his face with a hidden blade when he embraced her, then cut her own throat (unsuccessfully) and was soon joining him for coffee again with a bandage around her neck. His second wife, Lupe Marin, was so enraged by their poverty that, when suppertime came, she served him a dish of the broken remnants of a number of clay Aztec idols he had bought using their food shopping money. Lupe didn't realize that worse things were in store for her. In true dramatic Rivera style, her parting shot to him was "Go to hell with your big-breasted girls!" Next, though, she went off to marry someone who was criminally insane, and she had a son with him, whom he immediately castrated, followed by himself. Not much luck for Lupe in the dating game, then.

Diego and Frida Kahlo were hell-bent on wedlock even though Frida's father warned Diego that he was marrying a devil. Not a bad guess, given that the couple discovered that when they kissed they could turn off and on electric lightbulbs, from streetlights to duller, domestic varieties. Frida was fascinated by Diego; she thought he looked like a large, standing frog. In turn, he thought Frida was wild and unpredictable—a taco, beans, and tequila girl. Maybe he was on to something; Frida kept brandy in a perfume bottle among her skirts. She pretended to dab herself with perfume, but instead took a quick swig. The wedding was an exciting one, tequila fueled, with lingerie hanging out to dry from the rafters. Lupe grabbed Frida's skirts and yelled, "Do you see those two canes? That's what Diego's going to have to put up with now and he used to have my legs!" Diego started firing pistols later on and even managed to break one guest's finger. Kahlo refused to move in with Diego for several days. Lupe eventually mellowed and, with great magnanimity, taught Frida how to cook the food closest to Diego's heart.

Diego often worked on scaffolding to create his huge murals, and Frida made up lunchboxes for him—a practice again taught to her by Lupe—complete with napkins embroidered with "I love you" and decorated with flowers. Diego gruffly liked to call them "laborer's lunchboxes." When he was diagnosed with cancer, the packed lunchbox's contents became very strict: two eggs, some meat, two slices of black bread, a cooked dessert, yogurt, six different fruits, and a thermos of black, unsweetened coffee. Through time, and at least by the time they remarried, Kahlo became increasingly maternal toward Rivera. When he was visiting Los Angeles without her, she wrote to his host, "Be sure that Diego sees the oculist in Los Angeles. And that he doesn't eat too many spaghettis so he won't get too fat."

Mexican food was one of the rich, sustaining influences in Frida and Diego's marriage. Rivera, if he had been drawing in the local market that morning, bought Indian huitlacoche for their cook to prepare. The derivation of the word *huitlacoche* can seem off putting: it comes from the Nahuatl word for *cuitla*, meaning "excrement" or "rear end," combined with *cochtli*, meaning "to sleep"—so that shakes out as "sleeping excrement." Not to be outdone, one determined body of etymologists insists on translating this as "raven's excrement." Splitting hairs? Also known as corn smut or corn truffle, huitlacoche looks like a mass of ovalish, pale-gray fungi on an ear of corn. Cooked, it becomes black and tarry with an earthy, mushroomy taste and a hint of corn. Diego's cook fried it with onion, chilies, and the herb epazote—which goes by the romantic pseudonyms of pigweed and Mexican tea. Along with the huitlacoche, Rivera and Kahlo lunched on jet black duck mole, with lime green guacamole on masa harina tortillas. Frida would down her tequila *copitas* from a red clay cup—she said, brilliantly, "I drank to drown my sorrows, but the damned things learned how to swim." Lunch was eaten off earthenware plates on a rough wooden table, overlaid with flowered Mexican oilcloth. Frida's parrot, Bonita, might try to tiptoe around the room to reach the butter, her favorite snack. Bonita has been immortalized in several of Kahlo's paintings, but without any incriminating butter. Out on the patio sat a much larger, dissolute male parrot, given to drinking beer and croaking, "No me pasa la cruda!"

Lunch with Frida and Diego—Duck with Black Mole

INGREDIENTS

3 wild ducks

THE BLACK MOLE

FOR THE CHILI PUREE . . .

6 dried chihuacle negro chilies (these have a rich aniseed undertone)
11 dried mullato chilies
6 dried pasilla chilies
4 dried chipotle meco chilies
1 corn tortilla, torn up into small pieces

FOR THE TOMATO PUREE . . .

3 green tomatoes, chopped (you can substitute red)
3 tomatillos, husked, rinsed, and chopped
1 tsp. oregano or ½ tsp. epazote
½ tsp. thyme
½ cup duck/chicken stock

FOR THE NUT PUREE . . .

2 cups chicken/duck stock
3 tbsp. sesame seeds
3 tbsp. each of sunflower seeds, pecan nuts, raw peanuts, and almonds

FOR THE BASE MIXTURE . . .

1 white onion, cut into thick rings
6 garlic cloves, unpeeled
2 tbsp. lard or vegetable oil
2 cloves, freshly ground
1 stick cinnamon
3 black peppercorns
1 tsp. fennel seeds
1 ripe plantain, peeled and cut into ¼-inch slices
2 slices dark brown, toasted, stale bread
1½ tbsp. raisins

TO FINISH THE MOLE . . .

3 oz. grated dark Mexican chocolate
2 tsp. brown sugar
6 cups chicken stock
Sea salt

METHOD

Clean the chilies; split them lengthwise, removing their stems and seeds. Unfurl the chilies and stack them, splayed out, ready for the next stage. As you do so, you'll begin to catch the scented character of each type of chili—the distinctive honeyed, paprika tones of the chipotle; the treacly, liquorice chambers of the pasilla. Heat an unoiled skillet, put the torn tortilla pieces into the skillet, and allow them to toast to a deep brown, with some blackening. Remove them, and keep the broken tortilla to the side. Next, pour the chili seeds into the pan. Shake the pan to loosen them as they go black—this takes about 20 seconds, and you'll know they're ready when you get spicy chili fumes rising. Next, remove them from the

Lunch with Frida and Diego—Duck with Black Mole *(continued)*

pan and pour the blackened seeds in a small bowl. Pour a little cold water over the chili seeds (just a little, not a pond!). After about 10 minutes, drain the seeds and reserve the chili water. Whatever you do, do not (as I did) scratch your nose or rub your eyes.

Put on the kettle. Heat the skillet again—get it nice and hot—then, in batches, place about 4 splayed chilies at a time flat on the skillet and press down on them for about 10 seconds each side, until they blacken—but don't carbonize them! You'll see the beautiful ebony mullato chilies move slightly in the heat, begin to blister, and release jet black chili sap. Prepare to cough! Place each finished batch in a large bowl and, when all the chilies are done, cover them in boiling water and use a plate to weigh them down. Let them soak for 30 minutes. When you drain them, reserve the chili liquid.

Put the oven on, to heat up to 350°F or 170°C.

Next, return the (still) unoiled skillet to medium heat and place the thick onion rings and unpeeled garlic in the pan. Roast them in this dry heat until they darken and soften. The garlic will take longer than the onion, so when the onion is done, remove it and place in a bowl. When the garlic has caught up, remove it and pop the softened, pulpy, sweet garlic out of their now woody carapaces into the bowl.

Now that the oven is hot, put the various nuts on a baking tray—keeping the sesame seeds in their own discrete strip—but also spread them thinly or some will brown while others will remain pale (and consequently be less tasty), and blast them in the oven until they become fragrant and alter in color—watch this carefully, as nuts can burn easily. As soon as they release their nutty aromas and take on a darker gold, remove them from the oven.

Allow the nuts to cool for 5 minutes. Reserve ¼ cup of the toasted sesame seeds for a final garnish and place the rest along with the other nuts in a blender. Add 2 cups of the chicken or duck stock to this and blend to a smooth nut puree (it will smell like roasted chestnuts!). Pour this paste into a bowl.

Next, puree the green tomatoes, tomatillos, oregano or epazote, and thyme, with a further ½ cup of stock, in the nut-soaked blender. Reserve in a bowl.

Now drain the chilies. Combine the fiery water from the soaked chili seeds and the soaked chilies. Put the chilies into the blender in batches to puree; with each batch, add about ⅓ of a cup of the chili water. When all the chilies are pulped, put a cup of this back into the blender; add the chili seeds and the toasted tortilla, plus a further ⅓ of a cup of chili water if necessary. Whiz this up until it is smooth. Combine all of this puree, and then sieve into a new bowl in order to remove chili skins and seeds.

Lightly crush the cloves, fennel seeds, black peppercorns, and cinnamon in a mortar and pestle. Heat the skillet and dry fry the spices for a minute. Next, add the oil or lard. Fry the sliced plantain in the oil, turning occasionally, for about 5 minutes. Remove the plantain from the heat. Next, add the raisins to the oil and fry them for a minute. Add the pieces of stale brown bread and fry them in the oil.

Lunch with Frida and Diego—Duck with Black Mole (*continued*)

Place the fried bread, plantain, banana, roasted onion rings, garlic gloop, and a ¾ cup of chicken or duck stock in the same, unwashed, nut-and-tomato covered blender. Once it has blended, place in a bowl.

You *are* getting there . . .

In a heavy-bottomed, large, and deep pot (I use a Dutch oven), heat 3 tablespoons of vegetable oil or lard until it is very hot. Add the tomato and tomatillo puree and stir constantly until this mixture becomes dark and thick (it should have the consistency of tomato puree; this might take up to 15 minutes). Add the nut paste and stir again until very thick (7 minutes). Now add the banana and spice mixture and stir until thick (7 minutes again). Finally, add the chili paste, turn the heat down to low, and allow this to cook for about 25 minutes, stirring frequently. Never take your eye off the pan at this time, as the mole can burn very easily; obsessively stir every couple of minutes. The resultant sauce/paste should be thick and nearly black.

Finally, add the remaining duck/chicken stock (about 6 cups) and the dark chocolate. Mix well and simmer on a very low heat for an hour. Add the sugar and sea salt. Now strain the mole through a fine mesh sieve.

Wash and dry the duck and heat 3 tablespoons of oil in a skillet. Brown the duck.

Now pour the mole back into the deep, large pot; heat it until it is simmering. Tuck the duck into the mole, cover partially, and cook gently for about 40 minutes.

To serve, place the duck on a plate, pour the tarry, treacle-brown mole over it, and scatter with the remaining toasted sesame seeds. Serve with homemade tortillas—and don't forget to make the sign of the cross!

Guacamole

INGREDIENTS

1 ripe avocado
Olive oil
1 lime
1 ripe tomato, finely chopped
½ red onion, finely chopped
1 red chili, finely chopped
1 tbsp. fresh green cilantro, finely chopped

METHOD

In a bowl, using a fork, mash the peeled and destoned avocado into a smooth paste. Mix in the tomato, onion, chili, and cilantro. Squeeze in the lime juice and add a drizzle of olive oil. Mix thoroughly and serve.

Huitlacoche Fry

INGREDIENTS

1 lb. huitlacoche
½ tsp. epazote
2 poblano chilies
1 garlic clove, roughly chopped
½ small onion, minced
2 tbsp. vegetable oil
Pinch of sea salt

METHOD

Heat the oven to 220°C, place the poblano chilies on a baking tray, and roast them for 30 minutes. Allow them to cool and then strip off their blackened skins. Open them up, clean out their seeds, and cut them into strips. Chop up the huitlacoche. Now warm the oil in your skillet and sauté the onion and garlic until they are golden. Add the huitlacoche, epazote, chilies poblanos, and a pinch of salt. Cook gently for about 15 minutes.

PABLO PICASSO

After 1936, lunch with Picasso was a calm and delicious experience. By then, Picasso had met Inès Sassier, who was to become his housekeeper and cook. Inès served toasted brioches for breakfast and offered a pleasant, sedentary undertone to Picasso's domestic existence. This was lacking in Picasso's amorous liaisons with haughty models and ballerinas or with flighty, culture vultures like the dizzy-headed Geneviève Laporte. Geneviève was always being transported by waves of poetry to reflect on the beauty of her horse's mane or some such thing. Fortunately, Inès was relatively indifferent to the lure of Picasso's striped sweater and "Andalucian stare" (he prided himself on a disarming, lidless stare, which set off the whites of his eyes against his tobacco-colored skin, and which he was convinced would undress you, if he chose). Instead, over the years with Picasso, she presented a steady run of delicious food, among them Cuban dishes, though Inès was Italian in origin. One dish that guests remembered fondly was fried eggs, pink sausages, and yellow, fried bananas decorating a turret of rice, almost resembling a still life. Inès could also adapt her cooking to suit Picasso's various moods, love affairs, interests, bids for good health or immortality, plus the frequent combination of ill-assorted foods sent by well wishers. There might be chocolate eels or rattlesnake in a tin to serve up, alongside whatever dish was most favored by Picasso at the time.

Before Inès, where Picasso ate—and what—depended on whether he could get food on credit: succulent Bayonne ham from the charcutier, and perhaps lunches in Chez Vernin on the Rue Cavallotti or in Azon's on the Rue de Ravignan; then he'd round off the day by looking in dustbins for food for his cat. Or Picasso ordered lunch to be delivered promptly at noon from a shop in the Place des Abbesses. Then, when the knuckle-headed delivery boy rounded the corner, Picasso fell completely silent. The boy knocked and knocked at the door . . . no answer. Reluctantly, he left his basket. Picasso sprang to the door to retrieve his lunch, to be paid for a day or two later when some cash came along. Picasso was also keen to swap his art for meals. To think what glories could have been yours for the price of a roast chicken. Best of all, Vernin of Vernin's restaurant had a spectacularly bad memory, which meant he never remembered if you had paid for your dinner the last time you visited—the possibilities for dinner on credit were endless, inspiring Picasso's friend, Max Jacob, to write this ditty (which they sang to a popular tune):

Ça m'ennuie d'aller chez Vernin,
Mais il faut y aller quand même,
Parce qu'on y prend des verres nains
Et des fromages à la crè-è-me!

Which translates as:

> I'm tired of eating at Vernin's,
> But that's where everybody goes,
> Because they serve wine in thimblefuls
> And helpings of cream cheese!

Then there was the large, butlerish Sabartés, a frequent eating companion at this stage in Picasso's life. On one occasion, Picasso and Max Jacobs had scraped together their last sou for some supper and sent Sabartés out to buy an egg, which they had resolved to cook over a candle stump. Triumphantly, after having been gone for some time, Sabartés headed home with the egg, a piece of bread, and two sausages. Weak with hunger, he tripped on the stairs to the studio, causing the egg to splatter on the stone. The others were furious: "You'll never amount to anything," Picasso hissed. "We give you our last penny and you can't even get back here with a whole egg. You'll be a failure all your life!" He stabbed his fork into one of the sausages. It exploded. Picasso stabbed the second—it discharged its stinking meat. The sausages were so fetid, their gases exploded through their pouches of skin. Picasso, who rarely spoke at meals anyway, became even more silent. He and Jacobs split the bread between them, and Sabartés got only a scolding for his supper. Any crumbs that were left went to his pet white mouse, which Picasso kept in a drawer. This was later to be replaced by a very smelly white owl, which, incidentally, only ate mice (but not, hopefully, the mouse in question). A continuous napkin joke circulated among Picasso's friends; there was always a shortage of napkins at Picasso's—in other words, there was one napkin. This led to one diner saying to his fellow eaters, "I've only got one napkin left; since there are four of you, you'd better have a corner each."

Kind-hearted models tried to feed the hungry artists: the hauntingly beautiful Benedetta, who stares out from Picasso's 1905 *Portrait de Madame Benedetta Canals*, rolled up her sleeves to make everyone solid and unpretentious dishes based on traditional macaroni—she was a Roman, after all. Tragicomic artists abounded at the time, not always cooking but certainly eating, such as Henri Rousseau, the Impressionist painter. Picasso's one-time girlfriend Fernande, who could be relied on to make a good ratatouille, had a heart-to-heart with Rousseau one day after lunch. He gave a tragic account of a doomed love affair as he finished off his sugared pancakes (this in itself should have been a signal that his heart wasn't about to break). As the story unfolded it became darker and gloomier; the sugar from the pancakes spread over him until he looked like a large, sugared, weeping mouse.

The "at homes"—soirees—that slightly wealthier artists held offered an opportunity for a square meal. Picasso and Fernande went to Guillaume Apollinaire's Wednesday "At Homes." Apollinaire was a very colorful character who coined the term *Surrealism* and was arrested on suspicion of plotting the theft of the *Mona Lisa*; obligingly, he also managed to implicate Picasso in this. Appollinaire always prepared the same meal on Wednesdays of hors d'oeuvres, risotto, and braised beef, on one occasion aided by his girlfriend. The table was laid, diners were poised, forks raised above the hors-d'oeuvres when Apollinaire and his girlfriend started to bicker, a row that escalated so quickly they had to exit the room. One diner, Cremnitz, couldn't believe his bad luck and, deciding that Apollinaire's argument was taking too long, helped himself to a sausage. Apollinaire barged back into the room, his face contused with lover's rage, his hair wild, but he still found time to cast an eye over the table: "Someone," he roared, panting, "has eaten some sausage!"

Finer, more lavish dining could be had at the house of the wealthy German artist Henri Goetz. Parties there were so rowdy that neighbors peeped nervously out of their doors. This impression of recklessness was confirmed when Vighels and Braque slid down the banisters and landed feet first at the door to the flat below, just as its occupant, trembling beneath his nightcap, opened the door to see what was going on. Much of this banister sliding can be attributed to the huge silver basins of champagne that Goetz prepared, filled with several magnums and covered in jeweled, myriad islands of canary yellow chopped pineapples. Dinner was goose, crisp and burnished to a dark gold, carved with no less than a saw and an axe.

Braques's Downfall: Pineapple Champagne

INGREDIENTS

2 magnums champagne
1 pineapple, ½ chopped into bite-sized pieces, ½ crushed to a pulp
Ice, crushed
1 large silver bowl
1 large silver ladle

METHOD

Place two handfuls of crushed ice in the base of the bowl, top with the pulverized sweet pineapple, then top this with the canary yellow pineapple pieces. Pop open the champagne and pour each bottle (gently) into the bowl.

Serve yourself using an enormous ladle—it's what Picasso had to do.

Picasso's eating habits altered around the end of that decade, when he moved to Boulevard de Clichy and tried to fix his ill health through his diet. Gone were the sausage and the goose as he moved on to fish, vegetables, rice pudding, and grapes, all washed down with mineral water. This frugality in eating continued, at least into the 1940s, when Picasso is recorded as having for breakfast café au lait with two pieces of salt-free dried toast. No less. No more. Instead of Sabartés as a dinner companion, Picasso opted for his pet monkey, Monika, who loved to pester him at the table, stealing his cigarettes and fruit and nestling against his chest, tucked just under his chin, to enjoy her spoils.

When World War II broke out, Picasso staunchly chose to stay in Paris during its occupation by the Nazis and put up his own miniresistance, in part through food. Le Catalan restaurant, a new stomping ground on the Rue des Grands-Augustins on the Left Bank, was his battleground. Picasso had already been accused of being Jewish. It was possible that, despite his age, Picasso might be sent to the concentration camps of Eastern Europe. Suspected of Bolshevik sympathies, the Gestapo had raided his studio several times. He was to be watched carefully, and where better to spy on him than in Le Catalan? What was his crime? A chateaubriand steak! By 1943, the consumption of beef in Paris was strictly rationed, and Picasso was caught eating contraband meat. The authorities responded as harshly as they could—the diners were fined and reprimanded. Le Catalan had its license removed for a whole month. This has to be the first and last time in history that eating a chateaubriand was an act of Bolshevik resistance.

Alarm bells should have rung for twenty-one-year-old Françoise Gilot on that Wednesday evening in 1943 when the womanizing sixty-one-year-old Picasso offered her cherries at Le Catalan. Although he was with Dora Maar, who had been his "companion" since 1936, Picasso had tried to get Françoise's table's attention and now had to resort to approaching them, armed with cherries. He offered some to all, his best Andalucian stare fixed on Françoise, as she listened, panting, to his heavy Spanish accent drawing out the *s* sound in *cerisses*. Poor Dora was clearly left watching from the table, but she must have been used to such slights. Picasso's idea of a compliment was to tell her that she attracted him the way another man would.

When Dora later bumped into Picasso courting Françoise, she responded vengefully over lunch. "You don't mind if I order the most expensive thing on the card, do you? I suppose I still have the right to a little luxury, for the time being." What could Picasso say? Dora ordered the caviar.

In revenge, Picasso wondered if she would be able to find her way home. Dora pithily retorted, "I'm perfectly capable of getting home by myself . . . I imagine you need to lean on youth, though. About fifteen minutes ought to do it, I should think."

French Resistance Chateaubriand

INGREDIENTS
1 lb. beef tenderloin
1 tbsp. olive oil
1 tbsp. soft butter

FOR THE MADEIRA SAUCE . . .
2 garlic cloves, crushed
1 shallot, finely chopped
½ glass brandy
½ glass Madeira wine
3 tsp. finely chopped French tarragon
Tarragon leaves to garnish
Sea salt
Freshly ground black pepper

METHOD
Preheat the oven to 230°C. At a high heat, melt the butter and olive oil in a solid metal tray on top of the stove; the tray must be strong enough to withstand the heat on the stove and in the oven. When the butter is sizzling hot, place the chateaubriand on the tray; don't turn down the heat. Do not move the meat for 1 minute, then turn, browning the meat all over. Now remove the chateaubriand from the heat momentarily and sprinkle with sea salt and black pepper. Place the meat in the oven. Leave in the oven for 10 to 15 minutes, depending on how rare you prefer your beef. Warm a plate.

Remove the chateaubriand from the oven and transfer it onto the warmed plate, place a tent of tinfoil loosely over it, and let it rest for 15 minutes. Retain the tray the meat had roasted in and, in the warm oils that remain, sauté the shallots gently for 3 minutes. Next, add the garlic. Turn up the heat, add the brandy, and use it to deglaze the pan, using a spoon to scrape together the beef fat, seared shallots, and garlic. When the brandy has almost evaporated, add the Madeira and allow this to reduce by half. Finally, add a tablespoon of butter and the chopped tarragon.

Carve the chateaubriand into diagonal, thick slices. Drizzle over the rich Madeira gravy.

Rice Pudding Fit for Picasso

INGREDIENTS

2 cups milk
½ cinnamon stick
3 largish strips of orange or lemon peel
Pinch of sea salt
½ cup short-grain white rice
¼ cup raisins
¼ cup light brown sugar
1 vanilla pod
1 tbsp. butter
1 tsp. freshly grated nutmeg

METHOD

Place the milk, rice, cinnamon stick, strips of orange or lemon peel, vanilla pod, and pinch of sea salt in a medium saucepan and bring slowly to boil. Stir frequently to make sure the rice doesn't stick. When it reaches a boil, turn it back down to low and let the spices slowly infuse the milk and rice over about 15 minutes. Remove the vanilla pod (if you wash and dry it, you can use it again). Next, add the raisins and the sugar; stir frequently to prevent the rice from sticking to the base of the pan. Remove from the heat and stir in the butter. Now serve hot or cold, with a dusting of grated nutmeg.

2

Dining with Famous and Infamous Movie Stars

The glamour and decadence of the jet set served up on a plate. On stage: Joan Crawford, Michael Caine, Laurel and Hardy, Cary Grant, Marlene Dietrich, Alfred Hitchcock, Liz Taylor, John Wayne, Marilyn Monroe, Humphrey Bogart and Lauren Bacall, and Woody Allen.

JOAN CRAWFORD

When Joan Crawford wasn't locking her adopted children into closets or tying them up in showers, she liked to present herself as the very flower of womanhood. She painted a brilliantly saccharine picture of herself as a mother; she read poetry with the children until their heads and hearts throbbed, they polished their little white shoes every day, and—get this—they washed out their shoelaces, too. Some of what she subjected them to was the standard stuff of childhood: they had to take naps during the day, and she insisted they brush their hair one hundred times a night (Crawford also recommended mayonnaise as a hair treatment—Katharine Hepburn used to rub six eggs, one by one, into her hair).

The children endured all the privations of Crawford's monstrous version of maternal love, combined with the independence and privilege of wealth. When left as nine-year-olds to design their own birthday party, the twins opted for vodka and caviar (I bet) followed by clear soup and New York cut steak. They even had a cheese board.

For her public, Crawford was full of disturbing Stepford wife–style snippets of advice about everything from how to look after number one (your HUSBAND!)

to how to keep your figure trim, with useful insights into how a celebrity would go about staying slim. When filming *What Ever Happened to Baby Jane?*, her character, the much-put-upon cripple, Blanche, was supposed to make short work of a box of chocolates. Crawford was having none of this, though, and rustled up miniature brown meatballs and ate these for protein rather than sugar! So, there's a great tip, dieters: substitute chocolate truffles with meatballs.

Married to her fourth husband, Alfred Steele, Crawford set about creating an idealized domestic retreat for Alfred after a long day at the office. When he rolled up at 4 p.m. every afternoon, he could enjoy a customary cup of turtle soup with Joan, in an effortlessly beautiful home—Alfred was unaware that such a thing as a feather duster even existed. The children were set to watch the telephone and doorbell and answer these immediately after no more than one ring. When business associates bustled up at 6 p.m., if required, Joan would be visible, offering tea or cocktails and handing around the sort of homemade snacks that busy men deserve, made by her own fair hands—like her genius appetizer of peanut butter and bacon on black bread, the peanut butter gooey and the bacon popping with crunchy fat.

Busy Businessmen Snacks

INGREDIENTS

Crunchy peanut butter
Streaky bacon
Thinly sliced white bread
Butter

METHOD

Grill the bacon until it is crunchy; then crumble it into little fatty nuggets. Using a small, round cookie cutter, press out rounds of white bread. Butter these and then toast the rounds under the grill. Spread the rounds with peanut butter; return these to beneath the grill until they are piping hot, then sprinkle with the crumbled bacon. Serve.

If Alfred's business associates were kind enough to agree to stay for dinner, then Saint Joan of the Dishes had a freezer bursting with tasty, homemade meals from lobster Newburg to frozen aspics to beef bourguignon. If she had been negligent (God forbid), then she put a quick call through to the Casserole Kitchen, an obliging supplier of all stewed things wholesome, and they fired across an emergency casserole. Dinner was by candlelight, and Joan was ready to talk business if need be, but she never, ever, raised the unwholesome topic of children, which was woman's work to be reveled in only if you wore an apron.

Joan had all sorts of obsessive-compulsive ambitions when it came to buffets: twelve was the ideal number for a buffet of roast lamb, burnished squabs, cheerily smiling suckling pigs, and all accompanied by corn salad. Colors had to be matched: no white with white (like celery and cauliflower) and no yucky combinations of things like red and yellow. Textures must not be similar; whoever combined creamed chicken with mashed potatoes was an outright fool. Tastes must contrast; it wouldn't do to have sweet with sweet. Finally, balance was key; rich dishes must be followed by airy, light dishes.

She provided posterity (that's you and me and this page) with a blueprint for the ideal buffet (FOR TWELVE!!!). It goes roughly like this . . .

The buffet must have cheeky and eye-catching hors d'oeuvres like smoked salmon on pumpernickel bread, garnished with lemon slices and capers, or mustard and cheese puffs, or even highly seasoned meatballs with tomato sauce on the side—in case you mistake one of these babies for a chocolate truffle—to tempt the twelve guests into the meal (accompanied by brisk, boisterous, taste-bud-challenging cocktails such as Bloody Marys, Bullshots, Screwdrivers, a gutsy punch). Dishes should be temperature graded, for goodness' sake, you fool: one hot; one at room temperature; one chilled. A great "discovery" Joan made was that if you took a chunk of dry salami with a chunk of moist salami, slapped some mustard on them, and skewered these onto a cocktail stick topped with a pickled onion, this became an hors d'oeuvre that could make your taste buds sing.

The main should be two warm dishes—for instance, lamb curry or chicken breasts in a delicate, winsome sauce. Alongside can go salads. Joan recommends a wilted spinach salad—wilted because you pour hot bacon grease on it—or a bean salad, which had to be made the night before. This is made through combining leftover shards of fried chicken or baked ham with finely diced red onions, celery, green peppers, kidney beans, and chopped hot red chili pepper, and then dressing this with a combination of Tabasco sauce, vinegar, kosher salt, and black pepper. Joan was also boastful of her unique coleslaw, famed among a small circle of Alfred's business associates.

Dessert should be something gooey and sweet, as men are like this: "Pander to them, and let *them* worry about their waistlines."

She recommends, though, that you, humble housewife, not forget to introduce yourself at the outset to the assembled business associates. She said that she made a habit of saying, modestly, "Hello! I'm Joan Crawford."

To which, they'd chortle and reply, "You have to be kidding. We'd never know it."

But you, humble reader, can just go right on up and say, "I'm Anita Johnson. We moved here recently from Chicago." And off you go.

For the unmentionable children, tucked away by the telephone or doorbell, Joan rustled up "something simple," like her signature meatloaf.

No Mommie No Meatloaf

INGREDIENTS

2 lb. minced sirloin beef
1 lb. minced veal
3 eggs, beaten
Bottle A1 sauce
2 tbsp. Worcester sauce
Freshly ground salt and pepper
3 red onions, minced
2 green peppers, minced
4 hard-boiled eggs (or 8 quails' eggs)

METHOD

Preheat the oven to 180°C. In a large mixing bowl, combine all the ingredients. Place into a loaf tin the meatloaf mix; gently slip the 4 hens' eggs or 8 quails' eggs into the meatloaf mix; these will pleasantly surprise the children! Before putting the meatloaf in the oven, dribble over more A1 sauce, Worcestershire sauce, and (Joan advises, take it or leave it) salt. A crust will form. Cook for 50 minutes.

Once cooked, slice and serve.

MICHAEL CAINE

Born with the Dickensian name of Maurice Micklethwaite, Michael Caine grew up in an appropriately cold and grim London of the 1930s; his father had been a porter at Billingsgate market. Maurice never ate any of the fish that his father brought home but did remember the glow of dye given off by smoked haddock. There was no room in the fridge, and Mr. Micklethwaite decided to store a plate of fish on the floor at the foot of Maurice's bed. Young Maurice woke in the night and thought that a phosphorescent ghost was rising from the floor toward him. "You stupid sod," said Dad, "it's only the haddock." Chicken, according to Mr. Micklethwaite, was only eaten by "Nancy Boys," and so it never reached their table, leaving Maurice to be charmed by his mother's fried bread, sizzled in bacon fat.

During the bombing of London, Mr. Micklethwaite Senior was called up to serve in the Royal Artillery service, and the family were evacuated to the flat, windy stretches of distant Norfolk and the village of North Runcton Green. Maurice's mother, Ellen, got a job as a cook at the Grange, home to timber merchants Irwine and Constance English, and it was food heaven for young Maurice—Michael Caine the gourmet was born there, fed on the fish roe and pheasant leftovers from the English's table. There were black fish eggs that he wasn't at first keen on, plus a "paste" made of goose liver that, again, was initially disliked and later became a firm favorite. He immediately, however, took to wine and port.

Caine left military service in Korea in the 1950s after contracting malaria, which hit him every so often in terrible, delirious, sweaty bouts. While working at the Smithfield meat market by day and acting the part of Hindley Earnshaw in *Wuthering Heights* by night (and using another pseudonym, Michael Scott), Caine collapsed from a malarial bout. He convalesced under Ellen's care, and was revived by her bread puddings. Mother's bread pudding was legendary—in the 1960s she came close to winning the First International Bread Pudding Competition at the Playboy Club. She came in third because she'd been too heavy-handed with the cinnamon.

The world of acting offered many eating surprises. Even when Caine was locked up for the nonpayment of maintenance to his first wife, Patricia, and their daughter, there were still benefits to be had. The slot on Caine's door opened, and a quiet voice asked, "Are you an actor? Were you in *Dixon of Dock Green* the other night?" It was the warden, and Caine, of course, was a big hit with the authorities because *Dixon of Dock Green* portrayed the police in such a positive light. For the rest of his sentence, Caine got an extra slice of cake with his tea.

There was very little money for food when Caine and Terence Stamp shared a flat on Harley Street and were often hungry until Caine spotted a recipe for egg custard in the papers. *I'll have that*, he thought, and he made it for them every evening.

Bread Pudding Recipe . . . a Cure for Malaria

INGREDIENTS

½ lb. white or brown stale bread, made into breadcrumbs
½ pint milk
1 oz. butter, melted
3 oz. brown Demerara sugar
1 tsp. cinnamon
½ tsp. mixed spice
1 beaten egg
6 oz. mixed, dried fruit
Grated rind and juice of ½ a lemon
Grated rind and juice of ½ an orange
Freshly grated nutmeg

METHOD

Place the breadcrumbs in a bowl, pour the milk over them, and leave them to soak for one hour. Preheat the oven to 170°C. To the soaked, milky bread, add the melted butter, beaten egg, cinnamon, mixed spice, and Demerara sugar. Mix well and then add the mixed fruit, orange and lemon rinds, and juice. Line and butter a square or oblong baking tray. Pour the mixture into the tray, and sprinkle on a little Demerara sugar for extra crunch. Grate the nutmeg over the whole. Bake for 1½ hours. If it seems to be browning too quickly, cover the pudding with tinfoil. When the bread pudding is ready, cool it on a wire rack.

Fortunately, a reprieve from the egg custard diet was offered when Stamp became embroiled with a gorgeous and wealthy neighbor of theirs. Realizing the actors were hard up, she began regularly posting raw steaks through their letterbox. Their food problems were solved, but with the egg custard recipe came the revelation to Caine that he really enjoyed cooking.

When he moved to Grosvenor Square in the early 1970s, he instigated special Cockney fry-up evenings (at which he imagined his father watching him with deep, paternal pride).

A Cockney Fry-Up

Eggs, fried
Pork sausages, fried
Bacon, fried
Tomatoes, fried
Drippings (to fry all of the above in)

ACCOMPANIED BY . . .

Sliced white bread and butter
Tea with full-fat milk and refined white sugar

On one fateful evening in 1971, Caine settled down in front of the TV with his friend Paul, their stomachs full of the Cockney fry-up. They drew the curtains so that no one with binoculars could spy on them (I have this problem, too). There were two channels available on the TV and no remote control, so Caine had rigged up a cunning method of changing channels without moving an inch. He kept a long broom handle at his side, ready to poke the TV with. A Maxwell House Coffee advertisement came on, shot in Brazil, and Caine saw a girl dancing with maracas; she was the most beautiful girl he'd ever seen. Heart palpitating, sweating, he knelt down in front of the TV to see the girl more closely, but she was obscured by a close-up of Maxwell House Coffee.

"I want to meet her."

"She's in Brazil," Paul replied.

"Do you want to come to Brazil with me?" Caine asked. He was determined to storm Maxwell House Coffee as it opened the next day. But that very night, he and Paul went to Tramp, a good disco hangout, and he bumped into a guy named Nigel Politzer, whom he vaguely knew. Nigel worked for the company that made the ad, and it turned out the model wasn't Brazilian—she was Shakira Baksh and she lived on Fulham Road.

The rest is history.

LAUREL AND HARDY

"I don't eat much, I'm just big boned," Oliver Hardy liked to tell interviewers. Darker accounts also contributed to the mythology surrounding Hardy's weight; he had to watch his twelve-year-old brother, Sam, drown in front of him in the Oconee River, as he panted and struggled uselessly to pull him out. Hardy's response was to eat his way out of loss and misery, until he was 250 pounds by the time he hit fifteen. His widowed mother, Miss Emmie, sent Norville Hardy (he took the name Oliver later in memory of his father) to military school, Georgia Military College in Milledgeville. A fat boy in a military school stuck out like a sore thumb.

Hardy loathed drilling, didn't give a damn about discipline, and once was so exhausted that he dropped to the ground and refused to move. The other cadets were ordered to cart Norville off the parade ground, but, try as they might, he was just too solid to budge. He simply lay in the middle of the dusty parade ground until he felt strong enough to go to his room. That was it, he decided, and he ran away—across the street—to his mother. The food at the Georgia Military Hospital was not good enough, he argued, and he would never go back! Well . . . he might: on one condition! Only if she baked a whole batch—perhaps even a couple of batches—of his favorite biscuits, Miss Emmie's special baking powder biscuits, would he even contemplate returning. She did. He ate at least twenty and returned to boot camp.

It was really two years after meeting Stan on the set of *Lucky Dog* in 1918 that Hardy, having escaped the clutches of his first wife, Madelyn (both Laurel and

Special Baking Powder Biscuits

INGREDIENTS

2 cups all-purpose flour
1 tbsp. baking powder
1 tbsp. butter, melted
½ tbsp. sugar
½ tsp. sea salt
4 oz. butter, cubed
¾ cup milk

METHOD

Preheat the oven to 190°C. In a large bowl, combine the sieved flour, sugar, baking powder, and salt. Add the 4 ounces of cubed butter and rub this through the flour until it has the consistency of breadcrumbs. Now add the milk, a little at a time, combining the whole into a batter (this should not get too wet, though). Flour a board and turn out your dough. Try not to handle it too much, as this will affect its ability to rise. Roll it to a thickness of ¾ of an inch and then cut into biscuit shapes. Brush a baking sheet with a tablespoon of melted butter. Place the 8 to 10 biscuits on the baking sheet and bake for about 15 minutes.

Hardy had doomed marriages until their final ones: wife number four for Laurel and wife number three for Hardy), took to the gourmet cooking that was to so endear him to his friends—that is, if they managed to survive their first experience of his cooking. He invited everyone out to his bachelor pad at Cahuenga Pass in Hollywood Park, on the promise of dishing up stuffed fish broiled in his very own special sauce. All ten of Hardy's friends sat down at the table, rolled up their sleeves, and got on with eating. It wasn't too long, though, before they all became aware of the strange pong rising from the fish, cutting like sweat through the delicious scents of Hardy's sauce. Ptomaine poisoning struck the table like lightning. There was a wild scrambling mass movement toward the one small toilet, but most didn't make it and instead rolled around the floor, awash with their own vomit.

There were similar slapstick moments throughout Hardy's cooking career. By 1926 Hardy had been ensnared by his second wife, Myrtle. She had damaged her leg as she ran away from a rattlesnake, and Hardy decided to take charge of the cooking while he nursed her back to health. A leg of lamb was the order of the day, and, as Hardy removed it from the oven, his oven glove proved too small; it slipped and heat welded the roasting pan to the skin of his palm. Transfixed by agony, Hardy dropped the pan, but not before the scalding juices of the pan had spilled down his arm, blistering the skin. Nearly blinded by pain, he tried not to wail, as he didn't want to disturb Myrtle. He staggered to the kitchen door, preparing to let rip with a wail of pain once he was out of earshot. Instead, just as he reached the door, he slipped and fell, twisting his leg and bruising it. He had to be hospitalized.

A cheerful, final marriage to Lucille meant that Hardy could settle into domesticity properly, doing showcase cooking when his card-playing friends turned up looking for a game; a tumbler of Hardy's favorite tipple, bourbon; and some good home cooking. There was a small theater at Hardy's house that he and Stan called the Laurel and Hardy Fun Factory. Stan Laurel's house, named Fort Laurel as a defense against the legions of ex-wives who liked to hound him, was where they held their joint birthday parties. Laurel had a passion for barbecues, claiming that he was so good at these because so many women had roasted him.

Stan Laurel was eventually to find happiness with wife number four, Ida Kitaeva (bizarrely, the widow of the world's greatest concertina player). When they got married in 1946, the newspapers carried the brilliant headline, "WHERE IS STAN LAUREL?" He was actually driving around Arizona with Ida (she called him Stanchka). Laurel was so poor (as a result of former marriages) that he hadn't the cash to buy Ida a wedding ring, but he more than made up for this romantically by telling the press, "They say I'm not a millionaire anymore. They're crazy. I got Ida."

Friends of Laurel and Hardy noticed that the diminutive Laurel ate more than Hardy, but, having said that, one fellow member of the Granada Club, a haunt of

Hardy's in the 1940s, remembered that the meal Hardy loved ordering was a vast thirty-two-ounce steak, accompanied by no less than twenty-four new potatoes fried in bacon fat (oh, with a salad on the side).

While Lucille did the day-to-day cooking, Hardy loved to showcase his culinary genius. The Hardys had a luscious, well-stocked fruit garden. Hardy kept a very large "Victory Garden" during the war and bottled their plums (of which they had four varieties), peaches, figs, apricots, and citrus fruits. This was Hardy's idea of contentment, and once, when canning some tomatoes, he looked long and deep into Lucille's eyes and cooed, "Oh, you don't know how happy I am just to be doing this. It's the exact opposite of my life with Myrtle. With her it was stress, strain, stress, strain. Now here I am putting lids on a jar of tomatoes, and feeling just like a kid let out of school!"

His waffles, one friend claimed, were too good even for the gods, and, according to columnist Henry McLemore, he was "a great cook of turnip greens." If you were lucky, you got to sample his secret hamburger recipe and rummage through his divine caesar salad or his spaghetti and meatballs—the sauce for which took Hardy all day to prepare.

Spaghetti with Tomato Sauce (Oliver Hardy's recipe, as found in an ancient and wonderful tome called *Famous Stars Favorite Foods*)

INGREDIENTS

1 lb. minced beef
2 tbsp. vegetable oil
2 medium onions, finely chopped
½ tsp. cayenne pepper
1 garlic clove, crushed
1 can of tomato juice
Sea salt and freshly ground black pepper

METHOD

Shape the minced beef into small balls. In the vegetable oil, fry the onion and garlic until softened. Add the cayenne pepper and tomato juice. Season to taste with salt and pepper. Bring to boil. Pop the meatballs into the sauce and cook over a very low heat for between 2 and 2½ hours. Cook the spaghetti and add to the sauce. Serve immediately.

Hardy was pretty passionate about learning the complex skills needed to successfully manage a Victory Garden and taught himself how to hand plow; he was a dab hand at woodwork, too. Hardy's wartime effort, though, led to a piggy love affair. Originally, Hardy acquired some pigs with a view to fattening them for slaughter, but being the softie he was, he bonded with the pigs until they delighted to hear his voice and wiggled and grunted when he was near. One commodious sow, Geraldine, stalked Hardy, following him about the garden, and when Lucille was around, Geraldine nuzzled her affectionately, knocking her over into the beds. The pigs got bigger and bigger and bigger, but the Hardys couldn't face the idea of slaughtering them, so they gave them away instead. The same happened with the chickens and turkeys they raised. As a friend, you could end up with one of these living feathered gifts. Indeed, the chickens ended up being too fat to get out of the elaborate chicken coops Hardy had constructed for them.

Laurel and Hardy also had their fair experience of British cooking during the postwar years; on tour in Britain in 1946 they were—all unknowing—served horse steaks. Lucille insisted that the steaks were not beef, and eventually, when Stan Laurel got hold of this information, he suffered from retroactive nausea. There were other gristly surprises, too, like the deceptively familiar-sounding Hamburger a l'Américaine on the menu at the Hotel Métropolein Brussels. Beautiful, hand-painted Sèvres plates arrived at the table, each sporting an individual silver dome as a modest covering for what each of our diners hoped was a burger, a little bit of home. "What is this?!?" exclaimed Hardy when he lifted his dome to reveal a ghastly cone of raw mince, holding a raw egg in its cup. Steak tartare going by another name—it was sent back to the kitchens to be cooked. Stan and Laurel, though, were lucky to get anything to eat in postwar Europe. Hardy lost a pile of weight and told journalists that he'd have been happy to eat anything in Europe, but there "wasn't anything in sight."

Then there was the enormous haggis that an official offered them in Scotland, which had been kept for so long waiting for just such an occasion that it exploded from its own pent-up gases, throwing oatmeal and offal over Laurel and Hardy. "I picked haggis off me for a week," Hardy liked to groan. Harry Lauder entertained them at Sunday lunch by singing "A Wee Deoch an' Dorris" in his Glaswegian home, Lauder Ha'. Hardy went on to sing this regularly in the bath. By far one of the most exciting things that happened to Stan Laurel, though, when he hit those northern shores was his first taste of British fish and chips. Was this heaven? he wondered. What magic of batter and cod and deep fried, beef-dripping-coated potato chip could this be?

Nevertheless, when the boat they were on arrived in New York, Laurel and Hardy stepped off to celebrate their return. The Hardys decided to celebrate with a little room service: a genuine American meal of hamburgers, apple pie, and pints of milk.

Food still featured in the final days of Laurel and Hardy's relationship. When Laurel was ill, Hardy visited him and they shared lunch together—though history doesn't tell us what this last supper was. They laughed together when Hardy teased

Laurel, saying, “Well, here’s another fine mess you’ve gotten yourself into!” The men shared more than an ordinary bond, right down to the wordless, pantomime gestures they could use to “talk” to each other. When Hardy was diagnosed with aphasia, a cruel consequence of a stroke in which coherent speech, reading, and writing become impossible, the two friends met. Hardy could no longer talk and could only weep as he made a movement that Stan understood: “Look at me. Isn’t this appalling?” he’d gestured to Laurel. And that was the last they ever saw of each other.

CARY GRANT

A terrific insight into the world of Cary Grant as penned in the memoirs of his erstwhile lover, Maureen Donaldson, will put paid to romantic longings any one of us could harbor about Cary Grant. While she was working as a magazine journalist, Maureen managed to secure an interview with Grant—then aged sixty-nine. She felt pretty gooey about him, despite a forty-year age gap, and her eyes lit up when, over dinner and white wine at the French restaurant where they'd arranged to meet for the interview, he crooned, "I have something very important to ask you."

Maureen broke into a light, anticipatory sweat and said, gently, helpfully, "Yes?"

"Do you know where you can get some decent bangers and mash in this godforsaken city?" Grant asked.

Hmmm . . . bangers, for all you Americans, are sausages and were extremely hard to come by in the early 1970s. But it just so happened that Maureen, ever the intrepid journalist, knew of a British restaurant in Santa Monica that dished up bangers. "Will you take me there?" he whispered. Who could resist? Like fellow British actor Richard Burton, Grant always hankered with the longing of an exile for the nice, crisply brown British banger (though salmon cakes and sardines on toast were also in the top ten), but never a barbecued banger, as Grant thought (quite rightly) that charcoal-based cooking could contribute to cancer.

Maureen and Cary's conversation moved on next to fish and chips in California (a few years later, the first thing Grant did when he got to London was to get skate and chips from the fish and chip shop). The next day Maureen bit into turkey sandwiches on Cary's bed—but before that sounds raunchy, they ate them off white wicker trays while sitting on the bed and watching TV. Yes, like a relationship with Lady Di, if you were eating at home with Cary Grant, no matter how raunchy things might get later (fingers crossed), you'd find yourself eating dinner in front of the TV off a tray. And if you played your cards right, this might be in Cary's

TV Dinner Turkey Sandwiches

INGREDIENTS

Thinly sliced sourdough bread
Roast turkey
Smidgen of butter
Smidgen of mayonnaise
Freshly ground black pepper
Watercress

METHOD

Ask Doris Day or use your common sense.

Now cut the sandwiches into small diamond shapes (yes, that's right!). Switch on the TV, get a white wicker tray, and kick back.

bedroom. There were no plants there, though, as Cary thought they were robbing the air of oxygen. What arrived on your TV lap tray also tended to be what Cary liked best, and it wasn't usually sausages but, instead, specially prepared by his chef, Willie, the recipe scrawled down by Doris Day on a piece of paper during the filming of *That Touch of Mink*, came (drum roll) . . . turkey sandwiches.

In fact, a few weeks later it was Maureen's act of tidying away the dinner trays that convinced Grant of her worth: Grant watched open-mouthed as Maureen hopped off the bed and put the trays into the kitchen. "You are a dear, *dear* girl," he said. "Do you know how many women I've had in my life who have expected me to wait on *them*? I think they thought if Cary Grant waited on them, then they really were something." But it wasn't all cold food at chez Grant; a hot meal might well be lamb chops, followed by a toasted muffin topped with grilled Monterey Jack cheese and a slick of Worcestershire sauce. Dessert was often a babyish bowl of ice cream and wafers, never with raspberries, which he loathed—he reserved a passion for coconut, but Grant's sweet tooth was best pleased by chocolate-covered marzipan. Mmmm. Always, just before bedtime, Grant had a piece or two as a very special treat.

Bedtime Chocolate-Covered Marzipan

INGREDIENTS

- 10 oz. almonds, ground
- 5 oz. caster sugar
- 5 oz. finely sifted powdered sugar
- 1 tbsp. lemon juice
- ½ tbsp. orange juice
- 2 egg yolks
- 1½ tbsp. brandy
- ½ tsp. vanilla essence
- 4 drops almond essence
- 2 tsp. orange flower water
- 200 g. bittersweet chocolate

METHOD

To make the marzipan, sift the powdered sugar and caster sugar into a mixing bowl. Add the ground almonds. Now whisk the lemon juice, orange juice, and egg yolk together. Add the brandy, vanilla essence, almond essence, and orange flower water. Knead the marzipan paste until it becomes smooth. Using the palms of your hands, roll the marzipan into small Brazil-nut-sixed oblongs and place them on a baking tray. Place a Pyrex bowl over a pan of simmering water; don't let the water touch the base of the bowl, though. Break the chocolate into smallish pieces and melt these slowly in the bowl, stirring to help the chocolate melt easily. You need to temper the chocolate by lowering its temperature to 28°C and then gently reheating it to 31°C. Now dip the marzipan oblongs in the melted chocolate until they are fully coated and place on the baking tray to set.

The next step in the romance with Maureen was when he requested that, should she wake up to find him dead in bed next to her, she call his lawyer rather than an ambulance. So what does this suggest to you about the hero of *North by Northwest*, *Charade*, or *To Catch a Thief*?

Yes, he was a skinflint. So much so that he collected and used the plastic cups given out by Western Airlines. Ah, the glamor.

Grant collected discount coupons and hoarded the rubber bands that kept his morning newspapers rolled up. If his cook, housekeeper, or any of his secretaries wanted a soft drink in the course of the day, he insisted they bring it with them when they turned up for work in the morning.

MARLENE DIETRICH

As she sat in a drugstore in 1930, having newly arrived in America, cradling a wilting beef burger wrapped in some terrible, flabby bread, with a raincoat of wax paper around it, Marlene Dietrich vowed that the next burger to pass her lips would be made by her own fair hands. And she'd eat it when she wasn't facing rows of sanitary towels and deodorant. Typically, and this will be familiar to many a parent, Marlene's daughter, Maria, was bewitched by the waxy paper around great mysteries such as Egg Salad on White and thought that brown, fizzy bottles of Coca-Cola were nectar.

Americans, Dietrich decided, showing that irrepressible desire we all have to sum up other nationalities in one thought, "were not created to be cooks." At the kitchen stove was where Dietrich spent her first few weeks in America, cooking for her daughter, the governess, and Dietrich's assistant, saving them with whisk, sieve, and pan from the insipid darkness of American cookery. Her first move had been to write to her mother-in-law and ask her to send—as a matter of urgency—an Austrian cookbook.

To fill in the long, dull hours between shoots in Hollywood, Dietrich made her way systematically through the book, even mastering the art of Austrian baking, though good oven cooking, with its use of calculation, evaded Dietrich. Her daughter, Maria, watched Dietrich ranging restlessly about the kitchen wolfing down snippets of raw frankfurter, dill pickles, salami, and pickled herring, expecting her to die of food poisoning at any moment. Pop! In went some sauerkraut (interestingly, Marlene's own mother used sauerkraut to mothproof the family's Turkish carpets). Using her preferred method of open gas flame cooking, there was a world beyond wiener schnitzel, as she declared: "Ya lioublu tebya, I love you and good cooking!" The fame she gained in Hollywood as a great cook rivaled, she claimed, the legendary image she projected in film. "Cooking is an art. You must have a gift for it," she said grandly. "And, as with everything else, practice makes perfect. But talent comes first!" Only bores stuck to the exact measurements of a recipe, teaspoon by teaspoon. The best measuring cup, according to Dietrich, was the human eye. Eye, mouth, hand, and imagination were the ideal combination. And she hastily added, "If you find no pleasure in cooking, it's better to leave it alone."

Although she was drawn to Austrian and Swedish food, Dietrich's appetite was also for Russian food, which she learned to cook when Russians overran Berlin in the 1920s. Though she never managed to make the perfect piroshki, she reached a deep understanding of dill and always used it with fish. Both Austrian and Russian food were superior to overpraised French cooking, Dietrich proclaimed, and Austrian food was far better than German, which was the worst of all. In the end, Dietrich considered herself more of a country cook than an urban cook, and her pièce de résistance, no doubt showing the French how it's done, was her pot-au-feu, a deep, rich casserole, born of her "fondness for stews."

Pot-au-Feu

Pot-au-feu has the sort of magnificent simplicity that appealed to Marlene Dietrich. You should make pot-au-feu the day before you intend to eat it, as this allows you to remove the substantial quantity of beef fat that the stew renders. Pot-au-feu tends to be served in two sections: first, as a beef broth topped with garlicky croutons and grilled Gruyère. This is followed by the carved beef, served with scrumptious condiments such as pickles, Dijon mustard, and that most wicked of mayonnaises, aïoli.

INGREDIENTS

½ lb. beef bones (such as beef ribs)
4 split beef marrow bones
½ lb. chuck, blade portion
½ lb. brisket
½ lb. silverside
4 whole onions, peeled
4 cloves
10 black peppercorns
5 garlic cloves, chopped
5 leeks, chopped roughly
5 carrots, halved
½ bulb celeriac, chopped in two
3 parsnips, halved
½ turnip, chopped in two
3 potatoes
3 bay leaves
4 sprigs fresh thyme
Small bunch fresh parsley
Sea salt
Freshly ground black pepper

TO SERVE . . .

Homemade brown bread garlic croutons
4 tbsp. freshly grated Gruyère cheese

TO ACCOMPANY THE MEATS

Aïoli
Dijon mustard
Gherkins

METHOD

Place the beef bones in the base of a very large, deep saucepan. Put the meat on top. Peel the onions and skewer each with a dried clove. Add to the saucepan along with the black peppercorns. Cover this with water. Turn the heat up high and bring the pot-au-feu to boil. A surf of brownish scum will appear on the surface. Skim this off repeatedly until any scum appearing is white. Now reduce the heat until the water is just shivering. Allow this all to cook gently for 2½ hours.

Cool overnight and then remove the thick beef fat from the surface of the pot-au-feu. Remove the beef bones and add the marrow bones. Place the pot-au-feu back on the heat and bring to boil. Add the vegetables, cover, and cook for one more hour. While the pot-au-feu cooks, prepare the croutons, Gruyère, and aïoli. Heat the grill to a high heat. When the pot-au-feu broth is hot, ladle it into soup bowls, sprinkle these with garlic croutons, and put a thatch of Gruyère on top. Place under the grill, allow the Gruyère to melt and drip into the soup, and then serve.

Next, remove the meat, slice it, and lay it on a deep plate. Lay the marrow bones on a separate plate, ready for your guests to scoop out the delicious, buttery marrow. Surround the meat with the vegetables and pour over the remaining stock. Serve with aïoli, pickles, and Dijon mustard.

Croutons

INGREDIENTS

3 slices stale brown bread
3 garlic cloves
3 tbsp. olive oil
Sea salt

METHOD

Preheat the oven to 200°C. Break three stale slices of brown bread into bite-size pieces. Crush the garlic—with the sea salt to add grist—in a mortar and pestle. Now blend with the olive oil. Place the croutons on a baking tray covered with aluminium foil and brush them with the sticky, garlicky olive oil. Bake them in the oven for 5 to 10 minutes, checking to make sure they don't burn. You'll see they go to a hazelnut color and the garlic caramelizes. Remove from the oven and leave these to dry on some kitchen roll. The croutons are now ready to top the pot-au-feu soup.

Aïoli

Aïoli is a magnificent, roseate, and aromatic mayonnaise.

INGREDIENTS

5 garlic cloves
2 egg yolks
1 tsp. Dijon mustard
5 fl. oz. sunflower oil
5 fl. oz. extra virgin olive oil
½ tsp. sea salt
Juice of 1 lemon
½ tsp. saffron threads, soaked in 1 tsp. water
1 tsp. cayenne pepper
Freshly ground black pepper

METHOD

In a mortar and pestle, crush the garlic with the sea salt; reduce the garlic to a pulp. Add the Dijon mustard, blend, and then add the egg yolks. Now equip yourself with a handheld whisk. Drop by drop add the blended oils, whisking the oil into the eggy garlic ooze. As you whisk, a mayonnaise-like texture will form. Continue until you have used the last of the oil. At this point, you will have a scrumptiously gloopy, green-yellow garlic mayonnaise. Whisk in the lemon juice, saffron, cayenne, and pepper. The aïoli is now ready to accompany the pot-au-feu beef. Should you want the aïoli to thicken further, put it in the fridge for an hour.

This sort of bossy kindliness meant that Dietrich was given the job of taking care of Jean Gabin when he turned up in Hollywood; she was to speak French to him and find him French food. Of course, she couldn't resist cooking him French food—though at first, she jokingly claimed, he'd hide in the garden bushes to try to escape her, by the end he "clung to me like an orphan to his mother." Or, rather, like the passionate lover he became. Jean Renoir, the film director, liked to dine with the pair, too, and both Frenchmen were very partial to Marlene's stuffed cabbage—so much so in Renoir's case that he made himself a frequent guest, eating huge quantities of the cabbage and leaving almost immediately after. When John Dos Passos became ill working with Dietrich on the set of *The Devil Is a Woman* (Dos Passos wrote the screenplay), she rolled up her sleeves and made him chicken soup, which her daughter, Maria, decided to call Poet at Death's Door Chicken Soup.

Food and wooing went hand in hand for Dietrich; in the early days she kept herself skinny on a diet of tomato juice and soda biscuits but wooed her lover, the director Josef von Sternberg, with Hungarian goulash and egg noodles. Maria always remembered her mother making scrambled eggs for men who would, strangely, have turned up at the door fully clothed and coated up very early in the morning.

Renoir's Temptation: Stuffed Cabbage Rolls (Krautwickel)

INGREDIENTS

2 dry rolls
½ cup milk
1 tsp. caraway
1 head of white or Savoy cabbage
2 onions, finely chopped
2 garlic cloves
2 tbsp. butter
400 g. mixed ground beef and pork
½ tsp. each of paprika, thyme, and marjoram
4 tbsp. parsley, finely chopped
1 egg
4 rashers bacon, chopped
2 carrots, peeled and sliced
2 onions, roughly chopped
¼ pint beef stock
2 tbsp. soured cream
White cotton string
Sea salt and black pepper

METHOD

Crumble the bread rolls and soak them in milk. Bring a large pot of water to boil, and add the caraway seeds and salt to the water. Remove the central stalk of the cabbage and discard damaged leaves. Plunge the remaining cabbage leaves into the boiling water with the caraway seeds; stir to separate them. Allow them to cook for 10 minutes or until they soften. When you remove them from the cabbage water, reserve a ¼ pint of the water.

Melt 1 tablespoon of butter in a frying pan and sauté two finely chopped onions and the garlic until the onion is golden. Squeeze the excess milk out of the bread. In a large bowl, combine the bread, minced beef and pork, onion, garlic, parsley, and dried herbs. Add the egg, mix, and season with pepper and salt.

Renoir's Temptation: Stuffed Cabbage Rolls (Krautwickel) *(continued)*

Preheat the oven to 200°C. Butter an ovenproof dish.

Place the drained cabbage leaves on paper towels. Put one or two smaller leaves on top of the large leaf. Into the center of each cabbage leaf, place a tablespoon or two of the meat mixture. Fold the edge of the cabbage inward over the meat, and then roll the cabbage into a neat parcel shape. Tie each roll with a piece of string. Nestle the cabbage rolls side by side in the ovenproof dish.

Now heat 1 tablespoon of butter in a frying pan; add the bacon lardons and strips of the remaining cabbage. Fry the bacon until it is golden brown. Scatter the bacon and cabbage over the cabbage rolls; add the onion, carrots, and the cabbage and beef stock. Cover and braise in the oven for 45 minutes. When ready, remove the cabbage rolls from their braising liquid and strain the liquid. Melt a tablespoon of butter in a saucepan; add a tablespoon of flour and blend to form a roux. Remove from the heat and slowly add the cabbage/beef braising liquid. Return the pan to the heat and bring to boil, stirring constantly. Once it has thickened, take off the heat and add the 2 tablespoons of soured cream. Pour this over the cabbage rolls and serve with buttery mashed potatoes.

ALFRED HITCHCOCK

Where once there had been the sweaty tangle of sex, there would be food—this was the key to a successful marriage in Hitchcock's world. And the sight of his wife, Alma, carving a duck, while Hitch uncorked a good wine, looking for all the world like a grocer in his apron, was emblematic to friends of the couple's long and happy marriage. Hitch explained his views on food and marriage to one journalist as follows: "As they get on, after five or six years, in most married couples 'that old feeling' begins to dissipate. Food oftentimes takes the place of sex in a relationship." Thus spoke an expert. And Hitchcock's waistline is enough to tell you that he thought food was pretty damn sexy—even down to the slight flutter of earthy, intimate repulsion he felt for what he most desired. To ingest, he liked to confide over dessert, as he slowly swallowed, was an act he found disturbing, linking it to sex and nausea. "I hate to say it," he might continue, "but I always thought a good red wine put into one's mind the thought of menstrual blood." No doubt one was left toying with one's wine. His blue meal was intended to challenge the senses and stomachs of his guests; they were guinea pigs, and he was testing out how they'd respond to blue soup and blue dessert. How macabre was a blue peach? An ambition of his, he told Françoise Truffaut, was to "do an anthology on food, showing its arrival in the city, its distribution . . . the cooking . . . the various ways in which it's consumed. . . . And, gradually, the end of the film would show the sewers, and the garbage being dumped out into the ocean. . . . Thematically, the cycle would show what people do to good things. Your theme might almost be the rottenness of humanity." What fun to have for dinner.

Being Hitchcock, of course, he invites dark psychological readings of his relationship with eating and playfully, gloomily, beckons us to speculate. For instance, his earliest memory of fear *and* comfort was food related. When he was aged five or six, Hitchcock's parents tucked him into bed, checked he was sound asleep, and went off for a stroll in Hyde Park (about an hour away by tram from the family home). Little Hitch woke to find himself all alone and wandered from cavernous room to cavernous room, calling out for his parents. Eventually, sobbing, he discovered the kitchen and a plate of cold meat, which he began to eat, slice by slice, each mouthful helping to stop the tears. His favorite room in any of his homes was to remain the kitchen.

Hitchcock was to pass his formative years in close proximity to food. First, there was his father's fruit and vegetable shop in Leytonstone, full of the tantalizing aroma of bananas, the metallic tang of tomatoes, the heavier zing of citrus fruit, the grassy aroma of green peas (Hitchcock was to write in 1920 a comic newspaper piece on "The History of Pea Eating"). He watched golf balls of green walnuts being husked, leaking their skin-blackening juices. The shop provided the Hitchcocks with a staunchly loyal supply of good potatoes, fluffy and buttery tasting, leaving Alfred with a profound love of tubers. If you were at the Hitchcock table in Hollywood, you could count on potatoes for dinner, in many incarnations—gravy-soaked roasted potatoes, or baked, fried, sliced, chipped, and, when Hitch's teeth gave way, mashed.

Mr. Hitchcock Senior decided to move into the fish business, and he opened a fishmonger shop at 130 Salmon Lane in London's Limehouse district, the mongers using up extra stock by doubling as a fish and chip shop. Deep vats of bubbling lard, crisp chips, the battered fan of fresh, crisp skate, and the immense joys of salt and vinegar now filled Alfred's life. There was a downside, though, in that Alfred had to endure a ribbing at school not only for being chubby but now also for smelling of haddock.

Having been reared in this culture of food, Hitchcock adored it, but, ever dramatic, he claimed immense loyalties and passionate dislikes. Cheese and eggs were on the firing line, but worst of all was the white, jellified shudder of a poached egg on a plate. He paid homage to Dover sole by eating it often; he also loved steak, and he was to say in later life, "There will obviously be a lot of drama in the steak that is too rare." Young Hitchcock's mother sent him off to convent school with a tuck box containing, believe it or not, a cooked fillet of Dover sole and some bacon.

Eating signaled the happiest of moments when Hitchcock married Alma Reville, his assistant director, in 1926. Staying in the Palace Hotel in St. Moritz, the newlyweds, happy to be in each other's company, washed down buttery local pastries with cups of hot chocolate and ordered long lunches. Hitchcock insisted on slipping into very fancy ski pants, wriggling into ever tighter pants in later, more portly years, not in order to ski, but in order to give the *appearance* of having skied or being *about* to ski as he sat perched on the porch smoking cigars. Hitchcock, sampling Swiss wines, developed a permanent love of *Apfelwein* on his honeymoon (he'd later have this cider delivered to the United States) with plates of *bündnerfleisch*. Before this leaves a misleading impression that Hitchcock's tastes were European, we are speaking of cider and a plate of cured beef here—there is a solid Anglo-Saxon conservatism to Hitchcock's predilections. He would navigate any menu by a rack of lamb with roast parsnips, even if he were staggering from one of his lethal White Lady cocktails.

Hitchcock needed the security of the British-style table, and he went so far as to secure storage space for himself at the Los Angeles Smoking and Curing Company, where he stashed survivalist quantities of Dover sole and English bacon, replenished several times a month. Alma and Hitch had fish and meat flown in weekly from Britain, these delicacies enhancing the menus Alma liked to compose.

White Lady

INGREDIENTS

Tanqueray gin
Cointreau
2 lemons
The white of one egg
Ice

METHOD

Place cracked ice in a cocktail shaker and add 2 measures of Tanqueray gin, ½ measure of Cointreau, ½ measure of freshly squeezed lemon juice, and one whipped egg white.

Shake through the ice. Serve in a sugar-rimmed glass with a twist of lemon rind.

Grilled Dover Sole (for two)

INGREDIENTS

1 large Dover sole (or two smaller sole)
4 oz. butter
1 lemon, quartered

METHOD

Your fishmonger will gut and prepare the Dover sole for you, but it should come trimmed, with its head on and its skeletal frame intact. Dover sole has a thick, coarse, gray skin that is packed with Omega 3 oils, so it is a crime to remove this natural, delicious packaging. The top side of the sole is a brownish dun color and needs to be thoroughly descaled before you grill the sole. (The top side has a pair of round, mournful eyes looking up at you!) You can either ask your fishmonger to descale the fish or run a knife against the direction of the scales.

Heat the grill. Melt 3 ounces of the butter in a saucepan and have it ready with a brush to apply slicks of butter to the grilling fish. Put a little dollop of butter in the grill pan and melt. Brush the fish with butter, and place the fish bottom side up in the grill pan. Leave the fish under the grill for about 4 minutes and then turn. Immediately brush the (eyes-up) side with more of the butter and grill for a further 6 minutes, until the skin is bubbly, golden, and spangled with rivulets of butter.

Serve immediately, with new potatoes and string beans. Drizzle the juices from the grill pan over the fish and finish with a dash of sharp lemon juice.

Alma and Hitch fit together ideally—Alma was a spirited and clever cook, and Hitchcock took considerable pride in washing up by hand afterward; much later in life he refused to allow their daughter, Pat, to help him with the washing up until she had demonstrated (he watched, and she washed) that she could meet his standards. Hitchcock liked to follow a daily routine that was in Alma's words "conducted like a railroad timetable": coffee for breakfast was followed by lunch on set. At three o'clock each day, he phoned Alma to discuss and plan what they would have for dinner. That way there were no nasty surprises. Alma liked to be very hands-on with cooking, and she did much of it herself; she made a homemade pâté that won Hitchcock's heart.

Although Hitch claimed that his very favorite dinner was roast chicken and boiled ham, this was not framed by any particular experience, unlike the one perfect evening he shared with Alma. He and Alma chose a fine wine from their cellar and ate roast duck and string beans cooked by Alma, followed by Hitch washing up. This they both universally declared the "Best Evening Ever."

Best Evening Ever—Roast Duck Dinner

To be true to the Hitchcock modus operandus, eat this promptly at a mutually agreed time (determined by a three o'clock phone call).

INGREDIENTS

A 4 lb. duck
Fresh thyme
Sea salt
Black pepper

METHOD

Preheat the oven to 230°C. Wash the duck, dry, and then, using a sharp fork, prick the duck skin all over—or score the skin lightly, but you don't want to penetrate the skin so deeply that the flesh is bared. This will allow all the delicious duck fat to render down and you can, then, pour it off and keep this dripping for the potatoes you'll roast to serve with the duck. Season the duck, inside and out, with sea salt and black pepper. Place a small bundle of fresh thyme in the duck's cavity. Take care to sprinkle salt liberally onto the skin, as this will help to ensure crunchiness. Place the duck on a rack in a roasting tray and put this in the oven. Allow the duck to cook for 1 hour and 50 minutes; after this, rest the duck for 20 minutes.

Although Hitchcock wasn't to move more permanently to America until 1939, he had still hand picked many favorite eating haunts before then. In New York, he loved the former speakeasy, the 21 Club, with its surreal row of iron-faced dwarf mannequin jockeys outside, and it was there, in August 1937, that he lunched with journalist H. Allen Smith. The two delicious American food greats, Hitchcock explained, leaning back in his chair, were steak and ice cream. What could be better than vanilla ice cream with a lick of brandy for breakfast, which he'd enjoyed that very morning? Hitchcock polished off his steak, set down his knife and fork, and called for ice cream. Then, before the incredulous journalist, Hitchcock ordered another steak. Then another ice cream. He called the waiter . . . was he going to

Roasted Potatoes

INGREDIENTS

4 large floury potatoes
3 tbsp. all-purpose flour
Sea salt
Black pepper
6 tbsp. olive oil
Duck fat, poured off the roasting duck

METHOD

Peel the potatoes, quarter them, and parboil for 10 minutes. Drain and allow them to cool. Into a plastic freezer bag, pour 3 tablespoons of all-purpose flour. Salt and pepper the flour. When the potatoes are cooled, pop them into the bag and shake—this floury crust will create the lovely honey-gold crisp mantle that every superior roasted potato has. After the duck has been cooking for about 1 hour and 15 minutes, place the olive oil for the roasting potatoes into a roasting tray and heat in the oven beneath the duck. The oil needs to get fully hot, so that when you test a shard of potato in it, the oil bubbles. When it does so, it is ready for the floured potato pieces. Add them to the oil, shaking off any excess flour, and return the tray to the oven. When fat comes off the duck, drizzle some of it into the potato tray. The roasted potatoes will take about an hour in the oven at 230°C—don't forget to turn them after about 30 minutes and keep them cooking right up until you intend to serve the rested duck.

Duck Gravy

INGREDIENTS

½ pint duck stock (or chicken stock)
1 glass port
1 tbsp. Seville orange marmalade

METHOD

When the duck is resting, drain most of the remaining fat from the roasting tray, taking care to reserve the delicious, caramelized duck juices and about a tablespoon of fat in the tin. Warm the roasting tin, scraping these juices from the base. Now pour in the stock and port, stir vigorously, and then transfer all of this to a smaller pan. Increase the temperature to allow this gravy to reduce by a third. Finally, add the port and orange marmalade. Season to taste and serve with green beans.

ask for his bill? No, you guessed it. Another steak . . . and an ice cream . . . oh, and a cup of tea. Dabbing his lips, he told Smith, "There are two kinds of eating—eating to sustain and eating for pleasure. I eat for pleasure." Hitchcock wasn't averse to secret eating, either; it was conducted like an extramarital affair, in his private rooms. Ice cream was often taken late at night, between the sheets perhaps—two-in-a-bed vanilla.

Vanilla Ice Cream (best eaten between the sheets)

INGREDIENTS

250 ml. organic full-fat milk
½ tsp. Maldon salt flakes
6 egg yolks—keep the whites to make meringues
150 g. vanilla caster sugar (keep a pot of caster sugar in your cupboard with at least 2 long black vanilla pods embedded in it)
500 ml. organic double cream
1 vanilla bean, split lengthwise

METHOD

In a medium-sized saucepan, gently warm the milk, *half* of the cream, salt flakes, and vanilla sugar. Plop in the vanilla bean (before putting in the vanilla bean, you could tease out its sticky, black seeds with a cocktail stick, allowing these to float through the creamy milk). When the milky mix is warm and the vanilla sugar has dissolved, remove the pan from the heat, cover it, and allow it to rest for about 30 minutes.

When the 30 minutes is up, place the egg yolks in a largish bowl and whisk them up. Gently and carefully add the warm, milky cream to the egg yolks—keep whisking—and then pour all of this back into the pan. Over a medium to low heat, begin to warm this mixture—use a wooden spoon or spatula because this mixture, which is in essence custard, will be ready when it coats the wood of the spatula or spoon. Never, ever, stop stirring or the mixture will transform into terrible scrambled eggs rather than thickening into custard. When it has custardized, then it is time to use the remaining *half* of the cream. Pool the cold cream into a largish bowl and pour the custard over the cream, stirring it in. Now you must cool this deliciousness for about 30 minutes. Use the freezer—but don't wander off and forget about it. Set a timer. It is ready for the next stage when it is cold. If you don't have a freezer, then you will have to leave it in the fridge for about an hour.

When it is cooled, remove the vanilla bean and start to churn the ice cream following the ice cream maker's directions.

By about 1939, Hitchcock had settled for the most part in America, and he set down his eating "roots" quickly. Their cook had fled, but Alma had memorized Hitchcock's favorite recipes, and all she needed, as Hitchcock put it, was an understudy, whom they found in an excellent German cook, Chrystal. Alma's menus make her mastery clear, listing Chrystal as her "extra help." They had moved into 10957 Bellagio Road in 1942 but then bought another property at Santa Cruz, and they transported their cook there from Bellagio Road. Chrystal sat in the rear of the car scribbling out menus while Alma drove.

An honor paid to anyone working with Hitchcock was to have dinner in the inner sanctum of Hitchcock's kitchen, seated at the kitchen table. When Prince Rainier and Grace Kelly turned up for dinner, they found themselves at just this spot. Hitch tippled on a predinner gin and orange and might make some of his wonderful own-recipe champagne punch, or share a brandy after dinner with his guests (watch how many of his films feature brandy drinking). He also had a wine cellar and considered himself to be a bit of a connoisseur.

Hitchcock could be pretty picky with his dinner guests, too. He didn't like Paul Newman's rough ways—Newman tossed his jacket over the back of his chair, turned down choice wine from the cellar, ambled across to Hitch's enormous walk-in fridge, got himself a beer, and then drank beer out of a can! But Hitch did like Ingrid Bergman and Cary Grant, and he loved Clark Gable and Carol Lombard (Gable was starring in *Gone with the Wind* at the time and Lombard was, tragically, soon to die). The Hitchcocks rented a house in Los Angeles for a period of time from Lombard ("The Farm" at 609 Saint Cloud Road) and really appreciated her story about when she found a shrunken head in Gable's possession. Completely spooked, she chucked it into a ravine; then, feeling pangs of guilt, she retrieved the head and buried it in the back garden of the house Hitchcock was renting. She couldn't quite remember where she'd buried it, though, and Hitchcock desperately wanted to hold a dinner party in which dinner guests were given shovels to exhume the skull.

If he were about some kitchen business himself at Bellagio Road, Hitchcock draped a large, white apron about himself, as if he indeed might also be a course. Predinner, Hitchcock secretly hit the bottle, wildly swallowing a tumbler's worth of Cointreau, keeping out of sight from Alma. Disarmingly, despite this secrecy, Hitchcock was always happy to attribute weight gain to booze rather than food, enjoying the wicked drama of claiming that he'd piled on the pounds since he "took to drink."

His food generosity could be staggering and whimsical. He sent one friend four hundred kippers. When Gregory Peck went to dinner with Hitchcock and Alma at Chasen's, Hitchcock was very interested in getting just the right match between the food and the wine. Soon after, he sent Peck a case of twelve assorted bottles of vintage wine, all individually labeled by him with handwritten recommendations of what to eat with each bottle—this is best with roast beef, said one; this with fillet of sole, said another. And there was his famous blue dinner: "It seemed such a pretty color, I couldn't understand why hardly anything we eat is blue," mused Hitchcock, and he served up a dinner at Bellagio Road with blue martinis, blue soup, blue steak, blue chicken, blue trout, blue potatoes, and blue ice cream. Jimmy Stewart showed up for this and was less keen on coming to dine ever afterward. In March 1953, on the brink of filming *The Wrong Man*, Hitchcock held a "Ghost-Haunted House Party" in a house he was renting on New York's East Eightieth Street, for which he sent out tombstone-shaped invitations with a "carte de mort" listing such lovely schoolboy nonsense as "morbid morgue mussels, suicide suzettes, consommé de cobra, vicious-soise, home-fried homicide, ragout of reptile, charcoal-broiled same-witch-legs, corpse croquettes, barbecued banshee, opium omelette, stuffed stiffs with hard sauce, gibbeted giblets, mobster thermidor, tormented tortillas, ghoulish goulash, blind bats en casserole, python pudding, fresh-cut lady fingers, Bloody Marys, Dead Grand-dad, formaldehyde frappe."

Beyond the Hitchcock kitchen in Bellagio Road, one of Alfred's great discoveries was Chasen's restaurant in Beverly Hills, where, when not on one of his parsimonious diets, he and Alma turned up on Thursday nights. They always ordered a steak fillet for their dog, which waited patiently for them in their car with the chauffeur for company. Chasen's was not so much Hitchcock's New World foodwise, as he tended to simply elaborate on old favorites there—a smidgen of lobster soufflé, fresh Dover sole, a couple of steaks. True to form, unable to tolerate alcohol well, Hitchcock nodded off during Chasen's dinner parties (he was also famed for snoozing after lunch every day—even in the middle of directing). When he had chosen Tippi Hedren for her part in *The Birds*, she turned up for dinner with the Hitchcocks at Chasen's, only to find at her place a box containing a pin—three seagulls—wrought in gold. Guess who had the part of Melanie?

LIZ TAYLOR

Reading Elizabeth Taylor's food biography is enough to give you heartburn. More than her relationship with her many husbands or alcohol or even Richard Burton, food was the great, unspoken, unacknowledged love of her life. In fact, so much did Elizabeth love her food that she inspired Montgomery Clift to exclaim, "Honey, you're the broadest broad I ever saw!"

Food was always there in the sidelines, but, in the beginning, Taylor was giving it rather than receiving it. A child star when filming the *Courage of Lassie*, Liz just so happened to have a fleet of chipmunks as her pets, all of which she fed chocolate ice cream sundaes. I wouldn't want to bet on the life expectancy of those chipmunks. Fellow child star Roddy McDowall was chummy with Taylor, as was future husband-to-a-Kennedy Peter Lawford. Roddy McDowall's mother made the best creamed spinach in the world, and sixteen-year-old Elizabeth loved having brunch at their home. Lawford cruelly and jestingly referred to her large breasts as her "pods." Because she had a crush on him at the time, and chubby legs, teenager Taylor went to great lengths to shape up, abandoning the peppermint milkshakes she loved and forsaking the counter of Will Wright's ice cream parlor and the dazzling hot fudge sundaes they served there (creamy inches of chilly vanilla ice cream, so cold they could make your head ache, melting under folds of hot fudge). Liz tried to stick to club soda and mint tea. It was hell, and her legs remained just as chubby as ever. Around this time, the eccentric millionaire Howard Hughes decided he was going to marry Taylor—he had clocked forty-four years, she was sixteen. When he happened on her sunbathing by the pool, he filled an attaché case with jewels and diamonds. Dragging the case up behind Taylor, he unclasped it and emptied it on her stomach. "Get dressed!" he bellowed. "We're getting married." It didn't work. Good old Liz.

Two years later and Taylor, aged eighteen now, had, unfortunately, fallen for Nicky Hilton, the son of the hotel magnate Conrad Hilton. The marriage, despite truckloads of rose petals, a five-tier wedding cake, three thousand witnesses, and a wedding dress provided by Metro Goldwyn Mayer, was doomed to end very quickly in violence and miscarriage. When Elizabeth expressed reservations about marrying her heroin-addicted, violent, and spoiled fiancé to Conrad Hilton Sr.'s administrative assistant Olive Wakeman, Olive's reply was to have a tasteful selection of cookery books delivered to Taylor, accompanied by a helpful note: "The way to a man's heart is through his stomach." And, indeed, Nicky was to claim that it was Taylor's inability to cook that drove him over the edge, into violence, in their dismal marriage. Family suppers with the Hiltons should have been warning enough for Taylor; they ate in silence off gold plates while Conrad Sr. belched in slow, regular waves, without apology. Nicky liked to chew on a brick of gum constantly, removing it at the table and storing it in his napkin, only to return it to his mouth after dinner.

After tying the knot, the groom slipped off on a drinking spree; there was no wedding night for Elizabeth. Similarly, when they headed off for their honeymoon on the *Queen Mary*, the night before they'd eaten a cake in the shape of the boat, complete with miniature portholes at each of which glinted a tiny electric light. Later Nicky set off on a drinking spree and lost a hundred thousand dollars on the gambling tables. Elizabeth, meanwhile, dined with the duke and duchess of Windsor. Furious at his losses, fuddled with drink, when Nicky came across Elizabeth in the shower, he punched her in the stomach.

Happier times lay ahead for Elizabeth. Following their split she found solace in joining the Fox and Lox brunch club that ran on Sunday mornings (Tony Curtis was also a member), and Taylor took her turn to make brunch from her home, marvellously making so much smoke and flame when she was frying her French toast that the Los Angeles Fire Department had to come to the rescue.

Marriage to Michael Wilding was a far more equitable affair. As if Taylor was trying to find the ideal counterbalance to Nicky's terrible, selfish immaturity, she married Wilding, twenty years her senior. True to herself, she came out with the great line, "This, to me, is the beginning of a happy ending," only for the marriage to dissolve five years later. Their wedding was very different: a quick, modest wedding in London, preceded by a dinner of duck and lobster in the honeymoon suite of the Berkeley Hotel. But note Liz's food passions beginning to burgeon. At midnight after the wedding the happy couple dined on pea soup, eggs and bacon, chocolate mousse, all washed down with lashings of champagne. Hollywood wackiness went down well with Liz, in a way it never did with Wilding. Columnist Donald Zec recalled going to the Wilding mansion in Beverly Hills for dinner. After tossing back champagne, they decided to eat dinner. To do so, though, Elizabeth had to find the secret switch under the carpet that activated the glass doors leading into the dining room. The food lay resplendent, dimpled, and tasty on the table beyond the impassive glass doors as the three of them hopped, stamped, and slid their way over the carpet, hoping to hit on the concealed switch, silent, half-drunk, and hungry.

Pregnancy gave Elizabeth a great eating opportunity—as she said, "My taste buds get in an uproar, and I get a lusty, sensual thing out of eating"—and the entry of children into her life gave her the opportunity to take in any number of pets (remember the chipmunks). Unfortunately, while Wilding may have enjoyed gazing affectionately at a distant dog or cat, nothing had prepared him for Liz Taylor's menagerie of ducks—not house trained—her pack of dogs, and array of cats.

While pets endeared her to the public, they put an extra strain on her marriage. She remembered once hearing a bus pull into her drive in Beverly Hills and the bus driver shouting at his cargo of tourists, "Up there is Liz's bedroom and over there behind the wall is the gravestone of her dog." Before long there were cockroaches in the kitchen of the Wildings' home, and it stank like an animal shelter. Elizabeth was rumored to be involved in a string of affairs with Rock Hudson, James Dean, and then Victor Mature, whom Wilding knew all about and who was leaned on to apologize to Wilding, which he did, to Wilding's surprise, while bending his knees, as if about to kneel.

Liz was having too much fun by half with the likes of Rock Hudson on the Texas film set of *Giant.* James Dean claimed that Rock Hudson only turned his attentions to Elizabeth when Dean turned him down. The heat and dust of Texas in August and through September were stifling, and Taylor, Dean, and Hudson drank like fish, staying up all night boozing during the shooting of the film, and Elizabeth vomited between takes. "How we survived I'll never know," Taylor said gaily. Many hangovers may all have been down to Hudson and Taylor's magical cocktail creation: the Chocolate Martini. Taylor claimed this was the best drink she ever had, quite a staggering claim, given her time in the Betty Ford Clinic, and definitely one to be imbibed by all serious drinkers.

The *Giant* Chocolate Martini

INGREDIENTS

Vodka
Kahlua
Hershey chocolate syrup

METHOD

Take 1 measure of vodka, a dash of Hershey's (or other brand) chocolate syrup, and 1 measure of kahlua.

Shake together through ice. Serve.

Husband number three, Mike Todd, was a wheeze: like Montgomery Clift and Richard Burton, Mike liked to poke fun at Elizabeth. On an early date, Mike told friends that he was bringing along a girl. When he and Taylor arrived at Mike's friend's house for dinner, he delighted in telling the assembled company that Taylor's name was Tondelayo Schwartzkopf. The hostess stared, bewitched, at Taylor. Eventually, she said, "I have to tell you something; you look a lot like Elizabeth Taylor, but you're heavier." Mike Todd wheezed with laughter and slapped Taylor on the bottom. "I told you you were getting fat!" he roared. They must have been a challenging couple to have over for dinner. They attacked each other violently at the dinner table or sexually mauled each other. At one Manhattan luncheon, with fellow diners present and buttering their rolls, Todd reached over the table and groped Elizabeth's breast. She didn't bat an eye. Indeed, Todd liked to gift to people tape recordings of him and Elizabeth making love; he gave one to Lord Beaverbrook to, as Beaverbrook put it, "warm him up." Todd even had a double bed installed in his private plane.

Taylor was filming *Cat on a Hot Tin Roof* in 1958 when Mike Todd died in a flying accident on the misnamed *Lucky Liz* private plane. Her fellow actors watched in agony as Liz mourned and starved herself. Weight began to drop off her; she was vanishing. Richard Brooks, the director of the film, hatched a brilliant plot to get her to eat again. Cast your mind back to the scene in *Cat on a Hot Tin Roof* when Big Daddy is greeted by a huge, festive spread of buttered corn on the cob and baked Virginia ham on his return from the hospital. As the character Maggie, Taylor had little to do in this scene; she had little dialogue but still had to appear occupied as a character. The filming began, and Brooks shouted, "Eat, Elizabeth, eat the food on the table." Gingerly, Taylor picked up some chicken and tried to eat it, her throat constricting. But Brooks wanted to shoot the scene again and again, exploring fresh angles and perspectives, and each time—during a long, long day—he'd bellow, "Eat, Elizabeth, eat the food on the table." By the end of the day, Elizabeth's appetite had returned and, when the cameras were switched off, all the crew applauded and cheered.

Elizabeth's appetite returned with a vengeance. By the time she was married to husband number four, Eddie Fisher, she was reaching entirely new heights of food decadence, as if to compensate for the listless core at the heart of her marriage. According to her biographer Donald Spoto, Taylor sat eating at the center of a whirlwind of food deliveries: there was Chasen's chili to be ordered (it must have been good—Clark Gable asked for it on his death bed); the best, juiciest steaks had to hurry their way from Chicago; pasta in several forms arrived from Italy; crabs were plucked from the Florida coast and taken to her table; even New Orleans dished up its shrimp creole. Her appetite was bottomless. The Fisher-Taylor marriage was immediately stuffed with children, pets, ducks, suitcases, assistants, and assistants-to-assistants. Eddie transformed from a singer into Taylor's personal assistant—one of his many roles was to keep track of the sixty-plus pieces of luggage Taylor needed on any trip. Cattily, Truman Capote, a friend of Taylor's, began to call Fisher "The Busboy," and the press referred to him as Mrs. Elizabeth Taylor. Everything about his kindliness made Taylor want to rebel against him.

Taylor fell ill with pneumonia in 1961, just before her involvement in the making of *Cleopatra* and what was to be the end of her marriage to Fisher. This led to a tracheotomy during which Taylor had a silver-dollar-shaped disk inserted into her throat; she was a patient in the London clinic and drank champagne secretly in the hospital with Truman Capote. They repeated this game a couple of times, hiding

Cat on a Hot Tin Roof Baked Virginia Ham

INGREDIENTS

5 lb. joint of Virginia ham
4 onions, quartered
3 carrots, halved
2 celery sticks, quartered lengthwise
4 bay leaves
1 large bunch parsley
3 sprigs thyme
3 mace blades
8 peppercorns

FOR THE GLAZE . . .

5 tbsp. maple syrup
4 tbsp. dark Muscovado sugar
2 tbsp. mustard
3 oranges, sliced
Toothpicks
A handful of cloves

METHOD

Soak the Virginia ham in cold water for four hours; drain. Now put the ham in a large, deep pot. Add fresh water, bring to boil, and then remove any scum from the surface. Now add the onions, carrots, celery, bay leaves, parsley, thyme, mace, and peppercorns. Cover and allow to simmer gently for about two hours.

Preheat the oven to 180°C. Now remove the ham from its bouillon. Put on a flat surface and, using a very sharp knife, score the ham fat into diamond-like sections. Place the ham in a large roasting dish. Brush it with the maple syrup. In a small bowl, combine the Muscovado sugar with the mustard. Brush this over the ham. Pierce the ham with the cloves. Now arrange the orange slices over the surface of the lamb and secure the slices of orange with the halved toothpicks. Bake for 30 minutes in the oven. Serve—but make sure you remove the toothpicks first!

the empty champagne bottle under the hospital bed. But Capote said, "She played a trick on me and yanked the plug out of her throat, spurting champagne all over the room. I thought I was going to pass out. I probably turned a few shades of green as I burrowed into my coat."

All too soon, after a pneumonia recovery diet of waffles and kippers, Taylor was back on her feet, ready to step into the lights with Richard Burton on the set of *Cleopatra*.

Taylor and Burton had first met in the 1950s, and it was a bland, vaguely negative experience, with each noting the other's shortcomings. It was a balmy Sunday brunch cocktail party, and a pregnant Elizabeth Taylor (she was married to Michael Wilding at the time) quietly observed the brunch and became aware of an annoying figure center stage, a real show-off, she concluded, who loved the sound of his own voice, whether it was booming, falsetto, or whispering—Richard Burton. He also had noticed her, and the qualities in her that were to hypnotize him—such as a deep, kittenish luxuriousness—were momentarily misjudged: she's so dark, he laughed with a friend, she probably shaves!

With gloomy and beautiful irony, it took until they worked together in 1963 on the doom-laden, tragic, and magnificent *Cleopatra* before each would get the other's full attention. Throughout the filming in Rome, though, it was Elizabeth's breasts that first got everyone's attention. "Just because Elizabeth's tits are bigger than mine," fumed Rex Harrison (he was playing Caesar), "doesn't entitle her to be driven around in a mile-long limo, while you restrict me to the backseat of a two-bit Fiat sedan." A crew member watched in awe as the costume designer struggled to zip Taylor's breasts into Cleopatra's corsets: "Her previously engorged breasts now looked like twin icebergs, large enough to sink the *Titanic*." It is almost as if she was ripening in preparation for the amatory onslaught of Richard Burton. "She is a wildly exciting lover-mistress," Burton confided in his diary. "She is beautiful beyond the dreams of pornography . . . Elizabeth is an eternal one-night stand." Burton adored Taylor's excesses, her breasts being one of them. "How I love arguing with her, especially when she's in the nude. Flailing around so vigorously, she positively bruises herself. Just look at those magnificent breasts!"

For these two, of course, any romantic entanglement would have to be seen through the lens of a cocktail shaker, and Zeffirelli recollected, "If the refrigerator in her dressing room wasn't stocked with her favourite goodies when she arrived for work, all hell broke loose." For Taylor, the road to love was paved with Vodka Collins, with vodka martini to follow; for Burton, it was straight Scotch. From that point onward, they developed their own private drinking rituals, like lovers, like alcoholics—from the salty dogs of gin and grapefruit juice they drank on their yacht, the *Kalizma*, to the Jack Daniels and vodkas of their sad and limping reconciliations.

Watching Elizabeth eat was Burton's passion: he would nudge someone in the ribs, "Look at this beautiful Jewess eating pork!" and there was Elizabeth, chewing.

Salty Dogs

INGREDIENTS

Juice of 4 grapefruits, yellow or pink
2 oz. gin
2 oz. vodka
Sea salt
Ice

METHOD

Wet the rims of two highball glasses and dip them in the sea salt. In a small shaker, combine the grapefruit juice, gin, and vodka. Add ice to the glasses and pour the zinging, salty dog cocktail into each glass.

"Over full of calories maybe, but still a total revelation!" This was the woman, after all, whom the Vatican denounced for "erotic vagrancy," and her sensuality also came by the plateful. When Taylor and Burton were filming *Taming of the Shrew* in Rome with Franco Zeffirelli, they enjoyed dining in the restaurant La Strega in the village of Practica de Mare, and, on one occasion, Taylor ordered for the entire table enormous potions of spaghetti with whiskey sauce, potatoes with coddled eggs, and crepes with lemon cream.

Spaghetti with Whiskey Sauce

INGREDIENTS

2 tbsp. butter
8 shallots, minced
1 tbsp. all-purpose flour
2 tbsp. Dijon mustard
½ cup whiskey
½ pint double cream
¼ pint stock, preferably veal
1 lb. spaghetti
Sea salt
Freshly ground black pepper

METHOD

Half fill a deep pan with water and salt and bring to boil. Add the spaghetti and cook for 10 to 12 minutes, until it is al dente.

Meanwhile, in a frying pan, melt 1 tablespoon of butter. Add the shallots, a pinch of sea salt and black pepper, and sauté until the shallots are softened and pale golden. Add the all-purpose flour and mix thoroughly. Turn up the heat and add the whiskey. Stir rapidly, and allow to cook for 5 minutes, until it is reduced by half. Add the Dijon mustard, double cream, and the stock. Cook rapidly for 5 minutes, allowing the sauce to further reduce.

Next, drain your spaghetti. Warm a large, wide spaghetti tray with hot water and then drain and dry. Dot the plate with small fragments of butter, and empty your drained spaghetti on top. Toss, glossing the spaghetti with butter. Pour the whiskey sauce over the spaghetti and serve.

Potatoes with Coddled Eggs

INGREDIENTS

½ cup milk
1 bay leaf
1 blade of mace
4 black peppercorns
14 oz. boiled floury potatoes
2 tbsp. butter
3 shallots, minced
1 tbsp. chives, minced
1 tbsp. parsley, minced
1 tsp. fresh thyme leaves
Sea salt
Freshly ground black pepper
6 eggs
6 tbsp. double cream
4 oz. Parmesan cheese, finely grated

Potatoes with Coddled Eggs *(continued)*

METHOD

Warm the milk, bay leaf, black peppercorns and mace blade in a small saucepan. Allow the bay leaf and mace to infuse the milk. Switch off before it boils and allow it to stand, cooling, for 30 minutes. Preheat the oven to 180°C. In a large bowl, combine the floury, dry potatoes with milk, butter, sea salt, black pepper, shallots, chives, thyme, and parsley and mash until smooth. Butter 6 largish ramekins. Divide the mashed potato between the buttered ramekins.

Next, crack each egg over its ramekin, taking great care not to break the yolk. Pour a tablespoon of double cream over the top of each egg and then top each with a thatch of Parmesan (about 1 tablespoon per ramekin) and dust with black pepper. Place the ramekins in a deep baking tray and pour hot water into the tray to reach about halfway up the ramekins. Place the tray in the 180°C oven and cook for about 17 minutes until yolks are set soft but not stiff. Remove from the oven and serve.

When they married in 1964, in a Montréal "hotel room," as one paper reported it (before you are tempted to attribute anything seedy to this, it was the Ritz-Carlton), Taylor was thirty-two and already on her fifth wedding in four years (sensitive to public opinion, she donned a yellow wedding dress), and Burton was thirty-eight, still sweating guilt over his divorce from Sybil Williams. Not the most auspicious of beginnings, the nervousness of their guests was compounded by Burton roaring after a forty-five-minute wait for Taylor, "Isn't that fat little tart here yet? I swear she'll be late for the last bloody judgment!"

Burton always had simpler tastes than Taylor. The food he was raised on in a Welsh mining community—faggots—tasty, macho nuggets of minced offal bound in a wrapping paper of pig's cawl and served with gravy, seaweed-enriched laver bread (which he called "collier's caviar"), potatoes, and Welsh cawl—remained his preference in adulthood.

Burton's favorite meal remained forever sausages and mash, as Susannah York discovered many years later when the Burtons came to call on her. They turned up, in the rain, in a lovely and enormous Rolls Royce—Taylor carted out four bottles of Jack Daniels whiskey, some serious drinking was in store. When York asked what Burton most desired for dinner, he replied without hesitation, "Sausages and mash."

Rather like the fabulous and doomed marriage of American writer F. Scott Fitzgerald and Zelda Fitzgerald, the marriage of Taylor and Burton went on to be full of gluttonous feasts and special cocktails, and through those luncheons you can also see the decline of a marriage. Novelist Edna O'Brien watched in awe as the Burtons lunched by her table at London's White Elephant Club. Taylor's

Crepes with Lemon Cream

INGREDIENTS

FOR THE CREPES . . .

10 fl. oz. milk
4 oz. all-purpose flour
Pinch of sea salt
2 eggs
3 tbsp. butter

FOR THE LEMON CREAM . . .

Juice of 3 lemons, plus the grated zest of 2 of the lemons
3 egg yolks
2 eggs
2½ oz. vanilla caster sugar
2 tbsp. butter

TO GARNISH . . .

Fresh green mint leaves
Powdered sugar

METHOD

Sift the flour and salt into a large bowl. Make a well in the center. Cream the eggs and add them to the well in the center of the flour, whisking them in. Now add the milk and whisk until smooth. In a frying pan, brown 1 tablespoon of butter and add to the mixture. Leave to rest for 15 minutes.

Meanwhile, in a bowl, whisk together the 3 egg yolks, 2 eggs, sugar, grated lemon zest, and lemon juice. Transfer this into a saucepan. Now place over a low heat and add the butter, cut into small chunks, to the mixture, stirring constantly. Now switch to your whisk and whisk gently, over a medium heat, until the lemon cream becomes thick and creamy. Remove from the saucepan and allow it to cool.

In a wide frying pan, heat the remaining 2 tablespoons of butter. Pour the butter back off the pan, reserving it in a little cup to add to the frying pan with each new crepe. Cook each crepe individually; allow about 1 teaspoon of lemon cream to one crepe.

To serve, rumple each thin, warm, honey-colored crepe on a plate, and smear with lemon cream, allowing it to pool in the folds. Garnish with torn mint leaves—these really are delicious in combination with the lemon—and sift a little powdered sugar on top.

plate was awash with spaghetti, pools of butter sauce forming, and, as she reached across to the bread basket for a roll to mop up the remaining butter sauce, Burton rapped her knuckles. "Aren't you fat enough already?" he scolded. And O'Brien watched Taylor's face—crimson, mute, and shamed. A relationship that began for Burton with adoration of his food goddess and her appetites had degenerated into an alcohol-fueled loathing of her excesses.

Taylor had her own moments of revenge, though—if she was a glutton, he wouldn't shut up, never losing an opportunity to posture intellectually, dragging out his recitation inventory of the literary canon whenever the dinner table presented an opportunity—Shakespeare, Burns, T. S. Eliot, and Dylan Thomas loudly intoned—and other diners couldn't talk, only listen. Elizabeth's comeback? It was short, succinct, and intended to humiliate Burton. Sensing perhaps her exasperation at his egotism, he demanded that she recite and she came out with a "poem by my father."

"What'll you have?" the waiter said, as he stood there picking his nose.

"Hard-boiled eggs," she said. "You can't put your fingers in those."

And yet, despite all the boozy rows over spaghetti, after his affairs—one of which was memorably with a Miss Pepsi of Butte County—and after their marriages to other people, they could never separate. It would take death to do that. As Richard's brother put it, "Part of Richard was always with Elizabeth. . . . He used to hold hands with her under the table when Sally [Burton's final wife] and Victor Luna [Taylor's fiancé] were there." Or, as Taylor put it more prosaically, they were stuck together like chicken feathers and tar.

After the emotional and physical chaos of the Burton years, marriage to quiet Republican Virginian senator John Warner must have had considerable appeal. It certainly started out well. Foodwise Liz started out slim in her relationship with John Warner; she was even determined to lose another ten pounds until he shared his wisdom with her. They were—of course—food shopping and passed the meat aisle. "Pick up that turkey over there, Elizabeth," he suggested.

"Boy, this is heavy," she replied, hoisting it up. He suggested that she look at how much it weighed.

She scanned the label and replied, "It's almost eleven pounds."

"Right, you can put it back," he responded.

"Aren't we going to buy it?" she asked naively (probably hungrily).

"No, dear, I'm just making a point. Do you realize you've already lost nearly the same weight as that bird you thought was so heavy?"

She took his point—and who could help but love a man who tells you to stop dieting?

Their love was finally sealed over a sunset picnic. There was lightning and rain, and they lay on the grass, full of joy. And then tucked into the picnic. Taylor was to claim she and Warner had chosen their burial sites in Virginia and liked to declare, "I belong in Virginia like fried chicken." Her nickname for him was "Stuffed Shirt"; his for her was "Chicken Fat" or "My Little Heifer."

Virginia got her hooked on eating high-calorie foods—fried chicken, creamed potatoes, corn, green beans, coconut cake—in fact, this is just what Taylor filled up on when working on the set of *Malice in Wonderland.*

The Taylor-Warner divorce in 1982 was quickly followed by Taylor diving into rehab at the Betty Ford clinic and, as if life was coming full circle, who should she meet but Peter Lawford? A week after Taylor had holed up there, Lawford tumbled out of a plane at the airport (having sunk twenty vodka miniatures on the flight) and into the Betty Ford Center camp car. Through a blur of vodka, he managed to focus on the car signage. "Ah!" he said, "Are we going to visit her? I've always liked Betty."

Treatment at the Betty Ford was an eye opener for Taylor. She had to wait on tables and wash piles of dirty dishes, and she was there (as she understood it) because for thirty-five years she had got stoned on a cocktail of drugs and alcohol to get over her shyness. She managed to go cold turkey—except that, foodwise, she'd get her maid to smuggle in vanilla ice cream and melon balls. On her next visit to the Betty Ford Center, Taylor's mother, age ninety-two at the time, was being treated in the hospital, the Eisenhower Medical Center, slap bang by the Betty Ford Center. Not only was Taylor cheating the health-conscious Betty Ford in-house diet regime by hoarding chocolates in her room, but she always turned up to visit her mother at mealtimes, just in time to dip into the French fries and chocolate mousse that were on offer for patients.

And guess who she met at Betty Ford? Husband number five, Larry Fortensky. Between them there was a connection greater than a love of the bottle—both seriously loved eating junk food, and postclinic, they toured local hamburger joints ordering hamburgers, with every conceivable garnish, and vast, creamy milkshakes. I wonder if Elizabeth still asked for peppermint flavor?

JOHN WAYNE

As if straight from the silver screen, cut from the film of one of his movies, the Duke, John "Marion" Wayne, met his third wife, Pilar, under the most romantic of circumstances. Straight after filming *The Quiet Man*, Wayne was talent and location scouting in Peru in 1952; his marriages so far had crumbled and, inevitably, involved food. His loathing of avocados came up in the divorce court. When he found these in one of his sandwiches he slapped his second wife, Chata. Fortunately, or unfortunately, this dark foodie fiendishness was nowhere to be seen when his eyes met those of Pilar's; she was an actress working on a film called *Green Hell* (and no, it wasn't about avocados) in a small town called Tingo Maria, which lay close to the fringe of the jungle. Morning came, and the news broke among the cast that the great John Wayne was coming to watch them in action. It just so happened that Pilar's scenes involved her skipping and writhing, barefoot and bare-shouldered, around a campfire, her tangled, black hair tumbling onto her bronzed, velvety shoulders, all set off by a low-cut gypsy costume. When, panting lightly, she finished dancing, the hot, blue gaze of Wayne was on her. "That was quite a dance," he drawled, his eyes looking her up and down. It was straight out of *Rio Bravo*. Cutely, and strangely like lots of his female costars, Pilar barely reached his shoulder.

The nights were warm and long in Lima in 1952, and that evening they held a dinner in honor of the Duke. Who should be there but Pilar, no doubt dressed recklessly in some feckless, sexy gypsy gear, trilling and crooning to Wayne such Latin American ditties as "Criolitta" and "Granada." Wayne was entranced, swooning as he downed Pisco sours. He asked coyly if she ever watched Westerns; she said, "Not really." I bet that went down like a lead balloon. They drank more pisco sours while they waited and waited and waited for the late Peruvian dinner hour.

At last it came: ceviche, zinging with fresh fish, chilies, and lime; pale hearts of palm salad; anticuchos, which are a playful shish kebab of beef hearts. Originally these would have been skewers of llama meat. Finally, picarones, scrumptious hoops of sweet potato doughnuts with aniseed-honey syrup drizzled over them. "Normally, I'm a steak and potatoes man," Wayne schmoozed. Note that he makes no mention of avocados. He stared at Pilar purposefully: "I won't forget my stay here."

"Nor will I," Pilar replied, and then, proving that she was good, staunch, 1950s marriageable material, she stood up, shook his hand—allowing for a short spell of palm-to-palm lingering—and said, "Unfortunately, I've got to be up by five."

"Then I guess this is goodbye," murmured Wayne.

But never say never again; they met next in Hollywood, she pushing open a door, he on the other side pushing in the opposite direction. They had dinner that night.

Pisco Sours (Wayne's favorite tipple was tequila, but these babies must have been a close second)

INGREDIENTS

1 egg, chilled from the fridge
1 measure of Pisco
1 tbsp. sugar syrup
Freshly squeezed juice of 4 limes
Angostura bitters
Crushed ice

METHOD

Separate the egg white from the yolk—reserve the yolk for later use; you're going to use the white. Whip the egg white until it is firm. Put the crushed ice, Pisco, lime juice, sugar syrup, and egg white in a cocktail shaker. Give it a good shake. Drain the delicately green Pisco mixture into a martini glass and add a few drops of Angostura bitters to the egg foam.

Ceviche

INGREDIENTS

FOR THE LECHE DE TIGRE (TIGER'S MILK) . . .

⅔ cup freshly squeezed lime juice
1 tbsp. finely chopped cilantro
3 garlic cloves, pulped
1 habanero chili, seeds removed and split lengthwise
3 large ice cubes
1 red onion, finely chopped
Sea salt

FOR THE CEVICHE . . .

1½ lb. fresh, high-quality white fish, such as halibut
1 cup freshly squeezed lime juice (Key limes are recommended)
1–2 habanero chilies, seeds removed and split lengthwise
1 red onion, finely sliced
1 tbsp. finely chopped cilantro

TO SERVE . . .

Firm, crispy, lettuce leaves
Some thin slices of red onion
1 tbsp. finely chopped cilantro
A dash of olive oil
1 ear of corn, cooked, kernels removed and cooked in a little oil
1 sweet potato, thinly sliced and deep fried
1 plantain, sliced and fried in butter

METHOD

Dice the fish into 1-inch cubes. Put them in a large, glass bowl. Add the onion, habanero chilies, and cilantro. Pour the lime juice over and mix well. Add a pinch of salt.

Ceviche (*continued*)

Cover the dish and refrigerate the ceviche for 15 minutes.

Now make the leche de tigre. Put the lime juice, cilantro, sea salt, garlic pulp, habanero chili, and ice cubes in a blender. Blend thoroughly. Now add the red onion and, using the pulse mechanism on the blender, pulse-blend the onion a couple of times. Strain the leche de tigre; you will be left with a beautifully green, milky liquid. Set aside and refrigerate.

Now remove the fish from its marinade. Arrange the small piles of ceviche on individual lettuce leaves, sprinkle with cilantro, and add a slice or two of onion. Serve with side orders of cooked corn kernels, fried plantain, and sweet potato crisps. Accompany with a shot of leche de tigre, which your guest can drizzle over their ceviche.

Anticuchos

INGREDIENTS

½ lb. ox's heart, cleaned of fat and membrane
2 garlic cloves
2 tsp. ground cumin
¾ cup white vinegar
2 dried, crushed small red chilies
Sea salt
Freshly ground black pepper

FOR THE BASTING SAUCE . . .

2 mild, fresh chilies
Juice of 1 lime
1 tbsp. brown sugar
2 tbsp. olive oil

METHOD

Prepare the heart by chopping it into 1-inch pieces. Using a mortar and pestle, crush the garlic, pepper, sea salt, cumin, and chilies. Now combine these in a bowl with the vinegar. Add the heart meat and allow this to marinade in the fridge overnight.

The next day, soak wooden skewers in water. Make a light, chili-based basting sauce by blending together the mild, fresh chilies with plenty of lime juice, some olive oil, and brown sugar. Thread the meat onto the skewers and grill over high heat for a few minutes on each side, basting the anticuchos with the chili basting sauce.

Picarones

INGREDIENTS

½ lb. sweet potatoes
½ lb. pumpkin
2 cloves
½ stick cinnamon
1 star anise
1 tsp. fennel seeds, crushed
½ tbsp. sugar
1 tbsp. fast-acting yeast
¾ lb. all-purpose flour
Sunflower oil for deep frying

FOR THE SYRUP . . .

200 ml. molasses
200 g. dark Muscovado sugar
1 stick cinnamon
3 dried cloves
2 star anise
¼ pineapple, cut into ½-inch pieces
1 banana, cut into ½-inch pieces
1 fig leaf or fig
1 orange
1 lime

METHOD

Peel and chop the sweet potatoes and pumpkin into 2-inch pieces. Place in a pan with the star anise, 2 cloves, and ½ stick of cinnamon. Cover with water and bring to boil. Once tender, drain—but keep the hot water, remove the star anise, and cool. In a blender, puree the sweet potato and pumpkin.

Using ½ a cup of the spice-scented warm water, combine with the sugar and then add the yeast. Put in a warm place until the mixture foams—this takes about 10 minutes.

In a large bowl, combine the vegetable puree with the yeast mixture, the all-purpose white flour, and the crushed fennel. Add a further ¼ cup of spiced water and knead to a smooth, stretchy, but slightly sticky dough. Be prepared to add a little more flour or a drop more water, depending on the consistency of the dough.

Put this dough in a lightly oiled bowl, cover with a towel, and leave in a warm place to rise for about 2 hours.

Now make the syrup. Cut four strips of peel from both the orange and the lime. In a medium-sized, heavy-based pan, put the orange and lime zest strips, the juice from each fruit, Muscovado sugar, cinnamon, cloves, star anise, pineapple, and banana pieces and the fig or fig leaf. Add water and bring to boil. Stirring frequently, reduce this to a syrup. Cool.

After two hours, when the dough has risen, heat the sunflower oil in a heavy-bottomed, large saucepan. It should fill the pan by a third. When the oil is silent and no longer crackles, it should be ready. Test with a small piece of dough. It should start bubbling immediately and rise to the top. Now you should wet your hands, take a small ball of dough, and gently force your finger through its center to form a dough ring shape. Do this repeatedly, dropping each picarone into the hot oil. Turn them as they fry with a slotted spoon. When each picarone is golden brown and puffy, remove it from the oil, drain quickly on some kitchen roll, and then serve piping hot, with a good drenching of the spiced syrup.

MARILYN MONROE

It is strange to think that, in 1962, when Marilyn Monroe whooshed, "Happy Birthday, Mr. President," on national TV to John F. Kennedy, her on-off lover of eight years, both of them were near their deaths, dissolving in the floodlights of their respective careers as Sex Kitten and President. Marilyn had two months to live; JFK some eighteen months.

Silence fell on Madison Square. "If I had been wearing a slip," gushed Marilyn, "I would have thought it was showing." Her second thought was, "Oh, my gosh, what if no sound comes out!" In her dress of "skin and beads," Marilyn's breathy surprise at the crowd's silence as she sang seems disingenuous, hiding the shiver of delight she felt at having trounced Elizabeth Taylor in her bid for the "Happy Birthday" slot.

But for me, it is sad and as strange to contemplate the stark, empty-cupboard loneliness of Marilyn's life that night in 1962. For instance, I ask you to think about the fact that Marilyn had in tow as her "date" her ex-husband Arthur Miller's old dad, Isadore, his glasses winking in the glitz. A kind act? Yes. The act of one with plans to spend the night with anyone who doesn't have varicose veins and a dodgy prostrate? No.

Throughout her thirties, loneliness left Marilyn desolate. Hollywood wasn't all it was cracked up to be. Where were the laughs? The love?

Enter food, our reliable friend. Yes, Marilyn was the ultimate comfort eater. Marilyn's regular cook, Hattie, supplied Marilyn with plenty of meat in bed. "The Romans used to eat like I do!" Marilyn exclaimed, dropping gnawed lamb chops onto her signature-white bed sheets. Then, wrapping two long noodles around her breasts, she'd giggle, "Look at me! This is my idea of wearing a bra!"

Always fun with food, Marilyn won Isadore Miller's love over a first course. Trial-by-soup dominated her first meeting with her future in-laws . . . who was this girl? Having downed two bowls of matzoh ball soup, Marilyn refused a third! In alarm, Isadore asked, "You mean, you don't like our matzoh ball soup?"

"Oh, I just love it," said Marilyn. "But gee, isn't there any other part of the matzoh you can eat?"

But Marilyn was always destined to belong to the president rather than the playwright. Growing up in the absence of her father, Marilyn told her maid, Lena Pepitone, "My father is Abraham Lincoln," and, before Lena began to do some baffling sums, Marilyn rejoined, "I mean I *think* of Lincoln as my father." It would be easy to dismiss this as frippery, which Lena probably did, until she cleaned Marilyn's bedroom later that week and discovered a photo of Lincoln by Marilyn's bed (alongside that of her sanatorium-bound mother). Yes, a president was always close by. JFK's wandering hand would usually be clambering about beneath her skirt at dinner parties—but he violently blushed, to her robust amusement, when he discovered that she wore no underwear. Of this, Marilyn quipped, "I bet he doesn't put his hand up Jacqueline's dress. I bet no one does. Is she ever stiff!"

Sharp and sassy, Marilyn was no fool. The difference, she said, between her early experiences prostituting herself and those of being a model was that in the latter existence you were paid for sex in pictures instead of dollars. The fact that she had had to wriggle about on so many casting couches meant that she fiercely pushed her preferred self-representation. When photographers suggested she do girl-next-door photo shoots, she'd retort, "I can assure you that I am *not* baking any cakes."

Marilyn knew she was eye candy for powerful men: warty Soviet president Khrushchev kept pumping her hand at one banquet—better, with true Marilyn sagacity, "than having to kiss him." And then she made a brilliantly empty point, which seems to level all political posturing: "Who would want to be a Communist with a president like that?"

She liked to study such men. Upon finding Bobby Kennedy "wise," she dogged his steps with a notebook, jotting down his thoughts. Before marrying Miller, she stayed with his family, rehearsing how to be a "proper" Jewish wife, as if it were a character part. She leafed through the Torah and practiced cooking borscht, gefilte fish, potato pirogen, and tsimis.

Marriage to stuffed-shirt Miller was mostly heartache, though, as Marilyn could never work out "what to do with nights" while Miller scribbled in his study, at Floor 13, 444 Sutton Place, New York. Rolling around the flat naked, flashing bright blonde pubic hair thanks to the self-administered application of peroxide with two toothbrushes, Marilyn saw in the mornings with poached eggs and Bloody Marys and saw through the empty nights with a bottle of Piper Heidsieck champagne to put her arms around.

Ever the romantic, she tried to woo Miller with intimate suppers—chicken cacciatore was put to just such use one evening. Miller emerged from his study, and Marilyn sat in her white toweling robe, her idea of dressing for dinner. Over the chicken Marilyn cast admiring glances at Miller, who chewed on silently, ignoring her. Eventually, Marilyn asked, "Arthur? You said something about going to a movie tonight . . . I'd love it if we could go somewhere."

"Maybe later," Miller replied coolly. Marilyn charged into her room, shook the bobby pins from her hair, slapped on some bright red lipstick, and dragged on a white silk shirt. But was Miller anywhere to be seen? No. No doubt he had other pencils to sharpen.

Chicken Cacciatore to Woo Arthur Miller

INGREDIENTS

4 chicken quarters, with skin
2 tbsp. olive oil
Crushed black pepper
Sea salt
1 yellow pepper, finely sliced
1 small onion, finely chopped
2 garlic cloves, finely chopped
1 glass of dry white wine
2 tbsp. white wine vinegar
1 cup chicken stock
½ tsp. crumbled oregano
2 bay leaves
1 cup mushrooms, finely chopped
1 can Italian peeled tomatoes, juice reserved
2 tbsp. fresh basil leaves, torn
1 tbsp. black olives, sliced
3 anchovy fillets
Freshly grated Parmesan

METHOD

Season the chicken with black pepper and a little sea salt. In a deep frying pan, heat the olive oil until a "haze" forms over it. Sauté the chicken quarters in the olive oil until their skin goes golden brown. Transfer onto a plate. Next, sauté the yellow pepper. Add the onion and garlic to the pan and cook over a moderate heat, stirring regularly, for about 8 to 10 minutes, until the onion is slightly caramelized and sweet. Add the vinegar to deglaze the pan, scraping any sticky browned bits off and into your sauce, and then add the white wine and boil briskly until this juice is reduced to about a ¼ glass. Add black pepper. Pour in the chicken stock. Turn down to low. Add the tomatoes, half their juice, oregano, bay leaf, half the torn basil, and the mushrooms. Return the chicken to the pan. Cover, reduce the heat, and simmer for 30 minutes. Transfer the chicken onto the platter. To the sauce, add the black olives, the remaining basil, and the anchovies; stir and cook for 2 minutes. Serve over the chicken and sprinkle with Parmesan. Serve with buttered spaghetti and watch out for Arthur Miller.

Miller, apart from being a cold fish, was, Marilyn decided, downright greedy, forcing her to make a movie she detested, *Some Like It Hot*, just for the bucks. She decided to eat her way out of the part of Sugar Kane, and one furious day of protest saw her down toast with three burgers, three eggs, three plates of home fries, a veal cutlet, two chocolate milkshakes, two helpings of aubergine parmigiana, and four bowls of chocolate pudding. "Call me Baby Elephant," she insisted, but "I'm going to get so fat they won't let me be in this awful picture." Fortunately for us, her plan backfired.

And always, vaguely, ominously, in the background of the Miller-Monroe marriage was "that big tease" JFK, with his dirty jokes, pinches, and squeezes. JFK was always late for meals and, like Marilyn, was a messy eater. Those who cleaned up after him often happened on half-eaten meals in unexpected places (Marilyn would *never* have left them uneaten). Granted, things weren't easy for him dietarywise;

Marilyn's Protest Diet: Aubergine Parmigiana

INGREDIENTS

FOR THE TOMATO SAUCE . . .

6 garlic cloves, cut into matchsticks
1 tin organic plum tomatoes
1 tsp. clover or heather honey
A handful of torn, fresh green basil
2 tbsp. olive oil
1 tsp. crushed black pepper

FOR THE AUBERGINE . . .

2 aubergines, sliced crossways into ½-inch slices
¼ cup all-purpose flour, with 1 tsp. coarse sea salt and pepper crumbled through
3 tbsp. olive oil
2 organic eggs, beaten
3 tbsp. freshly grated Parmesan cheese
2 packs of mozzarella, drained and cut into strips

METHOD

First, assemble the delicious tomato sauce. In a thick-bottomed frying pan, heat the 2 tablespoons of olive oil. When this is hot, throw in the garlic. Fry for about 30 seconds, then pour in the tomatoes. Then scatter with half the fresh basil. Now for the *top-secret* ingredient (told to me only by Sicilians): stir in a heaping teaspoon of rich clover or heather honey. This cuts through the bitterness of the tomatoes and gives the sauce a warm, golden, and aromatic undertone. Stir to help the honey dissolve, and add the black pepper. Allow the sauce to simmer for about 8 minutes at medium heat. Take off the heat and stir in the remaining torn basil.

Now it's time to assemble the parmigiana. Preheat the oven to 200°C. Heat the olive oil in a frying pan. Dip the slices of aubergine in the beaten egg and then in the seasoned flour. Next, fry each slice in the hot olive oil. (Test the oil before placing the aubergine in it—just shake a little of the batter mix into the oil and, if it's hot enough, it will make the batter ball and tighten immediately. If it just listlessly sits around the batter, then it's not ready.) Fry each aubergine slice for about 60 seconds on each side. Then, when it's golden, lift and drain each slice on paper kitchen roll. If the slices absorb too much olive oil, then add a little more.

Get a baking dish. It should be about 3 inches deep and 8 or 9 inches long. Place the aubergine slices in a single layer, drizzle with half of the tomato sauce, 1 pack of mozzarella, and half the Parmesan. Repeat, finishing with the last of the Parmesan.

Bake uncovered in the oven for 15 minutes.

his undiagnosed Addison's disease meant he was often on special diets to control his spastic colitis (lots of corn, peas, and prunes). But I get the feeling that, like the women in his life, food was secondary to power. However much he disappointed and dominated Marilyn romantically—using Bobby Kennedy to ditch her when she may or may not have been pregnant by him—at least in this one regard, the love of food, JFK could never step up to Marilyn's league.

No wonder, then, what with Miller's silent gnawing and JFK's prunes, that Marilyn pined, nostalgically, for the lost world of those Italian dinners she'd had with her ex-husband, faithful Joe DiMaggio. There was something trustworthy about all that Italian nosh. In fact, it was Lena Pepitone's account of her lasagne recipe that got her hired as Marilyn's maid, and, in a weirdly cyclical way, on the day of her death, August 4, 1962, Marilyn phoned Lena to arrange a lasagne party. More food fuel for the conspiracy theorists who mumble about Marilyn's abortive pregnancy by JFK and purported assassination, her table (always number 14) booked at her favorite restaurant La Scala on the night of her death, and all the reasons why she was unlikely to have taken her life. As if one could *never* say, "Now, for supper, I'll have two eggs, sunny side up, one rare steak, oh, and a smidgen of cottage cheese on the side," and *not* still feel clouds of despondency roll over you.

HUMPHREY BOGART AND LAUREN BACALL

When they finally met in 1944, Humphrey Bogart and Lauren Bacall seemed an unlikely pair. Bacall was so shy that she'd bring her own packed lunch to the set of *To Have and Have Not* so that she could eat in secret, squirrelly fashion rather than brave the throngs of the commissary alone. William Faulkner was rewriting the Hemingway story but battling with his own alcoholism, writing three pages of the story each day, which they'd hastily film, in case he lost or destroyed it, so that they'd have a safe second copy of it. And it wasn't just Faulkner's drinking. "Sluggy," Mayo Methot, Bogart's third wife, was encouraging Bogart to drink with her at every opportunity, hoping to drag him into the whirlpool of alcoholism that had already engulfed her. Alcohol, she calculated, would bind their marriage together (all in all, Sluggy wasn't good news; she was too handy with knives, paranoid, and tried to burn down their house). Bogart's health was rattling; he was a mess. In the mornings on set he'd drink coffee and orange juice, then vomit, and then go back for another orange juice. Drink had taken hold of him and was never to lose its grasp, but Sluggy was another matter. Bogart's marriage to Bacall was to prove gentler, more accommodating, but also less reckless: a Christmas tradition in the Bogart-Bacall family home was for the couple to make lovely, hot milk punch together. Bacall liked the punch because she couldn't taste the alcohol, and Bogart liked it because it helped him ease off his hangover.

Bogart and Bacall had three months to make *To Have and Have Not*. Cast opposite each other, there was a palpable electricity of desire, curiosity, and longing between Bacall and Bogart. For the first month they sat on the set in old camp chairs, watching each other's movements. By the second month they were popping in and out of each other's trailers for long "chats." No longer afraid she'd be alone in the commissary, Bacall started to leave her sensible packed lunches at home. Soon they took to cycling off together through the studio streets at the end of filming, through the love-charmed air. Or they'd start up Bacall's tatty Plymouth coupe and head off undercover to the Lakeside Golf Club—Bogart had bacon and eggs, and they'd share a cigarette and a cold martini together. Once, with typical Bogart-esque humor, he used prop handcuffs to handcuff Bacall to her dressing room, while he ran off for lunch to Lakeside.

Their life together at first was a relatively secret one: they'd abscond to *Sluggy*—the boat, not the wife, but named after her—and cook supper on a camp stove, the boat rocking under the stars while they imagined marrying each other one day; or he'd come around to Lauren's flat (still shared with her mother), where Lauren cooked European food, recipes borrowed from her Romanian Jewish grandmother who had been a wonderful cook, teaching Bacall how to make dishes of stuffed cabbage and kreplach (little knuckles of pastry filled with spiced chicken, meat, or cheese). Over the tiny stove of *Sluggy*, rocking in the water, Bacall rustled up creamed cauliflower and soufflé for Bogart, who secretly preferred roast beef and steak. Both were charmed by the other, play-acting the marriage they hoped to have one day.

Kreplach

INGREDIENTS

FOR THE DOUGH . . .

6 oz. all-purpose flour
1 tbsp. warm water
1 tsp. baking powder
½ tsp. saffron threads
2 medium-sized eggs
1 tbsp. olive oil
Pinch of sea salt

FOR THE FILLING . . .

¼ lb. minced beef
1 tbsp. olive oil
1 onion
1 garlic clove
3 tsp. powdered cinnamon
3 tbsp. walnuts, broken into small pieces
Freshly ground black pepper
Sea salt

METHOD

Soak the saffron threads in the warm water, allowing them to stain and enrich the water. Using a food processor, combine the flour with the baking powder. Add the eggs, oil, salt, and saffron water to the flour. Beat until you have a flexible, soft dough. Wrap the kreplach dough in greaseproof paper and chill it in the fridge until you are ready to use it.

Now prepare the filling. In a frying pan, heat the olive oil. Sauté the onions and garlic until they are golden, then add the minced beef and allow the mince to brown and cook. Next add the cinnamon, salt, pepper, and walnuts. Fry for a further 5 minutes and then allow to cool.

To assemble the kreplach, flour a board and rolling pin. Place the dough on the board and roll gently until the dough is very thin. Cut the dough into squares and then place little spoonfuls of the walnut mince in the center of each square. Wet the edges of the dough with your fingertip, wetted with water. Now fold over the kreplach and pinch to seal.

Drop into a pot of delicious chicken soup and cook for about 5 minutes. Serve with a scattering of broken walnuts on the top.

Cauliflower Cheese

INGREDIENTS

1 cauliflower, split into florets
½ pint milk
1½ tbsp. all-purpose flour
1 tbsp. butter
1 tsp. Dijon mustard
4 tbsp. freshly grated Parmesan cheese
Sea salt and black pepper

METHOD

Steam the cauliflower until it is barely cooked (it should still be al dente). Drain it well. Preheat the oven to 200°C. In a heavy-based medium-sized saucepan, melt the butter. Remove from the heat and add the all-purpose flour. Stir quickly to form a roux. Now slowly add the milk, stirring to blend the milk with the roux. Return the pan to the heat and, stirring constantly over medium heat, bring to boil. When boiling, turn down the heat and allow this white sauce to cook for a further 5 minutes over a gentle heat. Now add the Parmesan and a teaspoon of mustard. Salt and pepper to taste. Arrange the florets of cauliflower in a baking dish. Pour the cheese sauce over it and bake in the oven for about 20 minutes.

While you eat, you must try out on your guests some of the many jokes that Bacall and Bogart liked to share in an almost ritualistic joy: Bacall: "Know who's in the hospital?" Bogart: "Who?" Bacall: "Sick people." Or try this one—Bogart: "Did you hear what the ceiling said to the wall?" Bacall would reply, "No." Bogart: "Hold me up, I'm plastered."

When the day of their marriage finally came some eleven days after his divorce from Sluggy, it was Bogart who burst into tears of joy when they said their vows. Bacall, more comically, went quickly to the bathroom before the wedding and then was startled to hear the wedding march begin. Apparently, Bogart at this point had looked around desperately and said, "Where is she?"

Gesturing at the organist, the best man hissed, "Hold it! She's in the can!"

WOODY ALLEN

Conversation proved difficult when film editor Ralph Rosenblum met Woody Allen for a bite to eat. Every time Woody took a mouthful of food, he raised his hand to cover his mouth with near-bridal shyness, muffling every word he said. Eating is complicated for Woody Allen—of course. Doses of honey and incessant chocolate malteds are good for his throat. Boiled vegetables are always safe. Restaurants are visited again and again. When he started seeing Mia Farrow, they'd wear identical hats to go to his favorite Chinese restaurant, Pearl's, and they'd eat many of their other meals at the Carnegie Delicatessen on Seventh Avenue (they have created a Woody Allen sandwich in his honor of corned beef with pastrami).

The zoo of children and pets that followed in Farrow's wake tested Allen's phobia about infections of various kinds, and he took to using disposable paper plates and cups when he was staying in Mia's flat. When he was filming *What's New Pussycat?* in Rome in 1964, Allen was in deep trauma at the thought of European food. What was it? Was it dangerous? He decided to do two things: to only eat grilled fish *or* steak flown in from New York. The production eventually moved to Paris, and after a couple of run-ins with odd, foreign restaurants, Woody settled on just one restaurant and every evening enjoyed a dinner of poison-free grilled sole and, for some unaccountable reason, crème caramel. For several months.

Chocolate Malted

INGREDIENTS

3 scoops vanilla ice cream
¼ cup chocolate syrup
¾ cup milk
2 tbsp. malted milk powder

METHOD

Plop the ice cream, chocolate sauce, and malted milk powder into a blender. Slowly add the milk until your malted milk is just the right consistency. Serve in a disposable paper cup if you're at anyone else's house.

3

❖ ❖

Dining with Famous and Infamous Musicians

Bring pop stars into your parlor and divas into your dining room in these delicious meals. Appearing for one night only are: the Beatles, Louis Armstrong, Frank Sinatra, Woody Guthrie, Bob Dylan, Bob Marley, Michael Jackson, and the Rolling Stones.

THE BEATLES

Before the poppy seed haze of the Maharishi's ashram, funky vegetarianism, or even so much as a mung bean of John and Yoko's macrobiotic meditations—way back, before all that, the Beatles were a pack of very hungry boys, the same size and shape as a pack of scouts.

College students, John Lennon and his girlfriend, Cynthia Powell, must have seemed groovy and mature to those schoolboys, the fourteen-year-old Paul and his diminutive sidekick George Harrison, when they turned up at lunchtime, escapees from school, bundling up their blazers and tucking away their schoolboy caps to jam with John on the tiny stage behind the canteen at Liverpool Art College. John and Cynthia grabbed fish and chips from a nearby shop, and the four sat around a steaming pile of salt-crunchy and vinegar-sharp chips and potato scallops on crumpled newspaper.

Scallops and Chips—the earliest meal of the Beatles

And no, scallops are *not* of the shellfishy form; instead, they are dinky battered potato slices found in chip suppers in Northern English towns.

INGREDIENTS

2 large potatoes, peeled and cut into chips
2 large potatoes, cut into slices about ½ cm. thick

BATTER

4 tbsp. all-purpose flour
2½ tbsp. vegetable oil
4⅓ tbsp. cold water

FOR DEEP FRYING . . .

2-liter bottle of vegetable oil

TO GARNISH . . .

Lemon wedges
Vinegar
Sea salt
Ketchup

METHOD

Preheat the oven to 50°C.

Put the flour into a bowl. Slowly and carefully add the vegetable oil a little at a time and mix the two together with a fork or a whisk until fully integrated. Use this method to add the water until a smooth, runny batter has formed and bubbles of air start to rise to the surface.

Now, the trick about making good chips and potato scallops is that you have to have plenty of space in your frying pan *and* the oil must be hot enough. To that end, you should cook the chips in one deep pan and the scallops in a second. Heat one liter of oil—for your chips—in a large, deep pan. Do the same with the second liter of oil in another pan.

Once you have heated the chip pans for about 5 minutes, you should hear the oil crackle at first and then fall silent; it is when it is silent that it is ready. Try out the oil with one chip at first. It will sink but then very rapidly rise in the oil, surrounded by a "bubble-wrap" cluster of bubbling oil and air. When this happens, the oil is ready for the chips. Carefully empty them, a handful at a time, into the hot oil, stir once, and leave until golden brown (about 10 to 15 minutes).

Once the chips are cooking in the first pan, the second pan of oil should be ready for the same "chip" test—use a teaspoonful of batter this time around, and as soon as the batter rises in "bubble wrap" the oil is ready. Now swirl a raw potato scallop in the batter mix and immediately plunge it into the hot oil. Repeat with one scallop after another, and leave these, again, for 10–15 minutes.

Next, drain the chips and clouds of battered scallops, place them on paper towel (or a copy of the *Liverpool Echo*), and sprinkle with vinegar and sea salt.

Later on, but still fresh out of their childhoods, when they put on a gig at Liverpool's Jacaranda Coffee Bar, the Beatles' humble, boyish food was no more than fizzy sodas and beans on toast. Cheese roll lunches were called for at the Cavern, with mums and dads popping in to visit. In 1960s Hamburg, the band turned up so broke (pocket money doesn't stretch far) at the Indra nightclub that the cleaner, out of the kindness of her heart, lent them enough money to go across the street to Harold's Café for potato fritters, chicken soup, and cornflakes (eventually she got into the habit of giving each of them a chocolate bar for the day). Surprise, surprise, there was nothing to cook on in their digs, so they popped into the British Sailors' Society for cornflakes and milk, or, if something more substantial was called for, Paul's girlfriend, Liane, a Hamburg barmaid, cooked them Deutsch beefsteak (hamburgers) and coffee. Nor did the handouts stop in Hamburg: when John married Cynthia (wife number 1), Brian Epstein shelled out to take them to Reece's Café for a set lunch: fifteen shillings a head got them roast chicken (plus trimmings!) followed by a good, old, straight-laced fruit salad. And although the Beatles' passion for plain, big snacks could be put down to being short of a penny or two, it was also the order of the day for the lads from Liverpool. When the master of Brasenose College in Oxford invited them to dinner in the 1960s, rather than polish their forks at the prospect of what culinary delights the splendid and arcane kitchens of Brasenose might hold, the Beatles put in a request for jam butties—buns with butter and jam. There was often, as our Hamburg cleaner's chocolate revealed, something very parental in people's responses to the Beatles. When they turned up in Miami in 1964, touring America for the first time, their bodyguard took one look at them and decided they needed some American home cooking. He took the boys back to his house for a lunch of baked potatoes and beef, followed by a vast American strawberry ice cake. The boys were finally full: they couldn't eat until the next day.

There is a lovely naïveté about the Beatles and food: Lennon grew up on egg and chips, and he and Cynthia romanced over pints of Black Velvet—a half pint of Guinness and a half pint of cider. Paul decided that virginal Jane Asher was a good girl and the one for him after an evening spent exchanging notes on the best consistency for gravy and their favorite foods. For at least one of them, the realities of working-class attitudes to food set him on the long road to vegetarianism—George Harrison never forgot the sight of a slaughtered chicken hanging on the family clothesline to bleed dry (an interesting shared memory with American artist Jackson Pollock). Indeed, George seemed singularly unable to escape meat as a child; he even got a job as a butcher's boy, delivering meat parcels that he had to stow warm in the saddle bags of his bicycle. George grew up on teas of pork pie and ham, pickled beets and salad cream, and stolid tomatoes cut carefully in half and served alongside white sliced bread. In the early 1960s, George's idea of fine dining was

Steak Diane at Annabel's, but a book he and first wife, Pattie Boyd, read about veal farming put them off meat forever.

Through the early 1960s the Beatles became more aware of their culinary gaucherie, and Jane Asher showed McCartney the ropes foodwise—with Jane he even tried out the pastoral living that was to be his and Linda McCartney's trademark later on. McCartney bought a farm, and Jane, a gifted cook, rustled up delicious meals on the ancient electric cooker in the primitive farmhouse kitchen.

In 1965, when the Lennons moved to London, Brian Epstein, generally the food guru to the band, took John and Cynthia in hand to show them how the smart set lived in London. He swept them along on sort of London "taster" evenings: he took them to French bistro La Poule au Pot on Ebury Street, which was also a decadent, brocaded gay haven, with dribbling white wax candlesticks and festooned with baroque wine red, gold, and green drapes. Not one word of the menu, though, did they understand. Epstein made the dining decisions: honey-tendrils of French onion soup, coq au vin with its buttery sheen, followed by pale globes of pear and rivulets of chocolate—Poire Belle Hélenè. Bottles of tart, grassy Pouilly-Fuissé were consumed, and Cynthia spent the rest of the evening trying to say Pouilly-Fuissé (in truth, the Lennons preferred milk with their meals). No matter how many fine dinners they ate, the lads from Liverpool still got their chauffeur to pull up at a roadside café on the way home in the early hours of the morning for a bacon butty or a scotch pie.

The Brian Epstein Dining Experience . . . French Onion Soup

INGREDIENTS

2 oz. butter
2 tbsp. extra virgin olive oil
6 brown onions, sliced paper thin
1 tbsp. fresh thyme leaves
3 garlic cloves, pulped
1½ pints of homemade beef stock
1½ cups dry white wine
2 tbsp. brandy
Pinch of brown sugar
Freshly ground black pepper
Sea salt
1 tbsp. flat leaf parsley, minced

CROUTONS

1 narrow French loaf, sliced diagonally
2 garlic cloves, halved
Olive oil
200 g. Gruyère cheese, finely grated

METHOD

Warm the blob of butter and the olive oil in a large, deep pan. Add the onions and fry briskly for 5 minutes; now turn down the heat and add the garlic, brown sugar, and thyme. Sauté very gently for about 30 minutes—make sure you stir

The Brian Epstein Dining Experience . . . French Onion Soup (*continued*)

regularly—until the onion has released its sweet, caramelized sugars and is nut brown and sticky and filmy. Pour in the white wine and the rich, dark beef stock. Stir well, scraping up the onion caramel from the base of the pan. Bring to boil, turn down to low, and cook, uncovered, for a further 50 minutes.

Ten minutes before the soup is ready, drizzle olive oil on the bread, toast it under the grill, and then vigorously rub each slice with garlic. Leave the grill on at top temperature.

Taste the soup, season it, add your generous glug of brandy and ladle the soup into deep *prewarmed* bowls. Place a disk of toasted, garlicky bread on top of each bowl, sprinkle with a small thatch of Gruyère, and scatter with parsley. Now place under the very hot grill for 4 to 5 minutes or until the Gruyère bubbles and browns a little.

Serve immediately.

Coq au Vin

INGREDIENTS

1 chicken—ask the butcher for one that is as old as possible; the older the bird, the better the sauce—butchered into 8 pieces, but with the carcass and giblets reserved

1 carrot
2 tbsp. extra-virgin olive oil
1 onion, unpeeled
8 whole black peppercorns
2 bay leaves
1 tbsp. butter
1 tbsp. olive oil
Sea salt
Freshly ground black pepper
5 oz. piece of pancetta or green bacon, cut into ¼-inch-thick lardons
3 celery ribs, roughly chopped
5 garlic cloves, pulped
3 tbsp. cognac
4 sprigs fresh thyme
1 tbsp. tomato purée
1 bottle beaujolais, pinot noir, or burgundy
3 tbsp. minced parsley

FOR THE GLAZED SHALLOTS AND MUSHROOMS . . .

1 tbsp. butter
2 tbsp. olive oil
10 small, whole shallots
12 oz. small brown mushrooms, wiped clean
2 tbsp. softened butter
2 tbsp. all-purpose flour

Coq au Vin *(continued)*

METHOD

First, two hours before beginning the main preparation for coq au vin, prepare the chicken stock. In a deep-bottomed pan, heat the 2 tablespoons of olive oil until it crackles. Place the chicken carcass and giblets in the pan along with a whole, unskinned onion (this adds a beautiful bronze hue to the stock). Put a lid on, and shake the pan to brown the chicken. After 3 minutes of this, add the peppercorns, whole carrot, and one of the bay leaves. Now put boiling water over to cover—watch out, it will froth and bubble. Turn down the heat and leave the stock to simmer for 2 hours. You want to reduce this stock down to about one pint of rich, intense stock.

In a deep, thick-bottomed casserole dish, heat the oil and butter. Add the pancetta or bacon lardons and celery and sauté gently until they are golden. When they are golden, remove them from the buttery oil. Now salt and pepper the chicken portions and brown them in the tasty, buttery oils of the dish. When the chicken becomes golden, return the lardons to the pan; then, as these warm, get a match or lighter ready, drizzle the cognac over the pieces, and light with a match. The pan should now flicker with blue flame as the chicken flambés. After a minute, cover the casserole with its lid to extinguish the flame. Now add the red wine, tomato puree, garlic, remaining bay leaf, and thyme. Bring to boil, and then turn the heat down to a gentle simmer, leaving the casserole partially uncovered.

After 30 minutes, melt the butter and olive oil in a frying pan. Add the onions; season and sauté for 10 minutes or until they are golden brown. Next, add the mushrooms and brown them in the pan. Now add both the onions and mushrooms to the chicken casserole.

When the chicken is ready (after about an hour in total), strain the sauce from the chicken and vegetables. Lay them on a warmed platter. Return the sauce to the casserole and turn the heat up high; reduce the sauce until about 2 cups of the liquid remains. While this reduces, blend the softened butter with the all-purpose flour in a small bowl. Whisk this into the sauce. When the sauce is suitably reduced, drizzle it over the chicken, sprinkle with parsley, and serve.

Bespectacled Alf Bicknell, the Beatles' chauffeur, was often in charge of food supplies when the band was recording late in the Abbey Road studios. Alf zoomed to a favored little local Italian restaurant snuggled close by and picked up avocado vinaigrette for Paul McCartney. Ringo would call out, "I'll have anything, as long as it doesn't have onions in it." Rather a tall order for an Italian restaurant. The restaurant owner carefully placed the meals in a hamper, complete with wine, beaming crystal glasses, napkins, and polished cutlery. Alf would tootle back in the Beatle-mobile (an Austin Princess—Alf once had to swap cars, a humble little

Poires Belle Hélène

INGREDIENTS

4 ripe but firm pears
8 oz. caster sugar
1 vanilla pod, split
2 lemons, zested and then juiced
1½ pints of water

FOR THE CHANTILLY CREAM . . .

1 cup double cream
1 tbsp. powdered sugar
1 tsp. vanilla extract

FOR THE CHOCOLATE SAUCE . . .

10 oz. dark chocolate, broken into small pieces
7 fl. oz. heavy cream
3 tbsp. brandy

TO SERVE . . .

Sliced almonds
Very good vanilla ice cream

METHOD

Peel the outer skin carefully from the pears, leaving the stem intact and retaining the distinctive shape of the pears. Cut a small disk of pear from the base of each pear—this will allow your pears to stand upright. In a deep pan, combine the water and sugar, lemon juice and lemon zest, and, stirring constantly, bring to boil, until the sugar has dissolved. Now add the pears and the vanilla pod to the lemony sugar water. To ensure the pears remain submerged, cut out a disk of greaseproof paper and place this over the surface of the pan—it will weigh just enough to stop the pears from bobbing up. Simmer for about 20 to 25 minutes until cooked—a toothpick should run easily through each pear. Turn off the heat and allow the pears and syrup to cool.

Now make the Chantilly cream. Put the cream into a chilled glass bowl. Using an electric whisk, add the powdered sugar and vanilla essence; whisk for about 1 minute until the cream, although soft, dimples and can retain its shape.

Heat water in a small saucepan and place a heatproof Pyrex bowl over it; the base of the bowl must not touch the boiling water. Now add the broken chocolate, brandy, and cream. Stir constantly until this has melded into a dark chocolate, glossy goo.

It is time to assemble the Poires Belle Hélène. To make one: in the base of glass bowl, place a dollop of vanilla ice cream. Top with a drained pear, allow a spoonful of black chocolate sauce to tumble over the pear, sprinkle with toasted almonds, and put alongside a buttery dollop of Chantilly cream. Scatter an almond or two over the cream. Enjoy.

Honda saloon, to smuggle Pattie and George away on their honeymoon), trundle up the stairs with the hamper, fling a towel over his forearm, and announce, "Gentlemen, dinner is served!" The keyboard would stop tinkling.

It was after a dinner in 1965 with the Beatles' odd London dentist, John Riley, in his Bayswater Road flat that George and John first tried LSD. Cynthia Lennon had thought it was a bit strange when the dentist lined up four sugar cubes for his guests on the mantelpiece and then—carefully and elaborately—dropped one into each cup of after-dinner coffee (actually, it was the dentist's girlfriend who was the most insistent that they try the "delicious" coffee). George's girlfriend Pattie (soon to be his wife, and who had been the Smith's Crisps potato chip girl) hissed nervously, "What if it turns out to be an aphrodisiac?" Bravely, they drank the coffee; then the dentist told them what he'd just done—doctored their coffee with LSD. Alf came to the rescue, and they all sped off in the car, which seemed to be shrinking by the second, hotly pursued by the dentist in his.

There were many other dinners: with Joan Baez, Mike Nesmith of the Monkees (his devoted wife hovered at Cynthia's elbow while she cooked—"I always do it this way for Mike . . ." she'd aver, or "Mike doesn't like it like that"), and even Bob Dylan. He had introduced the Beatles to cannabis on that first 1964 strawberry ice cream cake visit to America. After smoking a joint, McCartney discovered the meaning of life and grabbed a pencil and paper. The next day, he scrambled through his notes to find one line, "There are seven levels," but nothing else. The Harrisons had a cleaner named Margaret at their house, whose macaroni and cheese they loved coming home to, and to whom John Lennon supplied pick-me-ups—uppers that Margaret would innocently refer to as "those lovely pills" and that would have her vacuuming the Harrisons' house wildly for hours. Then there was a Hampstead lunch at Peter Cook's house, when John was appearing on *Not Only . . . But Also* in January 1965 and the Lennons had their very first, electrifying taste of garlic; the assembled company drank liters of rich, warming, red wine, and the afternoon descended into hilarity with Dudley Moore. A week later, and it was the Lennons' turn to host dinner for the Cooks. Cynthia floundered, trying to cook up a three-course meal, but she realized that she had no idea how to cook anything very much. Prawn cocktail with frozen prawns and bottled sauce, a roast, and a packet apple crumble and tinned custard made it to the table—but John didn't, or didn't for at least two hours, by which time the food in the oven had hardened and darkened. Once John, however, had rolled a joint and they were all stoned, their guests devored their dinner, ignorant of its carbonized condition or the fact that their food was processed.

George Harrison was the driving force behind the famed Beatles expedition to India: he had been desperately looking for enlightenment, even spending several hours alone standing on top of a Cornish mountain, hoping to make cosmic communication with whatever lay beyond. But finally, George's cosmic longings led him to India, Ravi Shankar, and sitar playing at Shankar's school in Bombay in September 1966. *Forget Cornwall: this is it!* George must have felt. India was breathtaking, with its pink dust, the ghats of the Benaras, and the many gods and goddesses of Hinduism. It was his first real taste of Indian food, too; with its predominantly vegetarian dishes, Harrison learned to eat with one hand, Indian style, and the tastes he experienced must have lit up his taste buds and altered his awareness in ways he never expected (including one meal cooked by a chef who had been castrated so that he could work alongside women in the kitchen). Much later on, back in England and living in Friar's Retreat, George invited Ravi Shankar's nephew, Kumar, to stay with him and Pattie. Kumar proved such a whiz in the kitchen that George came to love his vegetarian Indian food above all others, alienating Pattie permanently by preferring Kumar's dhal to any of her cooking. And it was George who persuaded the rest of the Beatles to meet the famous Maharishi Mahesh Yogi.

During his speaking tour of the United Kingdom, the founder of transcendental meditation, the Maharishi, had been pulling in the crowds, and, having listened spellbound to him in the Hilton Hotel in London, the very next day a small cabal of Beatles traveled by train, a jaunty troupe, with Mick Jagger and Cilla Black in tow, to the somewhat incongruous venue of Bangor, Wales, to learn more about transcendental meditation and to eat Chinese food late at night in Bangor. They found that no one had enough money to pay the bill, so unused were they all to carrying cash.

The Beatles, wreathed with marigolds, turned up to stay with the Maharishi at the fifteen-acre ashram in Rishikesh, India. Mike Love from the Beach Boys, Mia Farrow and her sister Prudence, and Donovan, the folk singer (David Lynch was to become a follower later on), were fellow students. Photographers hung from the trees when the Beatles arrived. Cups of almond drupe tea were served to new arrivals. The Ganges lay, ancient and greening, over a hundred feet below, and Himalayan peaks, massed with jungle, towered around the ashram. The ashram itself consisted of long dining halls dedicated to vegetarianism, and small, twin-bedded cottages, in six of which the Beatles lived, composing such hits as "While My Guitar Gently Weeps" and "Revolution"—in fact, many of the songs for the *White Album*. Harrison sat on the roof of Mia Farrow's bungalow and played his sitar; the Beatles brought their guitars to the communal meals and sang among the plates. Halcyon days? Not quite.

As you'd imagine, getting up early wasn't expected of rock stars and hippies, so the open-air breakfast stretched out for a languorous four hours between 7 a.m. and 11 a.m. for whomever or whatever might emerge from behind the bedroom doors—which were tagged MEDITATING, PLEASE DO NOT DISTURB. Breakfast consisted of disappointingly un-Indian-sounding cornflakes and puffed wheat, Quaker Oats porridge, toast (made from Indian bread and soggy), canned juice, and jam. The Maharishi had never made too much of a fuss about a vegetarian diet (he didn't want to scare off meat-loving Western clients), but he was quite happy to go with the idea that meat excited the metabolism (as you'll see later, he tried to get more than a cuddle off a nurse by means of a chicken leg). Where the Maharishi bumbled, though, was in not employing one of the many wonderful Indian vegetarian cooks available, instead opting for two heavy-looking, white, English youths (like a pair of terrible, hormonally challenged dinner ladies), who dished up green-gray splodge by the ladleful (ashram regulars called it "glop"). The glop was boiled in huge, gray kettles, and the Maharishi banned the use of spices. Even Cynthia Lennon found it "surprisingly ordinary." The Maharishi was later to go on tour with the Beach Boys in America and drive everybody mad with his dietary stipulations about fruit. Dinner followed lunch, faithfully, unrelentingly, and taking the same form: a witheringly bad vegetarian dish, with carrots, turnips, and potatoes, as well as salads of tomato and lettuce—although no raw food was allowed unless washed by the ashram students themselves, as clean water could not be guaranteed. Not that this made much of a difference, as washing up in the kitchens was generally haphazard, with dogs on hand to helpfully lick the plates clean.

Ringo was a man who knew where he stood in life with steak and chips and Matteus Rose. He arrived with his wife, Maureen, and a suitcase of baked beans. To keep his spirits up at the ashram, homesick Ringo had eggs done in one of four different ways: boiled, scrambled, fried, or poached, usually cooked by Mal Evans, while Maureen swatted flies and missed Liverpool. Ringo was the first to go after ten days, announcing, "That Maharishi's a nice man, but he's not for me."

Baked Beans on Toast

INGREDIENTS

1 tin Heinz baked beans
1 oz. butter
White bread, as processed as possible
More butter

METHOD

In a small saucepan, warm the beans with an ounce of butter; stir to blend. Next, toast the bread. Cut the slice of toast diagonally in half. Butter liberally. Pour the hot beans over the bread and enjoy with a very hot cup of tea.

Onions and garlic pursued Ringo throughout his early years: Cynthia Lennon, experimenting with Vesta beef curries served with banana slice garnishes, was hurt by Ringo's rejection of the curry she made for his supper when he called on her and John. Did he think she was trying to be too posh? And if it wasn't spicy stuff waiting to surprise Ringo on his plate, it was many-legged, fishy stuff. In 1968, when Ringo was in the throes of leaving the band, he took off on Peter Sellers's yacht *Amelfis*. As if life were not complicated enough, the captain offered him octopus for lunch. In dread and horror, Ringo shrank from such perversions. The captain laughed merrily and told him about octopi decorating their front-of-house cave with shiny objects found on the seabed. Guess what? Ringo went off to his cabin and wrote "Octopus's Garden."

After Ringo left the ashram, the other students evaporated over a period of six weeks, leaving behind a hard core of John, George, and Mia Farrow. The Maharishi's ashram began to dissolve in a froth of rumor that he had been too free with his female disciples, *and*, despite the vegetarian ethos, it was rumored that he had offered chicken—clearly the ultimate in sexual enticement—to a female disciple (a blonde Californian nurse). Much to the alarm of Mia Farrow, he had tried to hug her, along with making her wear a little silver paper crown, accept fifty gifts, eat a dedicatory carrot cake, and then allow him to stroke her hair. Mia smelled a rat with the Maharishi when he started giving her mangoes and calling her to come for one-to-one meditation training. Eventually he suggested, "Now we will meditate in my 'cave,'" and led Mia into a small, warm, and dank cellar. After a twenty-minute meditation stint when they had been facing each other, he suddenly lunged forward to embrace her. Mia darted back up the stairs, leaving the Maharishi forlorn in his cave.

Stuff this, thought Lennon, and they got ready to leave.

"Why?" asked the Maharishi.

"Well, if you're so bloody cosmic, then you'll know, won't you?" Lennon retorted.

The late ashram breakfast would have suited John Lennon, who, back in England, always operated according to his whimsy when it came to eating and drinking, except for an unshakeable devotion to large bowls of Frosted Flakes. He was an unfaithful vegetarian, varying at different points between comic militancy. When he saw his friend Pete Shotton eating a hamburger, he'd challenge him: "You do know that's someone's mother you're eating, don't you?" Keen to justify vegetarianism, Lennon pored through the Bible, hoping to prove that Christ was a vegetarian and ignoring all references to fish and lamb. Lennon was keen to push meatless vegetarian substitutes of veggie burgers and soy sausages. And yet May Pang, his girlfriend during his brief escape from the clutches of Yoko Ono, always cooked him on Sundays what she described as a "total English breakfast," the implication being that there was a rasher of bacon in there somewhere but not, by that time, the tab of acid he used to place as an aperitif on breakfast trays. There were some of his beloved Hershey bars, and life was not without pizzas and cappuccinos in his marriage to Yoko, but the emphasis was on rice and raw fish. As he told an interviewer, "My diet's based on meal, bread which Yoko makes, rice and no sugar. We have honey if things need sweetening." From even before the ashram, Pattie and George had moved away from the cozy, early marriage lunches of cold chicken and spiced wine toward vegetarianism, and proselytising vegetarianism, as when Pete Bennett, a New York business executive, called in on them to broker some business and Pattie came in and offered everyone trays of raw broccoli, carrots, and celery sticks. Bennett thoughtfully chewed on it and then headed off to have a steak afterward. And everyone knows the story about the McCartneys' commitment to ethical vegetarianism and the Road to Damascus moment when, settling down to roast leg of lamb for Sunday lunch, the McCartneys looked out of their window and oohed and aaahed at some lambs gamboling nearby. They looked down at their plates and then at each other and said, "Wait a minute, we love these sheep—they're such gentle creatures—so why are we eating them?" It was the last time they did, with Linda inventing all sorts of vegetarian replacements, including a dish Paul described as "macaroni turkey," which you could carve into slices, just like turkey.

And, for old times' sake . . . Bacon Butty

INGREDIENTS

Streaky bacon
Butter
Butties (these are white morning rolls)

METHOD

Grill 4 rashers of streaky bacon under a very hot grill until they are crisp. Heat the butty in the oven at about 50°C for 10 minutes. When the bacon is grilled, split the roll, butter it, and add the bacon rashers. Top with a blob of ketchup, if you feel like it.

LOUIS ARMSTRONG

Back o' Town, the swampy quarter of New Orleans where Louis "Satchmo" Armstrong began life, and then the Third Ward of New Orleans, were full of tough, angular characters and honky-tonk joints. Family life for Armstrong was disjointed, hanging together in a piecemeal sort of way. From age seven onward Louis was aware of the anarchic life of his black community and of his family's slave origins, listening to his mother and uncle tell of slavery and the racism that made, as he put it, white men down mint juleps and hunt black men. The black communities of New Orleans, he felt, suffered more from a lack of brotherhood, family, and common purpose, qualities that he encountered in another stigmatized community, the Jews of New Orleans. Although Satchmo's grandmother sent him to school until he was eleven years old, both of his parents disappeared periodically and Louis had to do bits and pieces of work. One key job was working in the rag-and-bone trade for the Russian-Jewish Karnofsky family, who represented to young Louis a standard of decency and kindness he never forgot. Miraculously, he said that they woke the spirit and love of music in him; they sang Russian lullabies with him and complimented his voice, and he learned the thrill of blowing a little tin horn from their junk wagon, calling for old rags, bones, and bottles. The Karnofskys advanced him the two dollars to buy his first blackened, secondhand cornet, and even taught him to get up early in the morning. He grew very close to his Jewish employers and loved eating kosher food, having his first Jewish meal at age seven, which he considered far purer than the ham hock diet of poor blacks like his family. He even slept better after eating dinner at their house, and in later life he always kept a box of matzos in his breadbin for a late night snack. From age eleven onward, he'd rattle along at night in the coal cart with Morris Karnofsky, selling stone coal to "sporting women"—young, shivering prostitutes who worked the "white customers only" red light district, clad only in thin, silk "teddies" worn to pull them in, and who all kept little coal fires burning in their rooms.

Food, then, represented stability and pleasure to Louis; apart from his forays into a kosher diet, Satchmo was raised on steaming pots of red beans and rice, a meal so familiar that he described it as his "birthmark"—indeed, in adulthood, he often signed off letters with "Red beans and ricely yours." When he met his fourth and last wife, Lucille, a northerner who was some fifteen years his junior, the first question he asked *wasn't* "Are you too young for me?" but, instead, the far more pertinent "Can you cook red beans and rice?" Lucille laughed wildly at the joke, until she realized that, as a southern boy, he was being deadly serious. She said she'd try. Immediately, Louis said he'd come by the next night for dinner. Lucille rolled her eyes at his haste, brushed up on her red beans, and let him come round—in his best suit—a few days later. "I ate just like a *dog*," Louis confessed, and then apologized to Lucille for doubting her delicious beans. Then, flirtatiously, he suggested she put some aside for him to eat on his *next* visit.

Louis's mother, Mary Ann, was stoically brave, making ends meet. Any physical complaints were dealt with using homegrown remedies—Mary Ann, with her church sisters, gathered from the railroad track wasteland bundles of dandelions for cooking with delicious slabs of salt meat, as well as the toothed leaves of pepper grass that she'd bruise and rub her children's scraped knees with—Louis eventually favorably compared Mary Ann's soothing herbal remedies for the body to the psychological effects of the marijuana he came to love in his late twenties. His father, William, abandoned the family, and Louis began to think it was pretty odd that he had to call ever-varying men "stepfather" (Mary Ann passed on their trousers for Louis to wear, and he rolled up their bottoms, fancying himself in a pair of swank's plus fours), and then he thought it even more odd when he heard one of his "stepfathers" yell "black bitch" at Mary Ann and punch her face, knocking her into the canal. The "stepfather" then walked off without a backward glance, leaving Louis wailing and his mother, bloody faced, in the water.

It was customary in New Orleans to fire off a shotgun or pistol—whatever was available to make the maximum amount of noise—to celebrate the glorious days between Christmas and the New Year. Louis couldn't resist this and fired off his "stepfather's" old .38 revolver and was sent to the miserably named Colored Waifs' Home for Boys. At first, Satchmo swore off his beloved beans on a hunger strike to protest his innocence of any real wrong, but on day number four it all got to be too much: Louis cracked and ate. Finally, released from the Colored Waifs' Home at age fourteen, Louis was to realize his own unique talent for making beans himself. Although Louis wanted to stay in the Waifs' Home, he was released into the "care" of his biological father and his stepmother. Both William and his new wife were quite keen to leave Louis alone to cook and care for his stepbrothers, Willie and Henry. Louis cooked up a huge pot of rice, beans, and ham hocks, but he quickly realized Willie could put away as much as a vacuum, leaving very little food for the cook. Louis took emergency action and sneakily wolfed down a large plate of rice and beans before ringing the bell for Willie and Henry. Eventually, Willie spotted that Louis wasn't eating and asked why. "As I cook," replied Louis, "I like to taste from the pot, check my seasonings are right, so I've got little appetite by the end." He chortled inwardly as Willie fell for his tale.

Eventually, Louis got to return to his warmhearted mother, playing blues at night until early the next morning on his cornet in a local honky-tonk joint, run by a Frenchman—improbably named Henry Ponce. Louis's performances were fueled by the large bucket lunch Mary Ann made him. His wage was supplemented by another job driving a coal cart for Andrews Coal Yard (and writing "Coal Yard Blues"). He loved listening to and talking with the old hustlers at lunchtime in the coal yard, drinking his ten-cent cup of beer and eating a juicy po' boy sandwich, though he did lament the thinness of the ham and cheese cuts. An ingenious little piece of entrepreneurism supplemented his wage, which entailed Louis and his little sister, Mama Lucy, sorting through barrels of food waste, meat such as half-spoiled chicken and goose, old bread, and spoiled potatoes—the garbage left by the big produce houses in Front o' Town. Louis picked out the edible pieces and, with Mary Ann and the rest of the Armstrong clan, boiled these up, dressed them in a tasty sauce, and sold them on to posh restaurants, sometimes swapping them for sandwiches or a meal. Then again, finger food could always be picked up through attending wakes and funerals. Louis would show up, lead the hymn, and then slip off to the kitchen to load up on free coffee, crackers, and cheese. At other times, he picked up cash working as a dishwasher in Thompson's Restaurant, where part of his wage was made up of doughnuts, ice cream, and cream puffs—great at first, you'd think, but after a few weeks the very sight of a cream puff turned Louis green.

The deep, rich, Creole gumbo or cabbage and rice at home, cooked by Mary Ann, was much more delicious than doughnuts or funeral meats—Mary Ann's food was so ingeniously prepared that you'd want nothing else. And that was really saying something, given that Mary Ann called her children "the wrecking crew" because they ate so much. Mary Ann, though, had a particular remedy to the heavy "poor man's" black soul food they all ate—a nightly dose of laxative, a "purge" just before bedtime, along with this advice: "Son—always keep your bowels open and nothing can harm you." Armstrong swore by this for the rest of his life. The fact that Lucille would make him a perfect wife could only have been confirmed by her recommendation of the brilliant laxative Swiss Kriss. Along with the "red beans and ricely" salutation at the end of a letter, Louis wasn't beyond signing off with Swiss Kriss! It was far better than the purge he had been using, which made him "*sput* like a motorboat."

Mary Ann worked long, hard hours, as Louis put it, working so hard "in the white folk's yards, washing, ironing and taking care of the white kids," and every moment's labor was worth the sight of seeing her children eat. Mary Ann shoved fifteen cents in Louis's hand and sent him off to the chicory-scented Poydras Street Market, erected on the old plantation lands of Joseph Poydras, to buy catfish heads. From these she made vast pots of court bouillon. Armstrong, using New Orleans Creole patois, called this fish stew *cubie yon*, with which Mary Ann enriched a tomato sauce and served with soft, delicious, and fluffy white rice. From the simplest of ingredients, she could create the miraculous. Off she'd go to Zatteran's grocery to pick up rice, red beans, a large red onion, and a solid wedge of fatback. Then she'd move on to spend a nickel on stale loaves of bread at Stahle's bakery. All of these ingredients were reduced down to a rich, aromatic gravy that could be smelled a block away. She taught Louis how to cook their favorite dishes, a legendary Creole gumbo with its clouds of shellfish-scented aroma and delicious jambalaya packed with flavorsome lumps of pink bologna sausage, oysters, hard-shell crabs, and shrimp, with tomato sauce sweetening and moistening the rice. "If you ever," Louis claimed, "tasted Mary Ann's jambalaya and did not lick your fingers, my name is not Louis Satchmo Daniel Armstrong."

Jambalaya

INGREDIENTS

3 tbsp. oil
1 lb. shrimp, shelled and deveined
½ lb. crabmeat
6 oysters
¼ lb. bologna sausage, cut into chunks
1 cup rich fish stock
1 large onion, chopped
½ lb. smoked ham, diced
5 ripe tomatoes, chopped
2 celery ribs, chopped
3 shallots, chopped
1 bell pepper, chopped
3 tbsp. chopped parsley
2 bay leaves
2 tsp. dried oregano
1 tsp. Tabasco hot sauce
1 tsp. Creole seasoning
½ tsp. dried thyme
6 garlic cloves, chopped
2 cups cooked rice
Sea salt and freshly ground black pepper

METHOD

In a thick-based pan, sauté the onion in the oil over a gentle heat until it becomes golden brown. Add the ham and brown. Now add all the remaining ingredients—with the exception of the two cups of cooked rice, crab, shrimp and oysters—and cook, covered, on a low heat for three hours. Stir occasionally to make sure the jambalaya isn't becoming too dry. When the three hours are up, add the shrimp, crab, and oysters. Allow to cook for 4 minutes; then add the cooked rice and stir through to heat the rice. Serve.

Creole Seasoning

INGREDIENTS

2½ tbsp. sweet red paprika
1 tbsp. garlic powder
1 tbsp. onion powder
1 tbsp. dried Italian basil
1 tbsp. dried oregano
½ tbsp. dried thyme
½ tbsp. ground black pepper
½ tbsp. white pepper
½ tbsp. cayenne pepper
½ tbsp. celery seed

METHOD

In a bowl, combine all the spices together and store as you would any dried spice.

Red Beans and Rice

Three days before you want to eat red beans and rice, you need to make some "pickle meat," which is the delicious, aromatic, porky secret behind what makes red beans and rice so good. The brine pickle breaks down the pork, leaving it tender and scented.

Pickle Meat

INGREDIENTS

1 lb. boneless pork, cut into 1-inch cubes
½ liter distilled white vinegar
¼ cup yellow mustard seed
½ tbsp. celery seed
1 tbsp. red Tabasco sauce
2 fresh bay leaves, chopped
¼ tsp. cayenne pepper
2 allspice
4 cloves
4 garlic cloves, peeled and cracked
2 tsp. kosher salt
6 peppercorns

METHOD

Except for the pork, place all the ingredients in a large, deep saucepan. Bring to boil for 4 minutes, then take your pickle off the heat and allow it to cool. When cool, pour the aromatic pickle over the diced pork and mix thoroughly (mixing will get rid of trapped air bubbles). Cover and place in the refrigerator for 3 days.

At the end of the 3 days, assemble the ingredients for the main red beans and rice dish.

Red Beans and Rice Ingredients

3 tbsp. bacon grease
1 lb. red kidney beans, soaked in water overnight
3 pints chicken stock
2 onions, chopped
¾ lb. "pickle meat"
½ lb. smoked ham, diced
1 bell pepper, chopped
5 celery ribs, chopped
10 garlic cloves, chopped
Pinch of cayenne pepper
½ lb. Andouille sausage, cut into ½-inch chunks
½ lb. smoked sausage
2 tsp. fresh thyme
3 bay leaves
2 tbsp. fresh, chopped parsley
1 tsp. Creole seasoning
Worcestershire sauce
Red Tabasco sauce
4 cups cooked white rice
3 spring onions, finely chopped, to garnish
Creole hot sausage patties, served alongside

METHOD

Bring the kidney beans to a boil in a large pan with the 3 pints of chicken stock. Simmer for approximately an hour, until the beans are cooked but not crumbling.

Meanwhile, in a heavy-based pan, melt the bacon fat and add the chopped, raw, smoked ham and brown. Next, add the onions, bell pepper, and celery—the special "trinity" of New Orleans cooking. Sauté these until the onions turn a pale gold. Add a pinch of cayenne. Now add the two types of sausage. Give them 4 minutes to cook. Now add the garlic, fresh thyme, bay leaves, parsley, Creole seasoning, Worcestershire sauce, and red Tabasco sauce. Add the "pickle meat," the beans, and the remaining 3 pints of chicken stock. Bring to boil and then reduce the heat to a low simmer and cook, uncovered, for about two hours. Taste and adjust seasonings as the red beans and rice cook. Make sure to stir occasionally to check the mixture is not sticking—at the same time, top up with water if necessary to prevent it from becoming too dry. The beans will gradually start to thicken the sauce, making it creamy, as some of them crumble. About 20 minutes before the end, mash about a ¼ of the beans against the side of the pan. Put your hot sausage patties on to grill now.

When you are ready to serve your creamy, aromatic red beans and rice, garnish with the finely chopped spring onions and serve with a couple of hot sausage patties.

Homemade Hot Sausage Patties

INGREDIENTS

1 lb. minced, fatty pork
2 garlic cloves, minced
1 tbsp. cayenne pepper
1 tsp. freshly ground black pepper
1 tsp. sea salt
1 tsp. bay leaf, ground
1 tsp. fresh thyme
1 tbsp. paprika
Pinch of sugar
6 spring onions, finely chopped

METHOD

Mix well, form into patties, and grill.

Seafood Gumbo

INGREDIENTS

1 tbsp. sunflower oil
1 tbsp. all-purpose flour
1 green bell pepper, finely chopped
3 green celery ribs, finely chopped
1 large onion, finely chopped
4 garlic cloves, minced
½ tbsp. tomato purée
2 large tomatoes, seeded and diced
½ lb. okra, chopped—okra are really tubes of glue masquerading as vegetables, so don't be alarmed by the sticky ooze they shed—this will thicken your gumbo!
1 pint good fish stock
3 bay leaves
½ tbsp. Creole seasoning blend
1 tsp. cayenne pepper
Freshly ground black pepper
½ lb. small, fresh, peeled and deveined prawns
¼ lb. fresh crabmeat, both brown and white
6 oysters, freshly shucked, with their juices kept
Louisiana hot sauce

METHOD

In a large, heavy pot, heat the oil until it almost smokes, then add the flour. Stir constantly until a chocolate brown roux is formed; this takes about 5 minutes. Add the onions, bell pepper, celery, and garlic. Allow these to meld with the roux for about 1 minute, scraping the sticky, delicious roux from the base of the pan. Now add the tomato puree and tomatoes. Cook these in the roux for 10 minutes. The wonderful thing about gumbo is that you can smell each stage of the dish and savor the aromas of each new layer of the dish. Breathe in lungfuls of Satchmo's childhood. Ahhh . . . Then add the bay leaves, Creole seasoning, and cayenne pepper; season with sea salt and black pepper. Give these another 10 minutes in the roux. Add the okra, and cook this for 10 minutes. Now add the fish stock slowly and stirring constantly. Bring your gumbo base to boil, turn down to a gentle simmer, and cook for 25 minutes. Add the prawns, oysters, and oyster juice. After 3 minutes, add the crabmeat. The gumbo is now ready to eat: Satchmo said New Orleans gumbo "makes my big mouth run water just to think about it," even from a thousand miles away. Just give it a blast of Louisiana hot sauce and serve on top of fluffy white rice.

FRANK SINATRA

Food was about nostalgia, friendship, romance, and domination for Frank. Notoriously, he ate ham and eggs—using a knife and fork—off the naked breasts of a prostitute (even more believable, as Frank did enjoy a brunch of bacon, eggs, and toast almost every day of his life), but then he also raised a laugh with Humphrey Bogart when he stole brilliant talent scout Swifty Lazar's hat . . . and then reunited Swifty with his hat by serving him poached eggs with it.

Frank Sinatra would have sold his soul for good Italian cuisine, having been brought up on linguine by his mother, bossy Dolly Sinatra, who liked to meddle in local Democratic politics in Jersey City and then trotted out in Hoboken at night, with her black abortionist's bag—she was known as "Hat Pin Dolly." Dolly was quite a character: loud mouthed, opinionated, unreflective—she liked to dance the tarantella at weddings and arrived at local New Jersey funerals with a consolatory plate of sausages.

Home spelled spaghetti for Frank and holidays of the delicious crispeddi Dolly made: Italianate, sugar-dusted, deep-fried dough puffs, given out in the neighborhood at holidays and festivals. Best of all, though, was Dolly's lemon meringue pie, criss-crossed with kisses of caramelized meringue.

Frank's illiterate firefighter father, Marty, and Dolly were both wonderful cooks and taught Frank how to cook. Frank himself fondly recalled his father at the stove, face sweating, a towel thrown over his shoulder. Sicilian-born Marty could roll a mean gnocchi and, when visiting, loved to cook for Frank's parties. Then, a humble and modest man, Marty sat quietly in some corner of the room, watching with pride as Frank's friends ate his food. From northern Italy, near Genoa, Dolly spent hours slowly constructing a huge pot of deeply flavored, crimson "gravy" for the pasta. Mafia heavies and Frank's buddies, such as his best friend, restauranteur and bodyguard Ermenigildo "Jilly" Rizzo, wandered in, huge and boggle-eyed, jostled Dolly's elbow, and dipped bread in her gravy. Indulgently, Dolly scolded Jilly (she called him "Fuck Face") for eating out of the pot. Dolly even cooked for the petrifying Sam Giancana (who, incidentally, was mowed down by gunmen years later while frying himself a sausage and spinach snack).

Frank's long-suffering first wife, Nancy Barbato, was a much gentler character than Dolly and tried hard to please Frank with the sedentary, homely pleasures of spaghetti and lemon pie. She was sensibly frugal and devoted to her family, in hard times leaving the unaffordable meat out of their spaghetti sauce. Quiet, in the background, untouched and unnoticed, Nancy was dismissed as a little Italian housewife dishing out spaghetti to Frank and his pack. Once he'd lost interest in her, she tried to tempt him back to the marital bed and away from the embrace of Ava Gardner by keeping a jar of homemade spaghetti sauce in the fridge (assembled like a love potion, according to Dolly's instructions).

Finally, Nancy agreed to divorce Frank, and Dolly and Marty immediately invited the beautiful, straight-talking Ava for dinner to the house Frank had bought for them in Hoboken. Ava never forgot her first real Sinatra family food experience. The house was warm and generously full of life, laughter, and fun. An ancient uncle who lived with them appeared from nowhere, and a huge, brilliantly starched white sheet was draped over one of the large beds, as if awaiting a bride. But all over the sheet were scattered scores of tiny, uncooked ravioli shells, handmade by Dolly and Marty. Dolly's incredible Italian dinner charmed Ava—with, as she put it, "chicken like you've never tasted in your life . . . wonderful little meat things rolled in dough, and just about every Italian goody you can imagine."

Even Frank could solve their battles with food. After one fiery row during a New York performance of Frank's, Ava stormed out, jealously accusing Frank of crooning to an old flame. Ava eventually returned home, bedraggled and bewitching, after catching cold and wet trains back and forth across New York. Frank was waiting anxiously for her. "Egg sandwich?" he asked. She remained silent. Frank said nothing else, but quietly put a frying pan on the stove, heated a spoon or two of olive oil, and added a slice of snowy white bread. Then he dropped the egg into the oil, salted and peppered it, and sandwiched the egg in the fried bread. He poured Ava a big glass of milk, handed her the sandwich, and said he was glad she was home. Through a mouthful of egg sandwich, Ava agreed.

Although Frank and Ava were always fighting and cursing each other, then making up dramatically, Dolly was determined to help them stay together. Ava was her kind of lady. Indeed, Dolly resolved one of their famous fights by making them both swallow a big spoonful of her gravy. She invited them both for a cozy, intimate Italian meal. Ava and Frank were clearly delighted to see each other but tongue-tied. Dolly called for them both to come into the kitchen, where they stood on either side of her. "Taste this," she said, holding out her big gravy spoon to each in turn. They tasted the gravy, began to laugh, and hugged each other, and then the two of them grabbed Dolly as well in a bear hug.

Overcooked, flabby pasta or a blob of tomato ketchup was enough to incense Frank; a plate of soggy pasta in Matteo's Italian restaurant in Los Angeles, owned by his childhood buddy, Matty Jordan, had Frank storming into the kitchens. He looked around wildly, "Where are all the Italians?" he roared at the startled Filipino kitchen staff. Not content, he shot back upstairs and threw his plate of pasta against the wall. As he walked out, he dipped his finger in the tomato sauce and signed the smear: *Picasso* (Matty very good-naturedly put a frame around this later). He had fewer problems with the food in Jilly's restaurant/club being cooked by a Chinese chef named Howie. Late at night, Frank, his stomach rumbling, grabbed the funnel that Jilly used to communicate with Howie in the kitchen. He bellowed, "Howie! Send up some food!" only for the reply to come, "Fut you, Mr. Sinatra." This amused Frank, and he'd bellow back, "Fut you too, Howie!"

Frank, then, loved the pure, authentic tastes of Italian food, although he always kept an emergency supply of tins of his favorite Campbell's chicken soup with rice in his dressing room. Never did he lose an opportunity to feed his nearest and dearest Italian food—even as Frank comforted Judy Garland in the throes of labor giving birth to Liza Minnelli, Frank decided to order pizzas for everyone. He did, however, have an aversion to garlic; on the set of *Never the Few*, Gina Lollobrigida claimed she'd eaten raw garlic in order to make it difficult for Sinatra to kiss her. Frank attributed his garlic phobia to his boyhood experience of Dolly roping a head of garlic around his neck at the first sign of a cold or flu. He understood, though, that garlic was integral to flavor and would use it to flavor a dish, but then carefully fish out the garlic afterward.

Nights with broads and cards on the Strip mellowed in time to inebriated dinners at Chasen's in Los Angeles. Dean Martin, bored with martinis, asked the barman there to rustle up something new to titillate his taste buds, and the "Flame of Love" martini was born, a delicious concoction of ice, vodka, Tio Pepe, and flambéed orange rind rubbed on the rim of the martini glass.

After a long night raising hell with the Rat Pack, when the fun was exhausted and everyone stank of scotch and cigarettes, Frank—shaking off the effects of the Jack Daniels he loved so well—often made his speciality pasta dish at 3 or 4 a.m. He put a big pot of water on the stove, salted it, brought it to boil, and added pasta. This cooked until it was just opaque, with a good al dente bite to it. Then he'd drain the pasta. He'd crack two eggs into it, whirl them about—the warm pasta cooked the eggs—then add a stack of finely grated Parmesan cheese, with a drizzle of olive oil and some black pepper and sea salt. If Dean Martin was hungry, then Frank cooked up a pot of Dean's favorite, which he called *fajool*—in short, pasta fagioli, with barlotti beans, tomatoes, and elbow macaroni. They demolished it together.

Ever impressive in his excesses, be they underworld connections, women, music, or food, Frank Sinatra was brilliantly lavish with his gifts—although his diamonds had the effect of bewildering rather than impressing Mia Farrow—and 1966 was no exception. Over lunch in Palm Springs, Frank's friend Ruth Gordon ordered a slice of onion to go with her burger. "The onions here are nothing special," Frank offered, "you gotta try Maui burgers." Ruth had never even heard of them. "Oh, for crying out loud," moaned Frank, and he left the table. Was he in a huff? No. Secretly, he'd gone to order the onions flown in from Hawaii. Soon they arrived and everyone had Maui onions for lunch. Even Mia Farrow was impressed, but she was bored by Sinatra's interminable interest in golf. Indeed, although Mia officially met Frank Sinatra when she was nineteen years old—she dropped her bag in front of him and the jars of baby food she carried about for her cat rolled across the floor, along with her retainer and pictures of several horses—she had in truth met him first when she was eleven years old, dining with her father, John Farrow, in the famous Beverly Hills restaurant Romanoffs. "Pretty girl," Sinatra observed. To which Farrow replied, "You stay away from her." No sooner, however, had Frank scooped up Mia's retainer than he whisked her off to his bachelor pad in Palm Springs, where she drifted around, her cat tucked under her arm, mildly surprised to see Yul Brynner by the pool with a woman who was weeping (Frank's cook also took to weeping fairly frequently over her no-good husband).

Foodwise, things looked much less hopeful when Frank tied the knot with wife number three, Mia. Mia wasn't much interested in food, and Dolly knew in her bones that this marriage was doomed, telling Ava, "This one don't talk. She don't eat. . . . It won't last long . . . it's a good thing they weren't married in the church." Frank's guests were also bewildered by his timid, quiet bride, who was dressed in long, white stockings like a nurse. Nevertheless, Dolly bravely showed off her wares with a wedding feast of scungilli (large marine snails, usually served in marinara sauce); scallopine (cutlets of veal that have been beaten thin, doused lightly in seasoned flour, and fried in butter and drizzled with lemon juice); stick-to-your-ribs sausage gnocchi; and stuffed green lasagne noodles. In their prenuptial days, Frank asked his cook at Palm Springs, Elsie, to stand aside while he made his signature spaghetti sauce, with Mia perched on a stool at his side, eating potato chips.

Rat Pack "Fajool" (Pasta e Fagioli)

INGREDIENTS

8 oz. cooked barlotti beans
4 oz. elbow macaroni
4 oz. pancetta
1 celery rib, finely chopped
4 tomatoes, skinned, seeded, and chopped
1 onion, finely chopped
2 garlic cloves, halved
3 tbsp. olive oil
1 glass dry white wine
2 cups chicken stock
Fresh basil
Sea salt
Freshly ground black pepper
Freshly grated Parmesan cheese

METHOD

If cooking with dried beans, soak them overnight and then cook in boiling water for 1½ hours. Warm the olive oil in a deep saucepan and sauté the pancetta, onions, celery, and garlic. True to Frank Sinatra, remove the garlic from the pan. Now add the tomatoes and white wine. Add the drained beans, pour on chicken stock, and cook for 20 minutes, mashing some of the beans against the pan side. Now add the pasta and cook for a further 10 to 15 minutes, until it is al dente. Stir torn basil into the pasta minutes before serving. Salt and pepper to taste. Sprinkle with Parmesan.

Red Gravy—if your marriage is on the rocks, try this . . .

INGREDIENTS

FOR THE BRACIOLE (THESE ARE STEAK ROLLS) . . .

2 lb. thin, individual braising steaks
2 tbsp. flat-leaf parsley, finely chopped
2 tbsp. fresh basil, torn
4 garlic cloves, minced
6 tbsp. Parmesan, finely grated
4 tbsp. chopped raisins and pine nuts
Sea salt
Freshly ground black pepper

FOR THE MAIN BODY OF RED GRAVY . . .

Olive oil
Pork ribs, cut into sections
6 Italian sausages, spiced with fennel and red wine
2 onions, finely chopped
2 celery stalks, finely chopped
6 garlic cloves, minced
2 tbsp. tomato puree
3 tins chopped tomatoes
1 tsp. dried oregano
1 tsp. dried, crushed chilies
2 generous glasses of red wine
2 cups strong beef or chicken stock
2 cups water
1 tbsp. honey
4 bay leaves

FOR THE MEATBALLS . . .

2 lb. minced beef
1 cup ricotta cheese
½ cup Parmesan, grated
1 egg
¼ cup milk
¾ cup fresh breadcrumbs
2 tbsp. fresh basil, torn
1 tsp. sea salt
Freshly ground black pepper
Pasta

METHOD

Begin by making the braciole. Beat the steaks with a mallet to tenderize the meat. Sprinkle the steaks liberally with the parsley, basil, garlic, Parmesan, raisins, and pine nuts. Salt and pepper to taste. Next, roll each steak up tightly and secure each roll with either a toothpick or a piece of string.

In a large, deep pan, heat the olive oil and brown the braciole, pork ribs, and Italian sausage in batches. When they are golden, remove them. Now turn the heat down and add the onions and celery. Sauté them until they turn a rich gold. Add the minced garlic, crushed chili, and oregano. Stir in the tomato puree and cook until the puree darkens. Now add the tomatoes, beef stock, and red wine. Stir in the honey and add the bay leaves. Top up with water. Add the pork ribs and sausages and cook the gravy on simmer for two hours.

Now make the meatballs. In a bowl, combine the minced beef, ricotta, Parmesan, egg, milk, breadcrumbs, basil, sea salt, and black pepper. Shape these into 2-inch balls.

After the gravy has cooked for 2 hours, add the meatballs. Simmer for a further 30 minutes. Ten minutes before the time is up, put some water on to boil and cook the pasta until it is al dente. Serve it separately, buttered, and with a spoonful of red gravy stirred through it. Finally, remove the sausage, ribs, and meatballs from the gravy. Lay these on a plate. Put another handful of torn basil in the gravy. Serve up the three plates or bowls of pasta, meat, and red gravy.

Crispeddi

These delicious morsels come in both savory and sweet form, stuffed with either anchovies or ricotta.

INGREDIENTS

Sunflower oil for frying
1 lb. all-purpose flour
½ cup warm water
1 oz. fast-acting yeast
1½ tbsp. olive oil
¼ tsp. sugar
Pinch of sea salt

FOR SAVORY CRISPEDDI . . .

6 preserved anchovies, finely chopped
6 small cubes of mozzarella
Dried fennel seeds or oregano
A little chopped dill

FOR SWEET CRISPEDDI . . .

½ lb. ricotta
4 oz. sugar
Zest of ½ orange
1 tbsp. candied peel
¼ tsp. vanilla essence
¼ tsp. orange flower water
Powdered sugar to garnish

METHOD

In a bowl, mix together the fast-acting yeast with the warm water; put this in a warm place for 10 minutes, until it starts to bubble. Sieve ½ cup of the flour into a mixing bowl, and add the sugar, water, and yeast and combine to make a loose, wet dough. Put this in a warm place and leave it to rise for an hour.

After an hour, take the risen wet dough and combine it with the rest of the flour. Cautiously add more warm water, olive oil, and the sea salt. Now knead the dough until it is pliable and elastic. Place it in an oiled bowl, cover, and leave it to rise in a warm place for a further 3 hours.

Prepare the crispeddi fillings. In a bowl, mix chopped anchovies with chopped mozzarella. Add some oregano or a pinch of fennel seeds and some chopped dill. Reserve.

In a bowl, mix the ricotta with sugar, orange zest, vanilla, orange flower water, and candied peel.

When the dough has risen to twice its size, oil your hands lightly and divide up the dough, shaping it into smallish, egg-sized balls. Traditionally, an oblong crispeddi spells anchovies, while round crispeddi are sweet with ricotta.

To fill the anchovy crispeddi, take one of the oblong dough shapes, flatten it, and fill it with the anchovy mix. Moisten the edge with a little water and seal. Reshape. Do the same with the ricotta-filled circular crispeddi. Now lay the crispeddi on a surface lightly dusted with flour, cover with a tea towel, and leave to rest for one hour in a warm spot.

When the hour is up, heat 1 to 2 inches of sunflower oil in a deep, heavy-based frying pan until it is hot. Pop the crispeddi, a couple at a time, into the hot oil, turning them until they are uniformly a lovely, light-honey-brown color. Remove with a slotted spoon and dry on kitchen towels. Dust the ricotta crispeddi with a little powdered sugar; salt and pepper the anchovy crispeddi.

WOODY GUTHRIE

At first Woody Guthrie's childhood seemed to have all the makings of a gentle American idyll; he was raised in a fine house in Oklahoma by two loving parents, with a cheerful, jaunty gaggle of brothers and sisters. But his father, Charley, was in a risky trade—land trading—and a terrible shadow was about to fall across the family. Huntington's disease, put bluntly, is an inherited, degenerative madness leading to dementia, a time bomb that had begun to tick inside Woody's mother, Nora.

First there came fire. The Guthries' fine, brand-new house burned down. Not a single Guthrie was burned alive, but fire jumped quickly from room to room, leaving almost nothing but a pile of dust. Rumor had it that the fire and Nora's strange behavior were connected. Woody watched as his lovely mother was submerged by depression, her voice stilled, no longer singing to him the folk ballads he loved. The family moved into an eccentric-looking huddle of a house—Woody could see the dusty trail of the rail tracks from its high porch, and the snuff cans of its previous inhabitants lined the rafters like tinny bats. It looked as though the Guthries might pull together as they cooked up their first meal in the new house. Even though Woody's lovely, funny, older sister, Clara, moaned about the grumpy, old, dilapidated stove, little Woody savored the beefsteak and gravy, the green torpedoes of okra rolled in cornmeal and fried in grease, hot biscuits with a rich seam of melted butter through their middle, and all finished off with peaches. The house held more secret peaches; Woody discovered a tawny hoard of bottled peaches in the cobwebby basement, oozy with juice, on which he gorged. But then, with the timeless inevitability of tragedy, even as he sat with his new tousle-haired friend in the basement, licking the sticky peach juice from their fingers, the other boy asked, "Kids say your mama got mad an' set her brand-new house on fire, an' burnt ever'thin' plumb up. Did she?"

And fire came back again: Clara, ironing one day on an old kerosene stove, was swallowed up in a shroud of flame and died within hours. Her charred skin hung from her, and as she lay dying, her last schoolgirlish question was about her exams. She said to her teacher, Mrs. Johnson, "Do you—think—I'll—pass?"

"Yes, you'll pass," Mrs. Johnson replied, and she closed Clara's eyes.

Fire became a metaphor for Woody for the sort of energy that lit his music as well as the terrible force of the fires that consumed the Guthries. In a terrible, combustible finale to the family's collapse, Nora was committed to an Oklahoma insane asylum for setting fire to Charley, Woody's father, with a kerosene lamp. Perhaps Nora was as haunted as Woody was to be by the part Charley gleefully played in the Ku Klux Klan rape and lynching of African Americans Laura Nelson and her son, L.D. Poor Woody Guthrie. Thin times lay ahead in later childhood, because while his father was nursed far away, Woody survived by "junking"—going through piles of refuse and turning what he found into cents and maybe a dollar or two, washing dishes in a chili palace, selling root beer, and picking cotton. Food allowed him brief glimpses of the happier families and homes of other boys when he managed to beg a home-cooked meal from someone. Lungfuls of Bull Durham tobacco and a gulp of corn whiskey muted his appetite, but there was only so much moonshine could do to erase a boy's hunger. But hunger also taught him early on what he could get for his music, and he traded harmonica tunes for sandwiches, as he said himself: "I'd play fer my beans an' cornbread, an' drink branch water, 'er anything else ta play an' sing fer folks that likes it, folks that knows it, an' lives what I'm singin' 'bout."

During the lean years of the Depression, Woody met his first wife-to-be, Mary, and they dated on hot dogs and ice cream, too poor to afford the trappings of a real date. Then, a father of one, Guthrie managed to scrape a living somehow in the Dust Bowl of America, doing the rounds as a faith healer, traveling up and down America as a hobo—you can hear the rail tracks in his music—and Guthrie was still selling anything he could to fill his stomach. After one stint of two days without food, Woody found that he started to shake uncontrollably and was so intensely hungry that he "could smell a piece of bacon or corncake frying at a half a mile away. The very thought of fruit made me lick my hot lips," and he could only sit by the train lines and think of "homes, with ice boxes, cook stoves, tables, hot meals, cold lunches, with hot coffee, ice cold beer, homemade wine." Guthrie was never very picky with food after living for a time on ketchup sandwiches during the Great Depression. One day, after jumping off a Southern Pacific freight car, the best Guthrie could do physically was to stagger into a bean and chili bar, peel off the wet, green sweater he wore, sell it for one dime to a man too tall for it, and trade the dime for a plate of the patron's chili. Ever true, though, to his love for his fellow man, Guthrie never hesitated to share his bread with other hoboes and even pressed his own pay packet into the hand of a man he met who told Guthrie of his destitution. Despite all that poverty threw at him, Guthrie refused one thing: to change his music to suit the needs of the record companies. His soul was not for sale, even though, as he put it, "They try to tell me if I wanta eat and stay alive, I gotta sing their damn old phony junk."

One child became four children, and Guthrie struggled with the financial demands of fatherhood and his keen, desperate drive to write music: in a small, rough note to himself he said he could be a poet to match Walt Whitman were he not father to four children. Fatherhood kept Guthrie working in the poorest, most menial jobs, a day's labor given at the cost of who knows how many songs unwritten. With a parenting style that would have modern-day social workers knocking at his door, Guthrie kept his children quiet by any means possible while he worked, sedating them with breakfasts of hot dogs and orange juice stirred through with rum, buying their silence with candy through the day—anything to keep playing, strumming, jamming.

But children were not the enemy. Guthrie's alcoholism hit him hard, but behind it hid a far worse enemy: the Huntington's that had killed his mother revealing itself in strange, jerky movements and peculiar, physical twitches that the medical profession put down to alcohol abuse when Guthrie presented himself at the hospital. Doctors refused to listen to Guthrie's story about his mother. When the middle-aged, twitching, worn hobo that Guthrie had become exclaimed that he was enough of a musician to have written songs, played them, and appeared on TV, doctors attributed his claims to the delusional behavior of advanced alcoholism. Even Guthrie came to embrace this misdiagnosis—he'd rather be an alcoholic any day than the inheritor of the madness that had killed Nora.

No matter how little the medical profession appreciated the patient they held, members of the American population who had heard Guthrie play and recognized the genius of his style certainly did. They heard of his incarceration in a lunatic asylum, and one couple in particular, Bob and Sidsel Gleason, discovered he was being held in Greystone Park Psychiatric Hospital, an asylum only a forty-minute drive from their home in East Orange, New Jersey. Guthrie had bewitched them twenty years earlier when they listened to him play on the Woody and Lefty Lou KFVD radio station broadcasts. Now they realized their chance had come to care for Guthrie in some small way.

They contacted Guthrie's second wife, Marjorie, in 1959: Would it be possible, they asked, for them to take Guthrie out of the hospital on Sundays, drive him to their home on Arlington Avenue, and feed him a meal to please his soul? She agreed. And so it came to pass that every Sunday the Gleasons rolled up at Greystones, and Guthrie, gentle and grateful, would try best as he could to climb into their car, roll down the window, take a lungful of clear, free air, and ask (like all freed men), "How about a smoke?" Then they would trundle off in the car to the Gleason's apartment on the fourth floor of Arlington Avenue, where Guthrie might have a long, hot soak in their bath and a hair trim from Sidsel, and then, a root beer by his elbow (the doctors had banned alcohol), think up some replies to the fan mail he had crammed in his socks and shirt pockets. But the best thing in the day, the final kindness, was that Sidsel (known as Sid and from Montana) cooked Guthrie his favorite meal of cowboy stew on those Sunday afternoons. In a sense, Guthrie's music was still filling his stomach with someone else's taste of home—this stew of cheap beef cuts (kidney, liver, heart) stewed with onions, garlic, and canned tomatoes, with hot biscuits to soak up the gravy. Death was on its way, looking out for Woody Guthrie and finding him in his fifty-fifth year. Sidsel Gleason told a reporter, "I have never met a human being that has the courage that he has." And while the aroma of cowboy stew laced the air, visitors came. Among them one January was a young man, Guthrie's greatest inheritor, knotty-haired Bob Dylan, his guitar under his arm and inscribed with the self-same words that Guthrie had carved on his: "This machine kills fascists." They'd eat their plates of cowboy stew, and Dylan sang Guthrie's own songs back to him, even smoking the Camel cigarettes Guthrie liked. "I was there as a servant, to sing him his songs. . . . That's all I did," said Dylan. "I was Woody Guthrie's jukebox." On a card, Guthrie wrote, "I ain't dead yet," and Dylan carried it around with him, like a talisman.

Cornmeal Okra

INGREDIENTS

1 lb. okra pods, cut into sections
¼ cup buttermilk
¼ cup cornmeal
¼ cup all-purpose flour
1 tsp. onion or garlic powder
Sea salt and black pepper
3 tbsp. bacon fat

METHOD

Sprinkle salt and pepper over the okra and then soak it in the buttermilk. Drain and then roll the okra in the seasoned cornmeal and flour. Melt the bacon fat in a frying pan and fry the okra until it is golden. Dry on a paper towel and serve.

Home-Cooked Cowboy Stew (serve with Hot Biscuits)

INGREDIENTS

2 lb. cleaned heart, kidneys, and liver, cut into 1-inch pieces
4 tbsp. vinegar
Fresh thyme
2 bay leaves
2 tbsp. all-purpose flour
2 tbsp. butter
1 can plum tomatoes
3 medium onions, chopped
3 garlic cloves, crushed
Sea salt and freshly ground pepper

METHOD

The night before making this stew, marinate the diced heart in 4 tablespoons of vinegar, a rounded teaspoon of fresh thyme, and 2 fresh bay leaves.

The next day, drain the diced heart and dry it on kitchen roll. Salt and pepper the flour, and flour the pieces of offal. In a thick-bottomed skillet, melt the butter. Gently sauté the onions until they are golden brown. Brown the offal in the butter—you may need to do this in batches—and then add the tomatoes and garlic. Allow to cook for 20 minutes.

Pour yourself a root beer, put "This Land Is Your Land" on the gramophone, and plate up some cowboy stew, okra, and hot biscuits.

BOB DYLAN

One can almost taste the black coffee and thin red wine vibrate in Bob Dylan's early music. He always seemed to drink too much and eat too little, and his first tries at singing for his supper were so bad that, during his time at the University of Minnesota in 1959, local clubs and bars refused to let him play for his dinner, as he'd put other customers off theirs. Things improved marginally when Dylan arrived with his "scratchy" voice and his sloppy, wrinkled clothes to sleep on other people's couches and eat other people's food in New York. He was on a mission to find his hero, Woody Guthrie, and to learn from him as much as he could about folk songs, what Dylan called "handed down" songs. Dylan played a little at night in the eccentric Café Wha? (twitchy Woody Allen was cracking jokes on stage there, too). The floor was yours for a nerve-wracking ten to fifteen minutes. Café Wha? was host to eccentric acts during the day—Tiny Tim, the ukulele player who sang in a girlish falsetto voice; a hypnotist in a turban; a blind poet or two; and Billy the Butcher, who played only one song and was fresh out of Bellevue Insane Asylum. The resident cook, Norbert, had a face like a knuckle and wore an apron smeared with bloody whirls of tomato. Sweetly enough, though, Norbert was saving every cent he made to visit Verona and the graves of Romeo and Juliet. Dylan compared Norbert's kitchen to a cave, but Norbert's cooking was payment for his act—limitless supplies of hamburger and French fries. If this wasn't available, Norbert let Dylan and Tiny Tim heat up a frying pan for a tin of spaghetti or some pork and beans.

Dylan drifted from sofa to sofa, turning up inexplicably on the doorstep. Some hosts recalled him as maddeningly lazy, their hearts sinking when they found him on their doormat, while others—like the Gleasons, who made cowboy stew for Dylan and Guthrie—praised him for being the sort of guest who always did the dishes.

When he got his deal with Columbia Records, Dylan started to look for his own apartment to rent, with Suze Rotolo, his shiny-eyed girlfriend, in tow. 161 West Fourth Street was just the ticket, on a street that held the Music Inn, which twanged with every conceivable exotic instrument from dulcimers to didgeridoos. Junky metal stairwells traversed the red brick, and the tomato-and-oregano aroma of cheap and ancient pizza sauce wafted up to Dylan's $60-a-month flat. Tantalizingly, across the road stood the glass-fronted kitchen of the Bagel—a cook was always framed by the window, slapping burgers onto an open-flame grill. Suze and Dylan, wrapped in the thick sweaters the chilly flat forced them into, sat side by side, elbows on the table of the long, dingy counter, and ate the burgers, which were deliciously charred but moist and rare inside, packed into fresh crusty bread.

Or they staggered back after a night in the Village, with warm loaves cooked in a brick, coal-fired oven by Sicilian bakers, Zito and Sons, on Bleecker Street (Zito's bread was also an early morning favorite with Frank Sinatra and the Rat Pack).

Dylan's passion for Suze would be eclipsed all too soon by Joan Baez, with her limpid brown eyes and lank hair. She, too, came to be mesmerized by Bob Dylan, falling deeply in love with him eventually. When she first met him in Greenwich Village in 1961, though, he looked far from physically impressive. He had on clothes too small for him, and his cheeks trembled with puppy fat. He was really clever, though, full of raw, original ideas, with a dry and private humor that stemmed from his obsessive music and poetry-driven world. Talking to Baez, he'd absentmindedly pick at a stew she'd made, eating all the meat from it, leaving only potatoes and vegetables for Baez. Dylan's future wife, Sara, was, unbeknownst to Baez, already there on the periphery of his imagination and consciousness, but in the meantime the lovers, when in California, bought an upright piano together, drank coffee among the defunct sardine factories of Cannery Row, and zoomed by on a motorbike on the high, blue edge of Big Sur, where the Santa Lucia mountains plunge abruptly into the Pacific.

When Baez went to housesit a friend's place in Woodstock, New York, Dylan came with her and spent hours on his typewriter, drinking red wine, smoking, falling asleep, and then getting back up in the darkest hours of the night to start typing again. She'd ride his Triumph 350 out in the deep pine backwoods, surprised by the shock of love in her heart and discovering a fierce possessiveness inside, which led her to go to considerable lengths to keep Dylan's roving eye in check. This resulted in the infamous Baez-Dylan cake incident. They were eating in a restaurant one evening when Baez noticed a pallid, torn-about-looking girl staring mournfully at Dylan, and Dylan returning her stare. Baez decided drastic action was called for: she knew Dylan always gorged on food when he got drunk, and so she topped up his glass again and again, until his eyes were too pink and drowsy to roam. She then offered him dessert and, as soon as he'd licked the final spoonful of one irresistible custard pie, Baez called for a slice of pecan fudge cake and refilled his glass or called for another coffee.

But her plans were almost sunk when the girl wafted her way across the room to Dylan and sat down drunkenly, staring deep into Dylan's eyes. Furious, Baez stormed out to the alleyway and waited in the hope that the restaurant door would fly open and that Dylan would emerge, adoring and repentant. Instead, he rolled out groaning, holding his stomach, which was rotund and rock hard under his T-shirt. Baez drove him home, expecting him to throw up at every bend of the road. Instead, Dylan fell asleep, snoring peaceably. She even had to help him into bed, where he enjoyed the sleep of the innocents.

But all of Baez's machinations couldn't keep Dylan from his first wife, Sara Lowdnes, and the domesticity she represented. Although Sara may have seemed a slightly eccentric cook to more conservative guests—one recalled Sara making an unusual tuna salad with peanuts—Dylan's home life and kitchen was described by him in *Chronicles* as one of "the hot dogs with English muffins and noodles, the Cheerios and cornflakes with heavy cream—stirring flour into a large bowl for corn pudding and beating eggs."

Sara Oh Sara Corn Pudding

INGREDIENTS

- 6 ears of fresh sweet corn (enough for 2 cups of corn off the cob)
- 1 green chili, finely chopped
- 2 tbsp. butter
- Pinch of sea salt
- Freshly ground black pepper
- 3 eggs
- 2½ fl. oz. milk
- 200 ml. double cream
- 1 tbsp. all-purpose flour
- 3 spring onions, very finely chopped
- 1 garlic clove, crushed
- 2 tbsp. parsley, finely chopped
- 2 tbsp. finely grated Parmesan
- 1 tsp. fresh thyme, crumbled
- Pinch of grated nutmeg
- Pinch of cayenne
- Pinch of cinnamon
- 2 tbsp. grated mature cheddar

METHOD

Preheat the oven to 180°C. Set up a bain-marie in the oven. Butter a baking dish. Scrape the corn kernels from the cobs until you have 2 cups. Now heat the butter in a frying pan. Sauté the corn and the green chili in the butter with a little sea salt and black pepper. Remove from the heat and cool. Put 1 cup of corn in a food processor and blend into a mush; now add the eggs, milk, cream, and flour. Empty all this into a bowl and add the other cup of corn, diced spring onions, garlic, parsley, and Parmesan to the blended mixture. Now add the thyme, nutmeg, cayenne, and cinnamon. Pour the mixture into the baking dish, sprinkle with the cheddar cheese, and place the corn pudding in the hot water of the bain-marie and bake for between 30 and 40 minutes (until the corn pudding is firm).

You'll be glad to know that in his more mature years Dylan was reported as chewing on Red Man Tobacco, eating gumbo and crab legs on tour, and drinking brandy, whiskey, and Jack Daniels—all much more rock and roll than clingy girls and custard pie.

Custard Pie

8-inch pie dish, buttered

INGREDIENTS

FOR THE PIE CRUST . . .

9 oz. all-purpose flour
5 oz. butter, cut into sticks
4½ oz. vanilla sugar
1 large egg
1 tsp. grated lemon zest
½ tsp. ground nutmeg
Pinch of sea salt

FOR THE CUSTARD FILLING . . .

250 ml. double cream
250 ml. milk
Seeds scooped out of one vanilla pod
8 egg yolks
3½ oz. white sugar
Pulp and seeds from one scraped vanilla bean
Generous pinch of freshly grated nutmeg
¼ tsp. lemon zest

METHOD

First, make the pastry. With a hand-held electric mixer, cream together the butter, lemon zest, and sugar. Add the egg and beat until smooth. Sieve the flour with the salt and nutmeg. Gradually add this to the creamed butter, lemon zest, sugar, and egg. Turn the pastry onto a lightly floured surface and gently knead it until it comes together.

Now wrap the pastry in cling film, put it in the fridge, and leave it to chill for 30 minutes.

Butter the pie dish. Preheat the oven to 180°C.

Line a flan dish with the rolled-out pastry and trim the edges. Lightly prick the surface of the pastry. Now put a sheet of greaseproof paper over the pastry, pour in ceramic beans, and bake blind for 15 minutes. Then remove the paper and beans and return the pastry, uncovered, to the oven for a further 15 minutes. Remove from the oven and let it cool for 10 minutes.

Reduce the oven temperature to 120°C.

In a small, heavy-based saucepan, bring to nearly a boil the cream, milk, vanilla seeds, lemon zest, and nutmeg. Cream the egg yolks with the sugar, and then pour the hot milk mixture, in a thin stream, onto the egg mixture, whisking all the time.

Pour the custard mixture into the pastry case. Sprinkle on the top more grated nutmeg, and bake for about an hour or until a toothpick, inserted into the custard, comes out clean. Cool and serve.

Pecan Fudge Cake

INGREDIENTS

225 g. butter, softened
4 eggs, beaten together
4 oz. bittersweet chocolate
¼ tsp. sea salt
100 g. pecans, toasted
225 g. brown sugar
225 g. all-purpose flour
3 tsp. baking powder
1 tsp. vanilla extract
Milk (optional)

FOR THE ICING . . .

165 g. butter, softened
425 g. powdered sugar
2 tsp. vanilla extract
4 oz. bittersweet chocolate
2 tsp. lemon juice
100 g. pecans, toasted

METHOD

Preheat oven to 180°C, and butter two 8-inch cake tins. In a dry frying pan, toast the combined amount of pecans you need for the recipe. Set half aside and then roughly chop the remaining pecans. In a large bowl, cream the butter and sugar together and beat until fluffy. Melt the chocolate in a bain-marie. Add the beaten eggs and melted chocolate. Once incorporated, add the flour, baking powder, vanilla, and salt. Now add the chopped pecans. Try dropping the cake mixture from a spoon; it should fall slowly. If it is too stiff, add a little milk.

Pour the mixture into the buttered cake tins. Bake for 35 minutes. Allow the cake to cool.

Now for the delicious fudge frosting. Melt the butter and chocolate together in a bain-marie. Stir in the powdered sugar, vanilla extract, and lemon juice. Decorate the cake with the frosting and then place the toasted pecans on the top.

BOB MARLEY

Rita Marley was nineteen years old when she met shy guitarist Robbie Marley in the Trench Town ghetto of Kingston, Jamaica—Rita wanted to sing with his band, the Wailing Wailers, and she and some friends serenaded them on the dirt track. She had just had a child and was under the watchful eye of her aunty, who scolded, "Don't you dare stay too long because you have to give the baby titty when she wakes up!"

Rita finally fell for Bob when he noticed her breasts were leaking during a jamming session in Studio One, a studio on Brentford Road, owned by one of the Wailers, Sir Coxsone (a.k.a. Clement Dodd, local music entrepreneur), and told her to go home and feed the baby. Later that day, Bob turned up with Cow & Gate baby food for Rita's baby, five-month-old Sharon, and a drink for Rita's immensely formidable aunty, whom he plied with her favorite treat of Wincarnis tonic wine (in months to come he'd arm himself at every point with gifts of callaloo, oranges, and okra—Aunty needed no nonsense like chocolates or flowers in tough, poverty-ridden Trench Town). Bob, in the meantime, lived with his mother's ex-boyfriend, Mr. Taddy (Nesta), and his *new* girlfriend—an odd arrangement that meant Nesta felt he could impose upon Bob and wake him at ill-chosen hours of the night to demand his dinner with a cry of "It's Nesta, Nesta, wake up, hot up me food."

When they were not beneath the ireful gaze of Aunty, Bob and Rita courted at Studio One, the Wailers' jamming spot. Practices began at 9 in the morning, and then Bob, Rita, and the Wailers would break for a lunch of warm, white coco bread and meat patties. The fresh, hot coco bread was split in two, and pastry-lined, succulent, spiced meat patties were packed inside. These were all appraised by Bunny Wailer, who had the reputation of being a fearsomely good cook, and who sometimes rustled up daring soup concoctions for Bob and the Wailers. Food was to play an important part in the lives of Bob and Rita—eventually, desperate for some space they could call their own, they ended up living in Bob's friend Vincent Ford's kitchen, even making love there for the first time. Never did a word go into one of those Bob Marley songs composed in the kitchen or in Studio One that was not real and truthful, forged by the Wailers and Bob as they played the guitar and supped on cornmeal porridge—known in Jamaica as "cog" or "pop."

Love was alive in Trench Town, and Bob and Rita married on February 10, 1966, at eleven in the morning, just days after Bob's twenty-first birthday. Bob was kitted out at Aunty's, slipping into a black suit that Sir Coxsone had bought him, and a fancy pair of shoes that were much admired. Nineteen-year-old Rita, meanwhile, migrated to her Uncle Cleveland's house to don a knee-length white ruffle dress and veil, both made by Aunty. While baby Sharon nodded off in her chair, Bob and Rita tied the knot and walked down the aisle, husband and wife, toward Aunty's curried goat, rice with green bananas, and a delicious "three-sister" cake, made by the women.

A convert to Ethiopian emperor Haile Selassie's Rastafarianism, and with his awareness raised through the black consciousness movement, Bob followed Rasta ways, smoking pot—Rita shook baby powder around her room to disguise the stink of weed so that Aunty wouldn't pick up on it—and persuading Rita not to hot comb her beautiful Afro. He told her, "You're a queen, a black queen." And as in the early days, their chats turned to food and what should and shouldn't be eaten by Rastafarians. The common wisdom in Trench Town was that meals began and ended with pork: on the plates of Trench Town were always found pig's trotters and pig's tail—every pot of stewed peas and rice was flavored with ham stock—and when Bob suggested to Rita that they stop eating pig meat she scoffed, "What you talking about? The sweetest meat, and that's what I was grown on?" Rita also knew that poverty meant you couldn't pick and choose what went on your plate. The wrath of Aunty would have to be braved if Rita started refusing to eat pork. Aunty was deaf to the anti-swine arguments of the New Testament; she only saw in Rita's refusal evidence that the fancy Trench Town boys had got to her.

The day came when all hell broke loose over the porkiness of Aunty's cooking: callaloo and codfish were on the stove; the callaloo was being stewed with a pink wedge of ham. "Aunty," said Rita, "I won't be eating any of that callaloo today because of the pork." Aunty couldn't believe her ears: Had Rita lost her senses? She bellowed over the fence to her neighbor, Mother Rose, "You know Rita just tell me she not eating any of the dinner because pork in there!"

Mother Rose's less-than-helpful response was "I told you that boy . . ." and before you know it, Aunty and Mother Rose had pinned all the blame on Bob and Emperor Selassie.

There was no choice: Rita and Bob decamped to Nine Miles and set up a small holding, using the modest proceeds from Bob's share of each Wailers record sold to buy food and invest in buying potatoes, cabbage, and yams for the little farm, to eat as they chose, pork-free—plus any more left over would go on vitamins to feed their very own donkey, Nimble.

Coco Bread

INGREDIENTS

10 oz. all-purpose flour
½ tsp. salt
2 tsp. fast-acting yeast
1 tbsp. caster sugar
7 fl. oz. coconut milk
1 tbsp. butter, plus butter for oiling the bowl the bread will rise in and for brushing individual coco breads

METHOD

Sieve the flour into a large bowl and combine with the yeast, salt, and sugar. Gently warm the coconut milk; it should not boil but be of medium heat. Pop into this the tablespoon of butter—it will melt in the warm coconut. Now pour this liquid into the flour mixture. Mix all together until it becomes a pliable, slightly sticky bread dough. Remove from the bowl and, on a floured surface, knead until the dough becomes smooth and elastic. Now butter a clean bowl, put the dough in it, cover with a damp, clean tea towel, find a warm place, and leave it there to rise for 90 minutes, until it doubles in size.

Preheat the oven to 190°C. On a floured surface, knock down your dough and divide it into four pieces. Shape these into squares. Each square should be about 1 centimeter thick. Use melted butter to brush over the coco dough. Fold over and then use a smaller bowl to help you shape or cut a semicircle.

Once your coco breads are prepared, assemble them on a greaseproof, paper-lined baking tray. Return this tray to a warm spot for 10 minutes to allow the coco dough to rise a little more.

Now bake the coco breads in the oven for 20 minutes or until they have a lovely, golden sheen.

Jamaican Meat Patties

INGREDIENTS

FOR THE PASTRY . . .

1 lb. all-purpose flour
1 tsp. sea salt
1 tsp. turmeric
½ cup ice cold water
3 tsp. curry powder
3 tsp. onion seeds
1 tsp. baking powder
4 oz. butter
4 oz. shortening
Pinch of sea salt

METHOD

In a large bowl, combine the flour, baking powder, turmeric, onion seeds, curry powder, and salt. Cut the butter and shortening into sticks and work this through the spiced flour using your fingertips until the dough mix has the consistency of breadcrumbs. Begin to add small amounts of the iced water, and knead it in slowly to bind the pastry together. It should have a firm and only slightly sticky consistency.

Wrap the pastry in cling film and put it in the fridge and let it chill.

NOW FOR THE FILLING . . .

FILLING

1 lb. ground beef
1 tbsp. vegetable oil
1½ tbsp. butter
2 medium onions, finely chopped
4 garlic cloves, minced
3 stalks of fresh thyme
2 stalks of rosemary, chopped
1 scotch bonnet pepper, finely chopped
1 diced red bell pepper
1 tbsp. Tabasco
2 tsp. paprika
1 tsp. nutmeg
2 tsp. curry powder
1 heaped tsp. Muscovado sugar
2 tsp. cinnamon
1 tbsp. vegetable oil
6 finely chopped spring onions
Sea salt

METHOD

Preheat the oven to 200°C. Melt the oil and butter in a pan. Add the onions and cook gently until they turn golden brown. Add all the rest of the ingredients except the onions and fry from about 30 minutes until the mince mixture is quite dry. Finally, add the uncooked spring onions. Allow this to cool. Remove the pastry from the fridge and roll it out to a thickness of ⅛ inch on a floured surface. Using a saucer-sized plate, cut out as many circles as you can in the dough. Now place a tablespoon of mixture in the middle of each circle of dough. Wet the edge of the pastry circle, and then fold over each circle into a crescent shape. Finally, crimp the edge of each crescent with a fork. Arrange the meat patties on a greaseproof, paper-lined baking tray and bake for 30 minutes.

Serve the warm, spiced patties tucked into the warm coco bread, and you'll find yourself in 1966 on the streets of Kingston, Jamaica.

MICHAEL JACKSON

Growing up in Indiana, tucked up in a triple bed bunk with his brothers, young Michael Jackson already found life tough. Apart from the immense squash in the bunk bed, his father's temper was always paper thin, easily aroused by his wife and children and all too often resulting in physical violence. Whenever Joseph Jackson ran out of work and cash, he'd take work as a potato picker and bring home to the table potatoes of every shape and size that the Jacksons ate baked, boiled, and fried. His mother, Katherine, made the Jackson Five's clothes herself or browsed the local Salvation Army store for outfits. Poverty had its own miracles: when the TV set went bust, Katherine got the kids to sing. Happily, Katherine's inventiveness with clothes also extended to cooking. She went back to her black roots when cooking—but not without a fight. Eating soul food was, according to Joseph Jackson, his idea, and he liked to tell the family that they were eating soul food in order to be able to play soul. Katherine, he claimed, wanted to spend all the money they needed for guitars and drums on food. The family turned to collard greens and chitterlings to make ends meet. Deep, fruity apple pies and warm peach cobblers graced the table. Simple dishes like fish and rice fed the Jacksons at supper, with tomato soup and special egg and bologna sandwiches for lunch. Michael, however, was never going to be a hearty eater, and he needed special encouragement to eat properly.

Peach Cobbler

INGREDIENTS

FOR THE PEACH FILLING . . .

8 ripe, large peaches, their velvety skins removed, stones removed, and cut into generous chunks
3 tbsp. Demarara sugar
¼ tsp. ground cinnamon
Pinch of nutmeg
A squeeze of fresh lemon juice
2 tsp. cornstarch

FOR THE TOPPING . . .

1 cup all-purpose flour
½ cup brown Demerara sugar
1 tsp. baking powder
Pinch of sea salt
6 tbsp. cold butter, cut into sticks
¼ cup warm water

COBBLER TOPPING . . .

2 tbsp. brown Demerara sugar
1 tsp. ground cinnamon

METHOD

Preheat the oven to 200°C. Mix together the peach chunks, Demerara sugar, cinnamon, nutmeg, lemon, and cornstarch. Lay this peachy mess into the base

Peach Cobbler (*continued*)

of a baking dish. Bake in the oven for 10 minutes. Now for the cobbler topping. Mix together the flour, Demerara sugar, baking powder, and sea salt. Then, using your fingertips, rub the butter through the flour, until the mixture has the consistency of breadcrumbs. Add the water, a little at a time, until the cobbler topping is just beginning to clump. Remove the peaches from the oven, and drop the topping on them, allowing it to form big, uneven "cobbles" of crumbly topping. Finally, scatter the combined Demerara sugar and cinnamon over the top of the cobbler. Return the cobbler to the oven and bake for 30 minutes, until the topping is a rich gold.

Having just turned eleven, just as "I Want You Back" was being released, and on tour with the other Jacksons, Michael needed reminding when it came to food. Instead of staying with his father and brothers in the litter of motels that lay along the Jackson's tour trail in 1969, it was decided that eleven-year-old Michael should move in with Diana Ross for four weeks: she could act as his mentor. She treated him like a son. "You're going to be a great, great star," Diana crooned over breakfast. "Now eat your cereal."

Years later, it was Elizabeth Taylor's turn to cajole Michael into eating. He had been shedding pounds as he toured Bangkok and Taiwan. His family members were lurking nearby, waiting to see him. Just before lunch, Taylor rubbed down Jackson's shoulders as he confided his loathing of his father. "My father, I can't even stand to be in the same room with that man," he wailed.

"Neither can I, dear," Elizabeth replied, continuing to rub. When they made it to lunch, cradling a slice of frosted carrot cake in her hand, Taylor urged Jackson to eat it: "Michael, if you don't eat this cake, I swear to God," she threatened, "I will call your family in here and let them have a go at you. And you know I'll do it, too."

Jackson had to give in. "Give me that goddam cake!" Relenting, he took the gooey, frosted mess from her hands.

"Good boy," she whispered as he bit into the slice. "Good boy!"

All that bologna on the Jackson table was, eventually, to become a source of trouble; as a teenager Jackson was plagued with a rash of spots and blamed it on his greasy diet. As soon as he cut meat out of his diet, Jackson claimed in his autobiography *Moonwalk*, his skin improved—an improvement not, then, based on plastic surgery. Vegetarianism resulted in considerable facial change, Jackson hotly asserted. As one would expect with Jackson, the vegetarianism was a sign of greater food complications to come in Jackson's life. In his late teens he would go on to completely neglect food and eating.

Aged nineteen, Jackson was making the film *The Wiz* and staying in New York in 1977 with his sister, LaToya, but Katherine was so worried about Michael's disinterest in food that she gave strict instructions to LaToya to make sure he ate. "If I didn't have to eat to live," he told Katherine once, "I'd never eat at all."

Back at home, Katherine had been trying to tempt Michael's appetite with his favorites of sweet potato pies and sugared hot apple turnovers. Despite not being in the healthiest of food "mind frames" herself (she was addicted to chocolate at the time and had taken to downing straight Hershey's cocoa powder mixed with a dash of water), LaToya was obligated to rise before Michael's filming hour of 5:30 a.m. and rustle up plates of buttered toast and bacon, oatmeal porridge, and herb tea. No matter how ringing an example that may sound of sisterly devotion, one visitor did call around at the time and found Michael baking chocolate chip cookies in the kitchen and sleeping in a humble room with a little bed and desk, while LaToya occupied a very spacious, mirrored room.

Sweet Potato Pie

INGREDIENTS

FOR THE CRUST . . .

9 oz. all-purpose flour
5 oz. butter, cut into sticks
2 oz. Demerara sugar (this will give the pastry an extra crunch)
1½ oz. light Muscovado sugar
1 large egg
1 tsp. ground cinnamon
Pinch of sea salt

METHOD

With a hand-held electric mixer, cream together the butter and Demerara and Muscovado sugars. Pour in the egg and beat until smooth. Sieve the flour with the salt and cinnamon. Gradually add this to the creamed butter, sugar, and egg. Turn the pastry onto a lightly floured surface and gently knead it until it comes together into a walnut-colored lump that smells of cinnamon and treacle.

Now wrap the pastry in cling film, put it in the fridge, and leave it to chill for 30 minutes.

Heat the oven to 180°C. Butter the pie dish. Roll out the pastry into a circular shape on a floured surface to fit the dimensions of the pie dish. Place the pastry in the pie dish and lightly prick the surface of the pastry (try not to penetrate fully). Now put a sheet of greaseproof paper over the pastry, pour in ceramic beans, and bake blind for 15 minutes. Then remove the paper and beans and return the pastry, uncovered, to the oven for a further 5 minutes. Remove from the oven and let it cool for 10 minutes.

Sweet Potato Pie (*continued*)

NOW FOR THE SWEET POTATO FILLING . . .

3 medium sweet potatoes, baked
3 eggs, beaten
5 oz. butter, softened
1 cup light Muscovado sugar
¾ cup evaporated milk
½ tbsp. vanilla extract
Scant tbsp. maple syrup
2 tsp. ground cinnamon
½ tsp. nutmeg
1 tsp. grated lemon zest
1 tsp. grated orange zest
Pinch of sea salt

METHOD

Put on Jackson's electrifying song "Billie Jean." Bake the sweet potatoes for 45 minutes at 180°C. Cool. Scrape them out of their skins and mash until smooth. Leave the oven on. Next, cream together the butter and sugar until they are light and fluffy. Add the eggs and combine. Now add the sweet potatoes, evaporated milk, vanilla extract, maple syrup, ground cinnamon, nutmeg, grated lemon and orange zest, and pinch of sea salt.

Now pour the delicious, spiced, sweet potato gloop into the cooled piecrust. Bake for about 50 minutes, but keep an eye on the pie's crust. If it's darkening too quickly, cut out a strip of aluminium foil to protect it.

Serve warm, sliced, and with a gloop of whipped cream.

Perhaps he was off his food in 1978 because of his obsession with another older female icon, Jacqueline Onassis. He was apparently trying to date Jacqueline's daughter, Caroline, in order to make connections with Jackie. Every time he called her, he hoped that Jackie might pick up the phone; eventually Caroline agreed to a date and Michael whisked her off for a dinner of osso bucco (he'd never heard of it before) and a jaunt at the ice-skating rink. When he went to kiss her, she responded with "If my mother finds out I kissed a black boy, she will absolutely kill me." Michael retreated, mortified.

Six years later and Michael had become fully vegetarian—he hated the thought of any creature being killed for his dinner—but it remained the case that Jackson still neglected to eat. As he revved up for the Victory tour in 1984, his weight plummeted and his health suffered, and his cook, a Sikh named Mani Singh Khalsa, took to preparing dishes rich in high-protein pecan and cashew nuts and seeds.

As with any other vegetarian, Jackson lapsed at different points, one such infamous lapse being over Kentucky Fried Chicken, ever a temptress. But of course, being Michael Jackson, it had to be a complicated desire. He wanted it for every meal and made according to the top-secret KFC recipe, right down to the spray butter on the biscuits. "Strong-scented foods" were devil's fare. Michael's children, meanwhile, were on another Michael diet, with banned substances sensibly being sugar and chocolate, plus an unexplained directive that none of them be served so much as a shred of chicken skin on their KFC.

Fortunately for all of them, Jackson returned to his vegetarian diet, but, unfortunately for Michael, his grueling rehearsal schedule in the run-up to the massive O2 London tour meant that he again forgot to eat. Down to only one meal a day, his concert promoter, Randy Phillips, and the director, Kenny Ortega, had to resort to feeding him, cutting up into bite-size pieces small portions of his favorite dishes of tofu with chili sauce, vegetarian lasagne, and nut loaf. Michael died at age fifty shortly thereafter. Food to die for, surely? If only Liz Taylor had been on hand with her carrot cake.

THE ROLLING STONES

Perhaps the dining moment that is most remembered about the Rolling Stones is the notorious Mars Bar sex scandal of February 1967. The police stealthily planned an armed swoop on the Stones' smelly den of vice, Keith Richards's Redlands mansion (he'd bought it in 1966). No less than nineteen of Britain's finest police officers lurked around the shrubbery outside. Only the inhabitants of Redlands, high as rockets on Benzedrine and White Lightning, could fail to spot these bulky, blue-clad shapes in the privet hedge in front of Keith Richards's door, poised to swoop in on the groovy party inside. At their knock, Keith stumbled to the door to answer; in an unlikely moment of drug-induced, cross-generational gallantry, he thought that an elderly pensioner (and not a police detective) was rapping on his door to ask for his autograph.

Police bellowed and charged past Richards, only to screech to a halt before Mick Jagger, his head buried between Marianne Faithfull's legs, eating a *Mars Bar*. Never, ever, had Scotland Yard seen the like! It took all of about three hours for this to leak to the press; later a furious Jagger wanted to sue *News of the World*. But the chocolate story stuck (boom boom). When the court eventually listened to testimony about the Redlands raid later that year, the Stones' own lawyer, Sir Michael Havers, was forced to admit that when he'd prowled around Redlands post-raid he had, indeed, come across a stash of Mars Bars.

Mars Bar Love

INGREDIENTS

1 Mars Bar
1 Marianne Faithfull

METHOD

Work it out yourself, and enjoy!

Mick Jagger arrived for his court appearance following the 1967 Mars Bar incident, handcuffed to accomplice Robert Fraser, with whom he was being held in Lewes jail. It looked grim, but then Mick topped up the scandal by having lunch delivered by a local hotelier when the court had adjourned at midday. The press reported, in scandalized, admiring tones, that the unrepentant Jagger enjoyed a lunch of prawn cocktail and roast lamb with mint sauce on the side, followed by strawberries and cream, washed down with a bottle of Beaujolais. Very good at taking care of yours truly in tough times, even when he was studying as a student at the London School of Economics and sharing digs with Keith Richards and Brian Jones, Jagger enjoyed life on £2 a week on the combined income of parental handouts, a government student grant, and income from singing for Blues Incorporated. Meanwhile, Richards and Jones were on the verge of starvation, but did Mick share his spoils? No, he'd sneak off for restaurant meals while his flatmates resorted to stealing food from the local grocery. This meanness was apparent when he went out for dinner with fashion photographer David Bailey; Jagger was encouraged by Bailey to leave a tip of £10 for the waiting staff but, as they left the restaurant, out of the corner of his eye, Bailey caught sight of Jagger secretly retrieving the tip and slipping it back into his pocket. Lucky, then, that Mars Bars come so cheap.

Sneaky Mick could use food and drink to get what he wanted, too, as when he first met Marianne Faithfull in March 1964. Despite being in a torrid argument with his sweet-faced girlfriend Chrissie Shrimpton—she was so upset that her eyelashes had begun to slide off with her cascading tears—Jagger wanted to get Marianne's attention. Chrissie having abandoned him, Mick pretended to trip and, in doing so, emptied a glass of Dom Perignon over Marianne's thin blouse. Things didn't get much more glamorous for Marianne. She'd get stoned with the band at Brian Jones and Keith Richards's untidy, unsanitary pad at Courtfield Road, which was a mass of dirty dishes, and then about 10 at night, Marianne said, "We'd stagger out to Alvaro's for some wonderful pasta. But once we got there we'd be so stoned we could barely manage more than a mouthful. I'd stare at the exquisite china and watch the tiny dragons crawl over the fettuccine." Marianne seems positively streetwise compared to Jagger's future wife, Argentinian Bianca Perez Morena de Macias, whom he met in 1970 and wooed over caviar and Louis Cristal champagne. She's already been groomed for the high life by her well-to-do, doting parents and her previous lover, Michael Caine, with whom she'd lived in the Dorchester Hotel; as she reported of herself, "I never washed a dish, boiled an egg or cleaned."

Visiting Marrakesh in March 1967 must have seemed like a whale of an idea after the drama of the Redlands raid. The Stones drew up at a decadent hotel in Marrakesh, having migrated from London to Morocco. They arrived there complete with Brian Jones's swish car from his pad in the Swiss Cottage. They looked like a sulky, drowsy troupe of badly-stitched-together gypsies. White-faced Anita Pallenberg, her black hair hanging in big, dirty droplets, drifted alongside Brian Jones; Mick Jagger came with a wide-eyed retinue of Americans; and Keith Richards had turned his hand to making his own clothes and thus sported an eighteenth-century suit, his lavender-rose trousers bursting at the seams. Brian Jones appeared by the poolside, white trousers draped over his tight little buttocks, and a large, black square sewn over his rear. Photographer Cecil Beaton, who happened luckily to be in Marrakesh on the same night and in the same hotel, gravitated to Mick. Beaton was keen to photograph him, watching him elegantly drink cool Vodka Collins and set forth his case for why Britain had turned into a police state and about the pleasure he took in permissiveness. Eventually, they decided to go for dinner, and Beaton found himself tucked in the back of the Stones' Bentley, music booming in his ears, squashed into the litter of porn magazines, brightly colored fur rugs, and pop-art cushions they kept there. When they tumbled out of the car into the brightness of the Moroccan restaurant, Jagger taught Beaton how to eat tender chicken, Moroccan style, with his fingertips. Between mouthfuls, he asked Beaton, "Have you ever taken LSD? Oh, you should. It would mean so much to you: you'd never forget the colors. For a painter it is a great experience." The painter in Beaton noted that the next day Jagger's face had collapsed into a pale stew of tiny eyes, which Beaton memorably described as "albino-fringed, and widened nose—the only shade of pink on his face—and that none of the band seemed capable of speech, except in 'spasms'"; now what do you think they might have been up to overnight?

But before you imagine that that is the last we'll see of 1967, come July 1967 Jagger reappeared with Marianne Faithfull at a London party in honor of the return of American Beat poet Alan Ginsberg. They sashayed into designer Christopher Gibb's swish pad on Cheyne Walk, London (the street on which Jagger and Richards were to buy houses the following year). The sounds of *Sgt. Pepper* wafted through the air; MPs swayed to the music; a curator at the British Museum stood underneath the low lights; Princess Margaret toyed with her drink; and Paul Getty II was on his way. Come 10 p.m., someone had the bright idea that the butler

Vodka Collins

INGREDIENTS

A generous glug of Stolichnaya vodka (about two fingers)
Juice of 1 freshly squeezed lemon
1½ tsp. caster sugar
Soda water
Slices of thinly cut orange and lemon
A Maraschino cherry

METHOD

Put some cubed ice in a cocktail shaker; pour in the Stolichnaya, lemon, and sugar. Shake and serve in a Collins glass. Top with a splash or two of soda water. Garnish with orange and lemon slices and one provocative Maraschino cherry.

Moroccan Chicken

INGREDIENTS

1 medium-sized, organic chicken, cut into eighths (ask your butcher to do this)
2 tsp. powdered cumin
1 tsp. cinnamon
1 tsp. paprika
½ tsp. powdered saffron
Sea salt
Freshly ground black pepper
6 tbsp. butter
2 tbsp. olive oil
6 onions, peeled and finely sliced
¼ lb. chickpeas, soaked overnight and then drained of their water
Freshly ground black pepper
4 garlic cloves, sliced
2 pints strong chicken stock
4 tbsp. finely chopped flat-leaf parsley
4 tbsp. finely chopped fresh green cilantro
Lemon juice

METHOD

The night before, rub the chicken with the cumin, paprika, cinnamon, salt, and black pepper. Leave to marinade overnight. Soak the chickpeas in water overnight too.

The next day, melt the butter and olive oil in a Dutch oven, add the chicken, and brown it in the oil. When it is browned, remove the chicken temporarily from the oil. Now add the onions and soften them until they are a warm, golden color. Return the chicken to the pan. Add the garlic and soften this a little. Now add the saffron and chickpeas and cover with chicken stock. Simmer this delicious Moroccan stew for an hour, uncovered. Before serving, stir the freshly chopped parsley and cilantro into the sauce, but give it no more time to cook than the distance from stove to table! To further "lift" the flavor, sprinkle with freshly squeezed lemon juice. Use your fingers to eat!

should invite everyone to enjoy delicious hashish fudge, served on a silver platter. There was one small problem—although it was modish to rustle up hashish fudge according to the recipe given in the *Alice B. Toklas Cookbook*, on this occasion, some wrong-footed hedonist decided to double the amount of hashish in the mixture. What was on offer was hashish poison. All hell broke loose as Britain's finest in music and nobility swayed, burped, and collapsed about the room, overdosed on hashish. Stomachs were pumped that night, and Jagger and Faithfull took to running up and down the street in the dark again and again in order to fight the effects of hashish poisoning.

So here it is verbatim, word for word.

Hashish Fudge, courtesy of Alice B. Toklas
(which anyone could whip up on a rainy day)

Take 1 teaspoon black peppercorns, 1 whole nutmeg, 4 average sticks of cinnamon, 1 teaspoon cilantro. These should all be pulverized in a mortar. About a handful each of stoned dates, dried figs, shelled almonds, and peanuts: chop these and mix them together. A bunch of *Cannabis sativa* can be pulverized. This along with the spices should be dusted over the mixed fruit and nuts, kneaded together. About a cup of sugar dissolved in a big pat of butter. Rolled into a cake and cut into pieces or made into balls about the size of a walnut, it should be eaten with care. Two pieces are quite sufficient.

Disappointingly for Cecil Beaton, he met Mick Jagger again in the same month (September 1967) but found he bore little resemblance to the elegant and assured conversationalist of Marrakesh. With a face like suet, Marianne Faithfull stared up from beneath an odd cap of wispy, smothering hair while Mick made no move to be polite to Beaton, picking up a picture book to look at. Gone was the Bentley; instead, it was a taxi ride to Fulham Road for dinner in the inauspicious-sounding Baghdad House, where Mick ignored Beaton even more fulsomely, looking over his shoulder and mewing that he wanted some "fewd." So much for finger-licking chicken; Jagger shoveled a "cake of pap" into his mouth while Beaton looked on, his idol revealed as clay.

Jagger's long association with drugs and the immortality that seemed to ensure he never suffered the consequences lent him a dark, devilish glamour. Even when he had a secret snack about him it could be "read" wrongly, as when a friend of Andy Warhol's found a tinfoil-wrapped "package" in his pocket after a wild night out with Jerry Hall and Mick Jagger—what could it be, he wondered? A secret stash of heroin? Cocaine? No. As he carefully unpeeled the foil he exposed a Rice Krispie cookie! More famed for audacious acts when eating than for what was on his plate, one evening in a restaurant, when an older gent inquired of Jagger, "Are you a man or a woman?" his reply was to unzip his pants.

Alcohol also loomed large on the abuse list for the band. At the age of six, Jade Jagger amazed Andy Warhol by coolly inquiring what he'd like to drink when he visited the Jaggers in New York. When Warhol mumbled that he'd quite like vodka on the rocks, Jade called to the Spanish maid, "Dos vodkas con heilo." That was a Rolling Stone's child.

By the 1980s, alcoholism had Keith Richards in its tenacious grasp, and breakfast was burgers and Black Jack bourbon with an HP sauce chaser and maybe some home fries on the side. This predilection for HP sauce crops up much earlier in 1964, when the Stones were on tour in Brussels. An aspiring chef made the grave mistake of not researching their individual tastes and so missed Jagger's loathing of tomatoes, serving them up tomato soup and tomatoes stuffed with shrimps. His cooking was spurned but, even worse, he felt suicidal and murderous impulses when the Stones further offended by requesting chips and HP sauce (guess who for?). Indeed, Richards's HP passion was as much a part of 1960s Britain as Carnaby Street; HP was called "Wilson's Gravy" for a while, after British prime minister Harold Wilson. Wilson's wife, Mary, told reporters at the *Sunday Times*, "If Harold has a fault, it is that he will drown everything with HP sauce."

Even HP, or Black Jack, or orange juice and Stolichnaya, however, had not so great a hold on Keith Richards's affections as one particular dish. Wherever he is in the world, should there be a fridge in his room, look therein and, according to his closest acquaintances, you will find a shepherd's pie. Richards prides himself on his own belligerence (on the Brussels trip, for instance, he punched someone who suggested the Stones were actually the Supremes). So imagine what he's like if you go near his shepherd's pie—he'll experience tight-lipped anxiety if one (or several) isn't near to hand. Once one foolish, greedy member of his crew ate Richards's shepherd's pie, and he, spitting with rage, warned him that next time he would dice him into pieces and put his legs in the self-same pie.

Shepherd's Pie

INGREDIENTS

3 tbsp. olive oil
1 lb. minced beef
3 onions
3 garlic cloves, chopped
3 carrots, scraped and sliced into ¾-inch chunks
1 swede, peeled and diced into rough 1-or-2-inch pieces
1 green pepper, roughly chopped
1 tbsp. tomato puree
1 tbsp. Bovril
1 glass of red wine
Hot water
Sea salt
Freshly ground black pepper

FOR THE TOPPING . . .

1 onion, very finely chopped
3 lb. potatoes
3 tbsp. butter
2 tbsp. milk
Sea salt
3 tbsp. grated cheddar

METHOD

Warm the olive oil in a deep, thick-bottomed pan or Dutch oven. Add the onion and cook gently about 10 minutes, until the onions have turned a pale gold color. Add the garlic and allow it to cook for a minute. Add the minced beef and brown lightly. Now add the carrots, swede, and green pepper. Give this a generous

Shepherd's Pie *(continued)*

scattering of freshly ground black pepper and sea salt. Now put in the splodge of tomato puree, the red wine, and the marmite. Top with enough hot water to cover the mince stew. Let this bubble away on medium heat for about 1 hour, until the mince has a thickish gravy around it.

When the mince has been cooking for about 15 minutes, prepare the topping. Peel the potatoes, cut into quarters, and place them in a pan of cold, salted water. Bring to boil and cook for about 20 minutes. Keep testing the potatoes with a fork; they are ready when the fork can spear the potato. When this happens, drain the potatoes, put them back in the pot, place them over a low heat, and shake them gently to dry—you will see comforting billows of steam rising from the potatoes. Once they are dry, you'll see the outside of the potato fluff and scale. Now begin to mash them. Add the butter and mash through the potato, and then add the milk. Keep beating the potato until it is smooth and light. If the mince base isn't ready yet, then keep the potato covered and warmish until the mince is ready.

Heat the oven to 200°C.

When the mince is suitably thick, taste it to check whether it needs a little more salt or a splash more wine. Then, pour it into the base of a pie dish. Sprinkle the finely chopped onion over the surface of the mince—this will give a very faint oniony "bite" to the pie when it is ready. Now gently place modest spoonfuls of buttery mashed potato over the surface of the mince. Using a fork, gently drag these islands together to form a smooth crust of potato over the mince. Sprinkle over the cheddar cheese. Cook uncovered in the oven for 30 minutes.

Serve with cooked frozen peas and a generous dollop of HP sauce. Aaaahhhh!

4

❖ ❖

Dining with Famous and Infamous Writers

Read the menu written by Evelyn Waugh, C. S. Lewis, Ernest Hemingway, F. Scott Fitzgerald, John Steinbeck, J. D. Salinger, Ian Fleming, W. H. Auden, George Orwell, Agatha Christie, Oscar Wilde, and Sylvia Plath. You can soufflé cheeses with Agatha Christie, hiccup your way through F. Scott Fitzgerald's road trip truffled chicken, and end with C. S. Lewis's plum pudding.

EVELYN WAUGH

Cecil Beaton's diaries famously record the death of Evelyn Waugh in 1966: "Evelyn Waugh is in his coffin. Died of snobbery." Pomposity, according to Beaton, came upon Waugh when he was in his twenties and reached its full height by the time he had an ear trumpet in middle age. And it is certainly clear from Waugh's taste in food that he became more urbane the older he got. In childhood, Waugh was a simple little soul, wondering why sausages looked so very funny before they were cooked; by his forties, life's high point was a paunchy claret lunch at the Ritz, his "Marble Halls." But before we, like many others, decide that Waugh was just a selfish old bore, we should remember the tiny, stuffily kind moments in his life, as when he bumped into a penniless Graham Greene at a Catholic Mass in 1948. Greene had emptied his pockets, giving all his money to African causes, and Waugh took pity on him, lending him six British pennies for a new hat and treating him to a cocktail at the Ritz.

A youth of ginger beer, junket, hard-boiled eggs, ices, and half-penny buns was also punctuated by school dinners at Lancing Public School, which Waugh said would have had the occupants of a Victorian workhouse mutinying. Sundays were the darkest days, when nothing much happened, except performances from a terrible men's choir, preceded by queasy and spiritless breakfasts. The only food that was bearable at these breakfasts was plain bread, and young Waugh imagined a cheerless future of eating only that. Holidays and trips home were a chance to catch up with decent eating for all the Lansing boarders: Waugh drily noted that one boy, post-exeat, puffed to keep pace during a running game because of such dissipations. Pranks were rife, and Waugh poured cream into someone named Grimes's desk in the hope it would stink him out after a couple of days.

By the time he reached seventeen, out of school hours, Waugh was enjoying well-dressed crab, salmon mayonnaise, port, and iced coffee, and, by his twenties, he was quaffing brown sherry and smoking enormous cigars. The year 1924 was a year of discovery for Waugh—he had just turned twenty and turned up at Hertford College in Oxford to sit a viva voce: a gruelling oral "discussion" or examination of his academic work and performance with a team of worthy Hertford academics. Waugh braced himself with a quick whiskey—he always said his preferred sport at Hertford was drinking—and he needed it to face the shame. The viva, he believed, was a mere formality, as his dismal, sobering, third-class degree was already assured. He'd done all sorts of delightful things rather than study for "inconvenient" exam questions at Oxford—he'd tasted his first plover eggs, had lunches of hot lobster and unusual rums, and joined the Railway Club. This was founded on the bright idea of booking a rail carriage on a particular line and then ordering the five-shilling dinner on offer—this got you seven courses. The Railway Club's first meeting—and feast—was held on the mud-splattered Penzance to Aberdeen train. After they had gone down from Oxford and become men of influence in the world, the Railway Club dinners became increasingly elaborate. Cigarette boxes of silver were presented to puzzled engine drivers; celebrated London chefs hopped on the train; fine foods and rattling crates of mulberry-colored wine were loaded onto the carriage. The Railway Club was one of many wonderfully jaunty, perverse clubs in Oxford; there was one that ran at Balliol College, whose members lived the day in reverse, beginning with dinner jackets, cigars, and brandy at 7 a.m., dinner finished with soup at about 9 p.m., and breakfast by moonlight.

Having telegraphed his wilting parents with his forebodings about the Oxford viva, Waugh passed a reckless summer, part of which was spent in Dublin where all pubs closed at 9 p.m. Waugh claimed this was because all substantial political movements start in pubs in Ireland. Eventually Waugh and his companion, Alastair, happened on the town of Glenmalure—"happened" is perhaps too casual a word, as Glenmalure lies among some boulders in the Wicklow Mountains. They set up in an uncomfortable hotel where tea was served at dinner—could it be a temperance hotel, they wondered? But then they found to their relief that they "could obtain a ghastly sort of ale, very fizzy and tasting strongly of baking powder, or a spirituous liquor" and for company "a terrible woman with a bald husband and a friend called Mrs. Gwatkin." The year ended with gin and Benedictines and veal and ham pie in the Rising Sun saloon bar.

Rising Sun Veal and Ham Pie (wash down with Benedictine)

INGREDIENTS

1 lb. raw ham, cut into ¼-inch cubes
1 lb. veal, cut into ¼-inch cubes
4 rashers streaky bacon
1 large onion, sautéed in butter
4 tbsp. chopped parsley
1 tsp. shredded sage leaves
1 tsp. fresh thyme
1 tsp. finely grated lemon rind
3 tbsp. brandy
3 tbsp. chicken or ham stock
1 tsp. ground mace
½ tsp. ground bay
4 hard-boiled eggs
3 pickled walnuts
½ pint of chicken or ham stock
3 gelatin leaves
1 beaten egg
3 tsp. double cream

FOR THE HOT-WATER CRUST PASTRY . . .

INGREDIENTS

2 tbsp. water
5 tbsp. milk
6 oz. lard
1 level tbsp. powdered sugar
1 lb. all-purpose flour
1 tsp. salt

PASTRY METHOD

Into a large bowl, sift the flour, salt, and powdered sugar. In a pan, bring the milk, water, and lard to boil. Make a well in the center of the flour and pour the boiling lard/water mix into the well, stirring it through the flour with a wooden spoon. The dough should eventually form a smooth ball. Let it rest for 15 minutes. Grease a baking tin with butter and set aside.

Reserve about a quarter of the pastry for the pie lid, and shape the rest over the base and sides of your baking tin, using your fingertips to press the pastry into a crust. Avoid cracks, as these will allow the delicious veal and ham juices to leak out. On a lightly floured surface, roll out your pie lid to fit the top of the pie. Leave a 1-inch hold in the center of the pie lid crust—you'll need this to pour jellied stock into later. Place a rolled-up tube of card in this hole, so that it protrudes out of the pie to a distance of about 1 inch.

PIE FILLING

Preheat the oven to 200°C.

Mix all your pie ingredients together, apart from the boiled eggs and walnuts. Line the pie with the rashers of streaky bacon. Fill a third of the pie with the meat mixture. Now place the whole boiled eggs interspersed with the halved pickled

Rising Sun Veal and Ham Pie *(continued)*

walnuts. Now top with the rest of the meat mixture. Place the lid on the pie and brush with the beaten egg and cream glaze. Put the pie in the middle shelf of the oven and bake for two hours.

After two hours, when the pie has turned a lovely nut brown color, remove from the oven and allow it to cool.

Soak the gelatin leaves in cold water to soften. Drain. Heat the ½ pint of chicken/ham stock in a small saucepan, add the gelatin, and stir until the gelatin dissolves. Let this cool and, if it sets, simply warm it a little when you are ready to use it. When the pie has cooled completely, pour a third of the jellied stock down the cardboard funnel and repeat about every 10 minutes until the pie is full. Remove the cardboard funnel and return the pie to the fridge for an hour to allow the jelly to fully set.

After the wonderful disaster that was Oxford, Waugh looked for work teaching in private schools and eventually landed a job in 1925 in a private school, Arnold House, in Llanddulas, Wales. Mildly startled to be offered the job, Waugh thought being a school teacher would be difficult, but the £160 salary would be extremely useful to someone as poor as he. Not only that, but Llanddulas was also so far away from any pleasure, entertainment, or diversion as to be a great way of not spending any money. At Euston, he and other teachers met dispirited groups of boys in red caps and floods of tears, who then on the train set about drinking as much pop and ginger as possible; vomiting seemed likely.

On arrival at Arnold House, more grimness was in wait. The house the schoolmasters occupied was called the Sanatorium and sprang up amid some dung heaps and gooseberry bushes. In the boys' quarters, housemaids scurried about the corridors laden with urine. There were no timetables or syllabi. The headmaster wandered around saying things like this: "There are some boys in the classroom across the corridor. They are either History Set 2 or a dancing class. Either way, someone should teach them something." At which point the least lazy teacher laid aside his newspaper, stood up, stretched, and did just that. No wonder that one pupil named Howarth wrote in his history paper that James II gave birth to a boy. Waugh was exasperated by public school boys: he tried to subdue two boys simultaneously by beating them with a slipper but noted with disappointment that neither seemed to feel any pain.

Despite Arnold House being in the middle of nowhere, drink was needed to survive the boys and Llanddulas. Everyone in Wales, Waugh said, produced lots of black spittle, would spit on the ground by way of greeting, and say, "Borra-da."

The teachers spent many evenings in the local pub, where an ancient "eunuch" tried to teach them Welsh toasts but always got too drunk to speak, so all they learned was *Iechyd da I bob un* ("Good Health Everyone!") and the less decipherable *llywddiant ir archos* ("Success . . . ?"). Life, Waugh felt, might as well be over, and he made a failed suicide attempt on a nearby North Wales beach; his death bid was foiled when he was lanced by the sting of a jellyfish. Finally, at last, he was sacked from Arnold House for making improper advances to the school matron.

Oxford and London rescued Waugh from the doldrums, as did writing success. Oxford was always spectacular fun; for instance, one quick return visit to there later in 1925 gave Waugh the chance to enjoy an oyster omelette and mushrooms before going to the George Bar, where he bumped into a syndicate of homosexual business men—one of whom wore platinum suspenders and owned no less than 107 newspapers—and who bought Waugh several champagne cocktails.

A Decline and Fall Champagne Cocktail

INGREDIENTS

A brown sugar cube
Angostura bitters
Champagne
1 measure of cognac
Maraschino cherry

METHOD

Soak the sugar cube in Angostura bitters. Place it in the bottom of a champagne glass, add the cognac, and top up with champagne. Top with a cheeky Maraschino cherry. Drink and ponder the complexities of platinum suspenders.

Meanwhile, Waugh's adventures in London offered great material for his second novel, *Vile Bodies*; at one point Waugh went to lunch at the brilliantly named Gwen Otter's house but only found it with extreme difficulty. He got lost in the London fog and crashed into a wall at the corner of Kings Road, on which was chalked: ARE YOU WASHED IN THE BLOOD OF THE LAMB? Fortunately, lunch made up for all this, as all the other guests had gotten lost. Waugh was no doubt glad of this, because he had a terrible high-necked sweater on that made him look like a ten-year-old, though he also claimed Miss Otter looked like a Red Indian. Waugh and Otter ate between them a huge platter of gnocchi, intended to feed the vanished guests. Otter was also responsible for giving Waugh the best soup he'd ever tasted—chestnut. There was a brief low point in lunches when Otter's cook had to take a few days off to give birth, but Waugh noted in his diary that as soon as she'd picked up after parturition, the lunches got better again.

Chestnut Soup

INGREDIENTS

1 tbsp. butter
1 tbsp. olive oil
7 oz. cooked and peeled chestnuts (keep aside 2 chestnuts)
1 onion, finely chopped
1 celery rib, finely chopped
1 carrot, finely chopped
1 garlic clove, crushed
1 pint of chicken stock
Sea salt and freshly ground black pepper

TO GARNISH . . .

Dessertspoonful of crème fraîche
Crushed chestnut

METHOD

Warm the butter and the olive oil in a deep pan. Now add the onions, garlic, carrots, and celery and sweat these for 10 minutes. Add the chestnuts and chicken stock, season, and cook for a further 15 minutes.

Allow your soup to cool slightly, and then blend it. Warm your chestnut soup again; serve it in bowls with a swirl of crème fraîche and some crumbled chestnut.

C. S. LEWIS

C. S. Lewis always found the first dish of green peas in the year to be a moment to be treasured: indeed, the creator of Narnia was massively keen on peas and very discriminating about good pea quality. Conservative as a love of the British garden pea may sound, Lewis was not afraid of experimentation—in June 1922, he was found supping from his first ever glass of green, bittersweet, cowslip wine. Although as rich as sherry, it could play rough with your vocal cords; still, not all bad, thought Lewis. He was sharing a house at the time with the autocratic Mrs. Moore (in some ways, his adoptive mother) and her daughter, Maureen.

Mrs. Moore, known as "D" in his diary, made homemade strawberry jam, the fruity aroma greeting Lewis as he came home out of the rain, or rustled up for him a bowlful of mushroom stew, rich and delicious. In return, Lewis performed various chores around the house. He prepared Mrs. Moore's vegetables every morning, peeling onions or cutting up turnips.

Food on visits home to his bleak father in Northern Ireland was much less inspiring. He ate tepid and humdrum chops, mashed potato and cabbage, or boiled mutton, a dish Lewis loathed. Closer to home was another relative, his querulous Aunt Lily. In December 1922, he had chops and a "capital plum pudding" at her house; at another date she gave him an ambrosial bowl of strawberries and cream. Conversation was beautifully comical over dinner. Aunt Lily had been swamped by prams on a visit to town and equipped herself with a stack of leaflets from the CBC (Constructive Birth Control) society, which she was going to drop into every pram in Oxford. Lewis said uncharitably of Aunt Lily, "What I can't stand about her is that she knows everything: the Holy Ghost discusses all his plans with her and she was on the committee that arranged creation."

Plum Pudding

INGREDIENTS

1 tbsp. butter
12 oz. pitted prunes, chopped
3 oz. crystallized ginger, chopped roughly
5 oz. walnut halves, chopped roughly
7 oz. large raisins
Grated zest and juice of 1 orange and 1 lemon
4 oz. fresh brown breadcrumbs
4 oz. shredded suet
1 tsp. ground cloves
½ tsp. ground cinnamon
¼ tsp. grated nutmeg
3 large eggs
3 tbsp. brandy
2½ pints pudding basin

Plum Pudding ***(continued)***

METHOD

Butter the pudding basin. In a large bowl, combine the prunes, ginger, walnuts, raisins, orange and lemon zest, suet, brown breadcrumbs, cloves, cinnamon, and nutmeg. Whisk the eggs thoroughly, and then add to the plum pudding mixture. Finally, add the orange and lemon juice. In another bowl, whisk the eggs until frothy and slightly thickened, and stir well into the dry ingredients. Lastly, stir in the brandy.

Leave the plum pudding mixture for 30 minutes. Next, put a large, deep saucepan on the stove, and fill a third of it with hot water. Pour the mixture into the pudding basin. Line the top with pleated, buttered tinfoil or greaseproof paper. Secure this with a string; loop the string over the top of the pudding basin to form a string handle, which will allow you to lift the pudding basin out of the water. Carefully, using the string handle, lower the basin into the hot water. The water should submerge two-thirds of the pudding basin; if it doesn't, adjust accordingly. Cover the pan and bring to boil. Allow the pudding to steam for about 5 to 6 hours, topping up with the water when necessary.

Serve with homemade custard.

Lewis's taste in food was beautifully simple: he always ate a lunch of bread and cheese on a Saturday; the cheese had to be strong, like Stilton, or cheddar with resolve. He loved roast meat of any sort, but especially beef or chicken, and sherry was his favorite after-dinner tipple. Or Lewis might be found out and about in London, dining with his brother Warnie and other friends, where they ate, in Lewis's words, "kidneys enclosed, like the wicked man, in their own fat." When friends made him French food, the subtleties were lost on him, and he viewed with distinct suspicion the cooking of one friend's Italian servant. He liked egg sandwiches on picnics, but he wasn't generally keen on sandwiches. Plus he had a passion for pork pies, and nothing pleased him more for breakfast than home-cured bacon and eggs, with toast and marmalade alongside, although he preferred his bread untoasted. He had unusual views about boiled eggs, though; when Roger Lancelyn Green offered Lewis a hard-boiled egg on the train from Oxford to Cambridge, he refused. "No, no, I mustn't!" insisted Lewis. "It's supposed to be an aphrodisiac. Of course, it's all right for you as a married man—but I have to be careful."

Narnian Pork Pie (Not Made with a Talking Pig)

INGREDIENTS

FOR THE JELLIED STOCK . . .

1 lb. pork bones
2 carrots, roughly chopped
2 onions, stuck with 4 cloves
2 bay leaves
4 sprigs thyme
1 stalk rosemary
Small bunch of parsley
10 peppercorns

FOR THE FILLING . . .

2 lb. minced pork, a third should be pork fat (this keeps the pie moist)
2 dry cured, smoked bacon rashers, chopped finely
2 tsp. sage, finely chopped
1 tbsp. parsley
½ tsp. cinnamon
½ tsp. freshly grated nutmeg
½ tsp. ground cloves
½ tsp. allspice
3 tbsp. brandy
1 tsp. anchovy essence

FOR THE HOT-WATER CRUST PASTRY . . .

2 tbsp. water
5 tbsp. milk
6 oz. lard
1 level tbsp. powdered sugar
1 lb. all-purpose flour
1 tsp. salt
1 beaten egg
3 tsp. double cream
6 dry cured, smoked bacon rashers, to line the pastry

METHOD

Make the jellied stock a day in advance of the pie. Place all the ingredients in a pan and cover with cold water. Simmer for three hours; then strain through a sieve. Discard the solids. Reduce the remaining stock to ¾ of a pint. Season and cool.

The filling is beautifully simple: mix all the filling ingredients together.

Now make the hot-water crust pastry. Into a large bowl, sift the flour, salt, and powdered sugar. In a pan, bring the milk, water, and lard to a boil. Make a well in the center of the flour and pour the boiling lard/water mix into the well, stirring it through the flour with a wooden spoon. The dough should eventually form a smooth ball. Let it rest for 15 minutes. Grease a baking tin with butter and set aside.

Reserve about a quarter of the pastry for the pie lid; shape the rest over the base and sides of your baking tin, using your fingertips to press the pastry into a crust. Avoid cracks, as these will allow the ham mixture to leak out. Line the pastry with the dry-cure bacon slices and then fill the pie with the spiced pork mixture.

Preheat the oven to 200°C. On a lightly floured surface, roll out and shape your pie lid to fit the top of the pie. After placing the lid on the pie, brush with the beaten egg and cream. Leave a 1-inch hold in the center of the pie lid crust. Place a rolled-up tube of card in this hole, so that it protrudes out of the pie to a distance of about 1 inch. When the pie is cooked, you will need to add your jelly through this funnel.

Put the pie in the middle shelf of the oven and bake for 2 hours.

After 2 hours, remove the pie from the oven and allow it to cool. Get your jellied stock. If it has become too solid, warm it gently to loosen it. Carefully pour the jellied stock into the pie, a little at a time. Be patient; allow the jelly to slowly sink. Remove the cardboard funnel and return the pie to the fridge for an hour to allow the jelly to fully set.

When he wasn't enjoying ginger beer, drunk from a straw, or a cup of hot milk at night, Lewis was fortunate enough to be an undergraduate at All Souls in Oxford, where they served up red, strong beer that had been bottled and brewed in the nineteenth century and smelled enticingly of coffee. He walked between Mrs. Moore's house in Headington and All Souls, down Cuckoo Lane in the winter, where, he said, the snowy grass looked like gooseberry fool with cream. Lewis may well have been on his way to encounter one of the lively enemies he had at the university. He found himself plagued by an adversary called Onions, and he recalled one Onions-Lewis crossing-of-swords in the Bodleian Library on Friday, July 9, 1926: "Just before I came away for lunch Onions suddenly came upon me and said, 'You don't mean to say you're reading something, I thought you never read.' Went to [Magdalen] College for lunch where I met Onions who expressed equal surprise at my being there. I got it back on him by asking whether, reasoning as he did about my reading, he assumed I never lunched except on the days he saw me lunching."

In later years, Lewis and chums liked nothing better than to go walking over long tracts of countryside, the plains, and ancient English trails; he refused point blank to call such an activity "hiking," as this made going for a walk sound ridiculously self-conscious and contrived. Walking was not that complicated. If it was a hot day, and they came across an inviting pool or stream, they'd strip off and bathe in the cooling waters; apparently when swimming in the open sea, Lewis would dive about among the rollers like a dolphin, innocent of the Atlantic cold. Nor did he allow anyone to bring a packed lunch, as he insisted that they stop regularly at pubs to drink beer or cider in the morning, then some more at lunchtime, with bread and cheese this time. It had to be real ale that they drank; Lewis and his brother, Warnie, refused to touch "tinned" beer!

At one wayside inn, where they stopped for a midday drink, the landlord's wife, oozing decayed sex appeal with winsome smiles through heavy pan makeup and balancing a turret of peroxide hair on her head, kept calling Lewis "ducks" in a very familiar way. Lewis could hardly contain himself afterward and dug one companion in the ribs: "You know, old Morris," he spluttered, "there must still be *something* about me! Did you notice that that good lady called me 'ducks' three times in as many minutes?" On another occasion, when a reluctant landlady agreed to feed them only if Lewis and company removed their shoes and ate in the back kitchen, he whispered, "You know, I rather enjoy being ordered about like this. What would the psychologists make of it?"

A very kind postmistress gave them tea with boiled eggs (hopefully Lewis wasn't overcome with passion) and bread and jam on Salisbury Plane in 1929. Lewis felt as passionately about tea—it had to be peat-colored and strong—as he did about beer; he called bad beer "varnish." That same day for supper our walkers enjoyed cider, ham and eggs, cheese, bread and marmalade, and tea. Lewis liked tea at any time of the day or night, and meetings of the Inklings, as they called themselves, always began with the ritual of tea, though they might move on to rum and hot water.

The Inklings always met on Tuesdays in the back parlor of the Eagle and Child pub on Oxford's St. Giles, with a coal fire specially lit for them by the landlord, the crumbling coals glowing. During the course of an evening's fun, part of which was spent reading out the libretto of Wagner's *Die Walküre*, J. R. R. Tolkien and the Lewis brothers stopped for tea at Eastgate Hotel on the High Street to eat a savory omelette and fried fish, and then drink beer. Lewis probably lost his hat, which he was very good at doing. Out walking with a friend in the Magdalen College grounds, Lewis pointed out a sodden mass of velvet on the ground. "That looks like my hat," he said. Then, joyfully, "It is my hat!" and he grabbed the mess and popped it on his head.

Lewis had further great outings with friends. They made one memorable excursion up the Thames on a riverboat dramatically named *Bosphorus* (owned by Warnie), their return marked by the news that Hitler had entered Poland. Silence fell. Then, over dinner, Lewis tried to add some cheer by declaring, "Well, at any rate, we now have less chance of dying of cancer."

Postwar, between 1947 and 1950, the arrival of food parcels from one of Lewis's American admirers was very welcome. Lewis shared the food with the other Inklings. His method of distribution was novel: he tucked all the tins, packages, and parcels under his bed and his companions could choose between these humps. It was potluck; you might end up with something dreary like prunes.

Dr. Warfield M. Firor of Maryland, however, did the most to ward off the heavy tedium of rationing in Britain. His parcels always included the greatest prize of all—porcine gold in British terms—a large ham. Such was the joy that greeted the arrival of the ham that Lewis wrote to Dr. Firor, "To all my set you are by now an almost mythical figure—Firor-of-the-Hams, a sort of Fertility god." A private dining room in Magdalen College was turned over to Lewis's special "ham suppers," which a happy circle attended. There might even be japes such as raffles—one American admirer had sent Lewis a tuxedo, which Lewis was too large for, so this became the prize in the Great Tuxedo Raffle.

A ham supper would often be preceded by Lewis sidling up to you, a conspiratorial twinkle in his eye, addressing you by whichever nickname he'd gifted you, and saying, "I've got rather a nice ham in my room. Would you care to come up tonight and have some?"

ERNEST HEMINGWAY

Ernest Hemingway followed pure, clean-lined rituals in his early years of writing in Paris. He liked to work in solitude, sitting in a rented room high above the streets. Like many of us, when left alone he did two things: he became very self-conscious about when he'd last eaten and what he'd like to eat next, and he spent a lot of time thinking about his body temperature: Am I too hot? Am I too cold? Should I put on a sweater; should I take off my sweater?

All of this was solved quite simply: sitting at an appropriate distance from the small, crackling fire he had in his room and keeping a store of writerly snacks at hand. Because it was Paris and everything was beautiful, those snacks were chestnuts in pretty brown-paper bags, the nuts roasted by Hemingway on the fire. Delicate saffron moons of sweet winter oranges, the peel of which Hemingway liked to throw on the coals and smell the bitter tangerine oil curl in the smoke. Then, at least, he could worry about the perfect line on a full stomach.

The emptiness of hunger was also familiar and, in hindsight, Hemingway said it was lovely—as a young writer, he saw little financial return from his writing. Then, even to read the word *cassoulet* made his stomach ache; his appreciation of Cezanne, he said, was the sharper when he was famished. Hunger fed his fiction. He found he created characters with fierce appetites and foodie preoccupations. And whenever the day's writing was done, he knocked back a kirsch and slipped the oranges in his pocket or they would freeze on his desk in the night.

While Hemingway preferred to spend his time chasing the perfect line on cool blustery days, looking for the right words and drinking warm Martinique rum in cafés, other people had other plans for him; Ezra Pound had him delivering opium to other, distressed, poets. "Hem" and John Dos Passos met at the Closerie des Lilacs at the corner of Saint Michel and Montparnasse to drink vermouth cassis. They loved going to watch the six-day bicycle races—the Six Jours at the Vélo d'Hiver—and armed themselves with cold chicken, a pot of pâté, cheeses, wine, and freshly baked rolls at the stalls and barrows of the street markets and then head up to the gallery to watch the bicycle races. Another evening and they were able to eat, thanks to a horse-racing bet made good, Crab Mexicaine and oysters. Or Hemingway might wander the bookshops near the rue de Seine. He and Hadley, his wife, stopped to eat smooth mashed potatoes and veal liver, soaked in milk and perhaps cooked in brandy, shallots, and cream. Down by the Pont Neuf, Hemingway watched men fishing on the river from cranelike cane poles and bought their *goujons*, small, delicate roaches, and ate fried platefuls of *friture* made from fish such as these, sweeter tasting than sardines.

In the wintertime in 1926, Hem, Hadley, and baby Bumby went to the skiing resort of Schruns in the Vorarlberg in Austria. Fate was soon going to cast its shadow over the Hemingways: he would meet Pauline Pfeiffer, leaving Hadley far behind. But this last winter was a happy one; they skied across land, sleeping overnight sometimes in woodcutter's huts, the mattresses packed with beech leaves. They skied at night under the starry skies, the air prickling with pine scent, the snow squeaking under the skis.

They were permanently hungry and stoked themselves up with bread, fresh eggs, ham, and fruit preserves in the morning, and at night, warmed themselves with shots of Enzian schnapps, fragranced by mountain gentian, and ate jugged hare in deep, red wine gravy or venison in a chestnut sauce, topped up with red wine, of course. Hemingway grew a beard to protect his face from the damaging sun, and the local peasants called him "the black kirsch–drinking Christ," as he loved taking short blasts of the local Vorarlberg kirsch.

Jugged Hare

INGREDIENTS

1 hare, with its blood
2 tbsp. butter
3 rashers streaky, unsmoked bacon, cut into lardons
25 very small onions, blanched
1½ tbsp. all-purpose flour
1 pint rich, red wine
1 pint game stock
3 oz. button mushrooms

FOR THE MARINADE . . .

3½ tbsp. olive oil
4 tbsp. brandy
2 medium onions, cut into rings
4 shallots
3 tbsp. parsley
1 bay leaf
2 sprigs thyme

TO GARNISH . . .

Small triangles of bread brushed with oil and baked to a gold color in the oven.

METHOD

The day before you intend to eat the jugged hare, take the hare and cut off the legs, and divide the back section into three or four sections. Reserve the hare's blood. In a bowl, combine the marinade of olive oil, brandy, onion rings, shallots, parsley, bay leaf, and thyme. Allow to marinade for 24 hours.

The next day, using boiling water, blanch the bacon lardons by running boiling water over them. Do the same with the tiny onions. Preheat the oven to 170°C.

Jugged Hare ***(continued)***

Melt the 2 tablespoons of butter in a casserole dish. Add the tiny onions to the casserole and cook gently until they are a soft golden color. Reserve them for later. Brown the bacon lardons. Reserve them for later also.

Combine the all-purpose flour with the fat, stirring constantly, until the roux becomes a light golden brown. Taking them out of the marinade, add the sections of hare and allow them to brown. Add the game stock and red wine. Bring to boil, stirring constantly. Cut out a round of greaseproof paper to fit the top of the casserole, allowing for 2 inches of excess paper on all sides. Butter the paper, cover the hare stew, and then top with the casserole lid. Allow this to cook in the oven for approximately 1½ hours.

After the time is up, open the casserole and remove the hare. Stain the sauce through a sieve. Return the hare to the casserole; add the mushrooms, blanched onions, and bacon. Return the strained sauce to the casserole, and bake for a further 20 minutes.

Finally, remove the casserole from the oven and place it on a very low heat on the stove. Add the hare's blood—this will thicken the sauce. Serve with the triangular croutons.

And now for a shot or six of Vorarlberg kirsch.

When the Lost Generation (in other words, Dorothy Parker and the Murphys) met up for Christmas in Switzerland in 1929, Hemingway joined them. The Murphys were staying in the Swiss sanatorium, the Palace Hotel, in a bid to save their tubercular son. Dorothy Parker was there to cheer them up; she began by jokingly naming them Swiss Family Murphy. She wrote to Robert Benchley that she had always thought of Switzerland as "the home of horseshit" and hadn't changed her mind. Parker heard someone take their last breaths in the room next to hers, hated mountains, and thought she was courting death every time she stepped on to a funicular.

As the Lost Generation trundled about the Palace sanatorium, they noticed the temperature plummeted to the freezing point at night, and the Murphys set up a temporary bar in their room with a spirit lamp, wine, cinnamon, and lemons. They all wore gloves while they drank and spoke in whispers so as not to disturb the patients. For Christmas dinner, Hemingway shot an Alpine goose, which they roasted in the hospital kitchen.

Lost Generation Alpine Goose

INGREDIENTS

One 8 to 10 lb. goose
Butter
Sea salt
Freshly ground black pepper

METHOD

Preheat the oven to 190°C (ideally this will all take place while you are slightly drunk in a hospital kitchen). Combine black pepper and sea salt with softened butter and then massage this over the bird, applying this particularly thickly over the breast. Place the goose on an ovenproof tray and roast for 15 minutes per pound. When half the required time has passed, lower the heat to 180°C. Keep basting the goose every 20 minutes.

And now for a cup or three of mulled wine.

F. SCOTT FITZGERALD

The Fitzgeralds always looked as though they had just stepped in from the sun, so beautiful were they. At least, that's what Dorothy Parker thought. In truth, Scott and Zelda were trapped in an increasingly agonized, frantic whirl of socializing, which hid their essential despair—Scott sweating for his next drink, Zelda's sanity chipping away at the edges.

John Dos Passos turned up to dine with the Fitzgeralds, already starry young celebrities, in 1922, at the Plaza in New York. He rapped smartly on the door to their suite. Scott answered it, and Dos Passos fleetingly wondered whether the couple was just pretending to rent the suite: Had they just hired it for the day to impress visitors? The Fitzgeralds eventually ended up renting an apartment near the Plaza so that they could order food from there. From the start of their relationship, Zelda had made it clear that, as she put it, she was not the sort of person to be found in a kitchen.

The day kicked off: the Fitzgeralds, like a pair of unkind amateur psychologists, worked in tandem to ask annoying, leading questions in order to critique responses, revealing the potholes in their guests' answers. Dos Passos found it really trying. Sherwood Anderson was the other guest for lunch—Dos Passos may have been tempted to throw him to the wolves—and they sat at the gleaming table, toying with their Bronx cocktails and lobster croquettes, having difficult, testy conversations. The food was delicious, though, and the Bronx cocktails took Dos Passos's resentment out of the New York air.

The Algonquin hotel in New York offered the Fitzgeralds a very different sort of dining experience. Because she loved his writing, Dorothy Parker asked to meet Scott at the Algonquin, where they all sat in a row at one of the awkward tables that filled the dining room. The tables were too narrowly packed to have someone sit opposite you, so our happy group sat in a row, on a bench, their backs to the wall. Parker quipped, "This looks like a road company of the Last Supper."

The Fitzgeralds were always waiting for something fantastic to begin. And they found the fantastic to some extent in the protracted periods they spent on the French Riviera in the early 1920s. Summers with the Murphys at their villa were idyllic; the Fitzgeralds, slick with salt water and sunlight, lounged by the clear, blue water, drinking ice cold sherry or cassis and eating Sara Murphy's favorite meal of poached eggs, fresh sweet corn sprinkled with paprika, with plump tomatoes that had been sweated in garlic and olive oil. If things got too formal, the Fitzgeralds, again like conspirators, would begin to sabotage the evening. One night some very dull people came for dinner at the Murphys' (including a posse of duchesses); Scott and Zelda drank lots of cocktails and crawled among the vegetable foliage, chucking tomatoes at the guests.

Hemingway records a very funny eating journey with Scott in *Moveable Feast*, which bears all the hallmarks of Hemingway's good sense, Fitzgerald's scattiness, and their mutual fondness for the bottle. Hemingway had very kindly arranged with Fitzgerald to travel to Lyons with him to collect a car Fitzgerald and Zelda had abandoned there. Of course, Fitzgerald, in a fluster of lateness, had managed to miss the train to Lyons. Furious, Hemingway had to travel alone, using the meager pile of cash he'd saved to go to Pamplona later in the year. Fitzgerald then failed to find Hemingway in Lyons, but he appeared the next day, insisted on breakfast in the hotel, and that the hotel prepare them an extensive picnic for their forthcoming journey in the car—all of which was four or five times the cost of simply popping into a café en route. At least Fitzgerald took notice of Hemingway's advice that wonderful chicken was to be got in Lyons, requesting that the hotel put a chicken in their picnic hamper. It seemed an excellent plan to knock back a staunch whiskey or three after breakfast, and they wove their way through the streets of Lyons to get the car from the garage.

Hemingway stopped short in surprise when he saw the small Renault was open topped. It hadn't been before. Lo and behold, when the Fitzgeralds were in Marseille the car had been damaged. Zelda insisted that the mechanics remove the roof—given that Zelda's chief interest in life was learning ballet steps, no one should have listened to her. Anyway, Zelda's bright idea was fine while the weather was good, but the sky above Hemingway and Fitzgerald was overcast. The mechanic said, gently, "You gentlemen have no waterproofs?"

So Hemingway and Fitzgerald set off for Paris, squiffy with whiskey, in a strange, abbreviated Renault, the air about their ears. For about an hour, that is, until it began to drizzle.

They had no choice but to stop with the rainfall, and, eventually, in hungry desperation, they fell upon the hotel picnic, which turned out to contain one immaculately cooked, delicious, truffled chicken and gorgeous bread. Plus, Hemingway had managed to lay his hands on some very good white Mâcon wine.

Each time the rain dried up a little, they'd motor on, swigging even more wine, uncorking a further four bottles (it was, of course, a crate of Mâcon). Fitzgerald thought it very exciting to chug wine from the bottle and acted as if he were going skinny-dipping for the first time.

By the time that evening fell and they stopped at a roadside hotel, Fitzgerald decided he was dying of pneumonia. These were his final hours, he moaned, and demanded that Hemingway find him a thermometer. Hemingway thought he looked like a "little dead crusader" lying in bed and came up with the bright idea that he order drinks for them of whiskey and citron pressé to fight off any lurking pneumonias. The thermometer turned up, and Hemingway, wielding it over Fitzgerald, said darkly, "You are lucky it's not a rectal thermometer."

Truffled Chicken

Truffled chicken has the beautifully gloomy French name *poulet demi dueil*, which means "chicken in half-mourning," and when you see the white chicken with an undercoat of black, lacy truffle, it looks deliciously sorrowful.

INGREDIENTS

A 3 lb. free-range chicken
3 oz. black truffles, thinly sliced into discs
Freshly ground black pepper
Sea salt
1 garlic clove, finely sliced
3 tbsp. unsalted butter
2½ tbsp. Madeira
2½ tbsp. brandy

METHOD

Work under the skin of the chicken, gently easing it from the breast and legs and slipping the slices of truffle beneath the skin. Try to keep them in a single layer, covering the chicken. Now store the chicken in a sealed casserole pot, and refrigerate overnight.

The next day, preheat the oven to 200°C. Salt and pepper the chicken and pour the Madeira and brandy into the cavity of the chicken. Scatter the sliced garlic about the chicken. Lay the butter in slices on the breast of the chicken. Now bake the chicken in its sealed casserole dish in the oven for 1½ hours. When you open the casserole dish, you will be greeted by truffle and Madeira-rich clouds of scent.

Pneumonia Chaser

INGREDIENTS

2 measures of whiskey
Juice of 2 freshly squeezed lemons
2 tsp. sugar

METHOD

Combine all the above. Say a prayer and knock back.

Electrified by the thermometer and the pneumonia chaser, Fitzgerald suddenly recovered his health and insisted on going downstairs to call Zelda. This led them to the hotel restaurant, where they decided to have dinner. They ate snails in garlic butter, with Hemingway polishing off the remainder while Fitzgerald was on his call (for an hour!), using broken bread to mop up the buttery slicks of garlic and parsley. Fitzgerald, ever demanding, said that more snails would not do as a main course, nor liver, steak, or omelette—he had to eat something simple. This, in their world, translated to a marvelous French rustic chicken, poularde de Bresse, and a bottle of Montagny. Afterward, Fitzgerald very politely and gently passed out, his head in his hands, as if taking care not to upset the Montagny.

Shhh, let us leave and not wake him.

And for dessert we could have the cherry tart that they shared together at Michaud's restaurant on rue Jacob, when Fitzgerald asked Hemingway to look at his penis. Fitzgerald had never slept with anyone other than Zelda, and she had told him that he had such a small penis no woman would ever be pleased with him. Kindly, Hemingway led him to the "office," also known as the toilet, and had a look—his penis was fine, he reassured Fitzgerald. It's just if you look at it from above, you think it's small. And just to get the message across, he took Fitzgerald on a tour of the male nude statues in the Louvre.

Cherry Tart

INGREDIENTS

1 lb. bottled, stoned Morello cherries
1 lb. bottled, stoned sweet cherries
4 oz. brown-skinned hazelnuts
4 tbsp. butter
2 oz. caster sugar
2 tbsp. kirsch

AND FOR THE PASTRY . . .

INGREDIENTS

8 oz. all-purpose flour
2 oz. vanilla caster sugar
½ tsp. sea salt
Finely grated rind of one lemon
5 oz. butter, diced
2 egg yolks
3 tbsp. water

THE GLAZE . . .

3 tbsp. redcurrant jelly
1 tbsp. powdered sugar
1 tbsp. kirsch
1 tbsp. reserved Morello cherry syrup or juice

METHOD

Make the pastry first. In a large bowl, place the sieved flour. Add the butter, sugar, salt, and lemon zest, and rub all together between your fingertips until you have a biscuit mix. Add the eggs and 3 tablespoons of water. Now knead gently into a dough, cover in cling film, and allow the pastry to chill for an hour or two.

Cherry Tart (*continued*)

Now for the tart filling. If the Morello cherries are raw, cook them with a little water for a few minutes to soften the fruit. If bottled, drain the cherries and reserve the syrup.

Put the hazelnuts in a food processor and blitz them until they are finely ground. Then combine with the butter and sugar. Next, add the egg yolks and 2 tablespoons of kirsch and blend.

Preheat the oven to 190°C. Roll the pastry out on a lightly floured surface. Butter a flan dish and fit the pastry to the dish. Using a fork, carefully prick the base, taking care not to pierce it. Now line with greaseproof paper and baking beans. Bake blind for 15 minutes. Remove the foil and bake for a further 10 minutes, or until the pastry is golden.

Prepare the glaze. In a saucepan, melt the redcurrant jelly, kirsch, powdered sugar, and ½ cup of the cherry syrup. Simmer until reduced to a half. Brush this fruity, warm glaze on the base of the piecrust—but reserve some for brushing the surface of the tart. Now pour the hazelnut custard over it. Plop the little cherries into the custard. Finally, brush with the remaining redcurrant jelly. Cook in the oven for 20 minutes. It's so delicious, you'll forget about the size of anything—except your next slice!

JOHN STEINBECK

Like many writers, Steinbeck was hard up for a decade or two. Studying at Stanford University in the 1920s, he wrote to Florence, a girl he knew, about what it was like working in the City Café, Palo Alto, to finance his education. "I cannot step out much, Florence, because I have lots of ambitions and very little money so my fun from now on must be very prosaic . . . I am poor, dreadfully poor. I have to feed someone else before I can eat myself. I must live in an atmosphere of dirty dishes and waitresses with soiled ears, if I wish to know about things like psychology and logic."

By the 1930s Steinbeck was starving quite happily in Eagle Rock with his wife, Carol (Florence long since forgotten), robbing orange groves of their fruit and eating dinners of stolen avocados and hamburgers. The owner evicted them, and they moved into a house owned by Steinbeck's father in Pacific Grove, California. Steinbeck's cooking speciality at the time was a dish called Pacific Grove Starvation Special, but its ingredients are unrecorded. This may be a good thing, as Steinbeck said that the ingredients were top secret but would lead to nausea if known. Promising? Steinbeck couldn't resist populating the Pacific Grove pond with beautiful, iridescent green mallard ducks. They ate all the goldfish in the pond, and he then had to sell the ducks to pay for paper to write on.

By 1939, Steinbeck had made some cash from *Tortilla Flat* and *Of Mice and Men*, and he built a ranch in Los Gatos. At last, the Steinbecks had their own vegetable garden. They made their own butter and cheese courtesy of the neighbor's cow, which gave them three quarts of milk daily in return for the chance to graze on their pasture. The cellar was pungently sweet with the smell of homemade wine brewing and crated apples. Carol canned her own tomatoes, and they laid out plums and grapes to dry into prunes and raisins in the warm sunlight. The frogs sang about rain, and even the birds were tipsy on the rich crops of wild berries.

Steinbeck was ever resourceful and seems to have belonged naturally to the landscapes he inhabited. In England, he thought nothing of picking bunches of dandelions from his garden and cooking them with a little butter. He ate the floppy, foul-smelling mess of white that was boiled turtle on the Sea of Cortez during his expedition there on a sardine boat called *Western Flyer*. Once, staying at a friend's ranch, Steinbeck took himself off through their grove of cottonwoods to go trout fishing. He found a pool that lay just beyond a grassed hill. There, he caught four rainbow trout, which he cleaned by the water. Having strung the fish, he carried them over his shoulder back to the ranch. While he hunkered over a mug of coffee in the kitchen, the cook dipped the rainbow trout in cornmeal and then fried them in bacon fat until they crisped. She put the plate of trout down in front of Steinbeck, the trout hot under a light, frangible cover of bacon-rich flour that crumbled in Steinbeck's mouth. "It was a long time since I had eaten trout like that, five minutes from water to pan. You take him in your fingers delicately by head and tail and nibble him from off his backbone, and finally you eat the tail, crisp as a potato chip. Coffee has a special taste of a frosty morning, and the third cup is as good as the first."

DIY Rainbow Trout

INGREDIENTS

2 plump, fresh rainbow trout
4 tbsp. cornmeal
Sea salt and freshly ground black pepper
2 tbsp. bacon fat

METHOD

Clean the rainbow trout, and then roll each trout in cornmeal, seasoned with sea salt and black pepper. Heat the bacon fat until it sizzles in a wide frying pan or griddle. Place the trout on the griddle, and cook on both sides for 5 minutes a side. The cornmeal makes the trout's oily, delicious skin even more crisp. When the trout's flesh is opaque (check the thickest section of the trout) and the skin is blistered and honey gold, serve with squeezed lemon and a knob of butter.

It is really at times like these when Steinbeck was on his own that we can see the man himself, as in 1960, when he traveled across America in an old bakery van with his ridiculous, long-nosed, brown poodle Charley (who looked as if he were wearing a dog toupee). Steinbeck claimed Charley was the only dog in the world that could pronounce the consonant *f*. Steinbeck also wondered if America smelled all the same to Charley or smelled "sectional."

Steinbeck's plan was to reconnect with America, to learn to write about it again, to make sure his "writer's truth" about the state of the nation was correct. So he began as all great writers do: he packed a wad of alcohol into the van, from bourbon to aged applejack and brandy. He was about to eat and drink his way across the continent, using this as a way of reconnecting with the America he felt he might have lost. He bought a gallon jug of freshly pressed cider, ate red apples so sweet that they burst with juice when he bit into them, and learned enough about America's food to be prepared to swear that dark-shelled Maine lobsters served with only lemon and butter were the best in the world. As he bumped his way through the world of motels, Steinbeck found himself resenting their sterilized world. He was amazed by a sealed toilet seat that boasted that it was treated with ultraviolet rays for his protection. Fondly, he remembered an Arab in North Africa handing him a glass of mint tea in a glass opaque with dirt. Steinbeck had loved this gesture of filthy companionability.

He found good breakfasts across America and bad dinners. America was a utopia of breakfasts, as long as you remained true to bacon, eggs, and crunchy, pan-fried potatoes. Whenever he saw a sign for "Sausage, Homemade" or "Fresh Laid Eggs," or, worse, "Bacons and Hams, Home Smoked," it was a sirenlike lure, and he had to pull over fast and buy some. The difference between motorway café wishy-washy battery eggs and the rich nuggets of yellow yolk on Steinbeck's plate was remarkable; sausage that was piquant and peppered with spices far surpassed the dulled links of sausage in the Steak n' Shake café refrigerator. And coffee—real coffee? It tasted to Steinbeck of mahogany-dark bliss and was the drink of working men. To make your coffee "shine," Steinbeck's top tip was that you drop an egg white and shell into the bubbling coffee pot. He liked truckers and listening to their voices, the words collected from the road. Coffee was their symbol of unity.

The food of America, Steinbeck felt, was becoming too much like its sanitized toilets and dispensing machines—lacking in humanity. Onto the spotless scallops of restaurant counters was delivered food, untouched by human hands. Steinbeck said he remembered with a pang dishes he'd eaten in Italy and France that had been crafted by many pairs of hands. But before Steinbeck sank too much into idealism, he checked himself: "Even while I protest the assembly-line production of our food, our songs, our language, and eventually our souls, I know it was a rare home that baked good bread in the old days. Mother's cooking was with rare exceptions poor . . . that good unpasteurized milk touched only by flies . . . that sweet local speech I mourn was the child of illiteracy."

He stopped at a German roadside restaurant in Mississippi, with sausages and sauerkraut draping the bar in an unused, edible bunting. The desiccated waitress took his order, and he saw the cook unwrap a cellophane-covered sausage and slip it into boiling water, the kraut pooled with old, gray, briny water. He asked directions and told his swart, crooked little waitress he had gotten lost in Minneapolis. "He got lost in Minneapolis!" she called to the cook, who bellowed back, "Nobody can get lost in Minneapolis. I was born there and I know."

Montana was a paradise of bubbling navy beans and fatback. There were brilliant signs on the motorway cafés, splattered by flies. Steinbeck laughed out loud at the national roadside humor on signage, which read like some God-like, divine commentary:

"Pies like Mother would have made if Mother could have cooked."
"We don't look in your mouth. Don't look in our kitchen."
"No checks cashed unless accompanied by fingerprints."

Montana Navy Beans and Fatback—they taste of America

INGREDIENTS

2 tbsp. oil
½ lb. strip fatback
½ lb. dried navy beans
3 onions, peeled and roughly chopped
2 carrots, chopped
2 celery ribs, chopped
2 garlic cloves, chopped
2 bay leaves
½ tsp. thyme
1 tbsp. chopped parsley
Sea salt and black pepper
2 pints ham stock

METHOD

Soak the navy beans overnight. In a deep pan, heat the oil. Add the fatback, skin side down, and brown it all over. Now add the onions, carrot, celery, and garlic. Sauté them for a minute or two, then add the bay leaves, thyme, and parsley. Salt and pepper to taste. Pour in the drained beans and cover with the ham stock. Bring to boil and then simmer slowly for 2 hours. If necessary, add more water as the bean stew cooks.

Finally, depressed in New Mexico, he and Charley parked the baker's wagon beside a huge, meaningless pile of bottles, and Steinbeck wondered if he had really learned anything about America, if he was even capable of seeing it anymore. Charley also seemed depressed (Steinbeck called depression "mullygrubs"). Drastic action was needed, Steinbeck thought, to raise their spirits. He decided it was Charley's birthday and that he would bake him a cake—hotcakes with syrup and a candle on top. The thump of Charley's tail seemed to be having a conversation with him.

Before you knew it, Steinbeck was ready to serve up: a straight whiskey for him and for Charley four layers of steaming hotcakes with maple syrup dripping between the layers, and on top the small, oily stub of a miner's candle.

They both felt better after this.

Mullygrubs Hotcakes and Maple Syrup (last enjoyed by Charley)

INGREDIENTS

1 cup all-purpose flour, sifted
¼ cup sugar
2 tsp. baking powder
1 large egg, beaten
1 tsp. vanilla essence
¾ cup buttermilk
Pinch of sea salt
1 tbsp. butter

METHOD

Sift the flour into a bowl. Add the sugar, baking powder, and a pinch of salt. Make a well in the center and gradually add the milk until you have a smooth batter. Add the beaten egg and the vanilla essence. Whisk this together and, if it seems too dry, add more milk, a little at a time. The hotcake batter should be relatively thin. Leave this batter to rest for a few minutes; it will thicken.

In a griddle or large frying pan, melt the tablespoon of butter. When the butter is hot, drop a tablespoon of hotcake batter into the pan. The first hotcake always has a sacrificial purpose; it's your trial run to make sure you've got the temperature right. Turn after a minute and cook the other side. Your hotcake should be golden brown. Drizzle some maple syrup over it, light a candle, and call Charley.

J. D. SALINGER

As the author of the rites-of-passage novel *Catcher in the Rye*, which tells the story of disaffected teenager Holden Caulfield, you'd imagine that J. D. Salinger might become a teen magnet. And he did become just that. And, like Holden, Salinger was drawn to teenage girls, too. Indeed, there is a great deal of Salinger in the uneasy pubescence of Holden. It is no accident that Salinger tried to insist *he* play Holden in any film version of the novel.

When fan mail turned up on Joyce Maynard's doormat in April 1972, she wasn't surprised. Her article "An Eighteen Year Old Looks Back on Life" had been full enough of youthful cynicism and angst to fire up controversy and admiration when it appeared in the *New York Times*. Her generation was that of Bob Dylan and Janis Joplin, wondering what had happened to that Mercedes Benz. They were the generation being sent to the hell of Vietnam.

Joyce turned the envelope over in her hands, ripped it open, and started to read. Quickly, she found herself charmed by the voice of the letter: the writer seemed to understand the sources of her disaffection. Then there was the final, sweet, surprising shock of seeing the closing signature: J. D. Salinger. Already an icon, Salinger had also been married twice and was thirty-five years older than Joyce. She had kissed someone. Once.

Having such a soulmate confess themselves proved too much of a temptation for Joyce. She wrote back to Salinger, their correspondence quickly becoming more passionate. He has a twelve-year-old son named Matthew, he tells her. She tells him she makes dollhouse furniture and rides a bike. He tells her she's a natural writer. He suggests that if they drank Scotch whiskey together, he would tell her many more stories. It's intoxicating. He loves his garden, his tomato plants; he has a dachshund, Joey. Joyce utterly adores Salinger. She is stung by poison ivy, mentions this in a letter, and he sends her a spotted jewelweed saturated in high-proof vodka; the poison ivy rash disappears.

To her, he's a magician.

She writes to him always as "Dear Jerry" and tries to convey a sense of ennui, but her innocence bubbles out in questions like "What is a day in your life like? Do you sit at a desk and write? Do you listen to music or visit and eat peanut butter sandwiches?" He sends her in return an account of the homeopathic treatment he's devised for himself and a list of the things he loves, and there is her name, last on the list.

The letter writing that began in April concluded in May. She had his phone number, which he suggested she call collect. They began to talk nightly by phone. He wanted to absorb her, know everything about her, and he was fun. He loved to gossip, telling her about Jerry Lewis, who had been chasing the part of Holden Caulfield for years. Actors of any kind made Salinger shudder. He said he'd prefer downing a glass of castor oil to hobnobbing with actor types.

Finally, in a romantic crescendo, they arranged to meet in Cornish, New Hampshire, where Salinger lived. She saw him from a distance; she recognized him from the cover of *Life* magazine, standing on the steps of the Hanover Inn. When she ran toward him his face lit up. They had already laughed together about how to recognize each other: he had told her the story about Lauren Bacall greeting him across a crowded street because she mistook him for her husband, Jason Robards.

Salinger made her lunch, all drawn from his special homeopathic mantra of good foods. In his basement he kept a vast chest freezer packed with homegrown vegetables, nuts, and fiddlehead ferns (more on these later). On her plate was brown, wholegrain bread, apples, a smidgen of cheddar cheese, and sunflower and pumpkin seeds mixed with unpasteurized honey. Ice cream, Salinger warned, was poison.

In a manner strangely reminiscent of the habits of another cold fish, Cary Grant, Salinger laid out two folding TV trays on the decking of his house. In my estimation, the separate TV trays should have been warning enough to Joyce that a deeply unromantic soul lurked within Salinger. The talk moved on to their given names; he moaned about being called Jerome, as it suggested he was a podiatrist or, even worse, a writer. She likewise complained that her parents handed over responsibility for naming her to her four-year-old sister.

By dinnertime, Salinger felt they were close enough to try out his fiddlehead ferns, and they ate those, steamed, plus more bread and apples, sliced this time. Then he rustled up his signature dish of homemade popcorn—not buttered, oh no, but drizzled with dark tamari soy sauce.

Finally, because she had a cough that worried him, he wrapped a blanket about her feet and placed her on the velvet couch—any intimations here of a controlling nature? Now it was time to watch movies (his choice): one of his favorites, Hitchcock's *Thirty-Nine Steps*, and the time was conjured away by Robert Donat. The next reel on the projector was *The Thin Man*, but Joyce nodded off during the showing. High times indeed. He tucked her in bed and straightened her sheets. When she took off her glasses, she joked that she could no longer recognize him: "You could be anybody," she said. "I'm actually Clark Gable," he replied.

Breakfast was more wholemeal bread, but with Bird's Eye tender tiny peas . . . hmm . . . Joyce may have begun to look perplexed, so, in their newly forming roles of teacher and disciple, he said (probably over his TV tray), "I want to teach you about this diet of mine." His intentions toward her were serious.

Salinger was obsessed with a raw food diet: no refined food should pass his lips, nor would anything that was cooked beyond a temperature of 150 degrees centigrade, like milk, for example. Cooked meat was death to the soul and the spleen, but one couldn't avoid having a little bit of cheese, if you were courting a young lady.

He had developed an unusual way of preparing meat. He bought organic minced lamb at the health food store, shaped it into patties, and froze these. The freezing process zapped any bugs and then, when he cooked the patties, it would be below 150 degrees centigrade. With this diet, he confided, he expected to live until he was 120 years old. She believed him.

His final gift to her when she left—he had kissed her once on the lips—was a copy of *Food Is Your Best Medicine* by Dr. Henry Bieler.

After this auspicious start, they were together again ten days later, and Salinger was doing his level best to take Joyce's virginity. Salinger's bedroom was sparse, with only homeopathic magazines for company. But sex was agonizing, as Joyce's muscles clamped. Rather than attribute any shortcomings to himself, Salinger decided to cure Joyce. She was his now.

Enter the TV trays.

He went down to the garden, fetched some summer squash, steamed it, tossed it in tamari sauce, and put it on a TV tray table. While she ate this, he rifled through the pages of *Materia Medica*. Eventually, he pronounced that her condition was vaginismus.

Every night, he made them lamb patties and vegetables, and every night they'd go back to the bedroom to reattempt sex (after watching more film reels . . . sitting on the velvet couch . . . wrapping her feet in a blanket). He reassured her that if all else failed, they'd write a play and then perform it in the West End.

Having eventually sorted out the vaginismus, Joyce and Salinger began to live together; he came up with a checklist of foods they could eat. But Salinger was hard to please and never hesitated to let his disenchantment be known. He complained about the apple cores she left around, the cucumber peelings, and the banana bread she baked. She thought she'd followed all the rules by using wholewheat flour and sweetening it with unpasteurized honey, but she transgressed by baking it at 350 degrees Fahrenheit! A crime had been committed. Perhaps the banana bread is the reason Salinger died at age 91 instead of the expected 120? Joyce kept Salinger happy with regular oral sex, which made him forget about the unwashed bowls in the sink and banana skins.

Salinger went to and fro the health store, controlling what they ate. Bread had been deleted from his checklist. Clearly, like cheese, it was a "courtship" food.

Unleavened bread was allowed occasionally and referred to as a "treat." Joyce looked forward more than anything to Salinger's trips to New York, when he brought back Bloomingdale's smoked salmon. The sheer luxury of a fleshy, fishy departure from lamb patties was too heady: Salinger and Joyce began to plan how they could smoke their own salmon.

Having picked up a basket at the local hardware store, Salinger stopped at the Purity Supreme store—Salinger liked to call it Puberty Supreme—and he picked up some salmon steaks. He motored home, donned a blue jumpsuit, dragged a ladder up against the wall of the house, and scrambled onto the roof with the salmon in the basket. He lowered the basket of salmon down the chimney. Down below, they lit a fire of hickory wood, as, theoretically, it would give a rich, smoky, hickory taste to the salmon. But the basket blocked the chimney, and soot coughed and billowed its way back into the house. Salinger, black faced, was left to ponder what a bargain Bloomingdale's salmon was.

Eventually, the Salinger-Maynard union came to a sticky end. Joyce was bulimic, weary of pumpkin seeds, and had begun to smuggle food into the house. She couldn't leave the cheddar alone and was secretly eating yogurt and granola in town, and oral sex no longer took Salinger's mind off her shortcomings. He threw her out.

A Romantic Meal with Salinger, Or Live Until You Are 120!

STEAMED FIDDLEHEAD FERNS

I have yet to come across a fiddlehead fern in a shop. What you must do is to take yourself to the woods in the early spring, when you can gather wild fiddlehead ferns. They are very beautiful, sage green, embryonic fern fronds, before they unroll into ferns. They resemble the scrolls of fiddles and look gloriously ornamental.

INGREDIENTS

¼ lb. fiddlehead ferns
1 tbsp. olive oil
2 garlic cloves, sliced

METHOD

In a frying pan, heat the olive oil. Add the garlic, then the fiddlehead ferns. Add a dash of water, cover the pan, and allow the ferns to steam for a few minutes.

Popcorn and Tamari

INGREDIENTS

Butter
Dried corn
Tamari sauce

METHOD

In a deep pan, heat the butter. Now add the corn. Put the lid on the pan, increase the heat, and wait to hear the quick-fire sound of corn popping. Vigorously shake the pan to keep on redistributing the unpopped corn. When the pan falls silent, remove from the heat. Pour the hot, buttery corn into a deep dish and sprinkle with tamari sauce.

IAN FLEMING

He had the suave ability to savor a canapé while simultaneously dodging a bullet, eyeing a woman, and downing a martini. Who? James Bond, of course, and his creator, Ian Fleming. Nowhere is the symbiotic relationship of Fleming and Bond more apparent than in their choice of a dish. Both loved caviar, sauce Béarnaise, broiled lobster with melted butter, and Jamaican curried goat stew. Indeed, Bond was conceived at breakfast time in Fleming's Jamaican retreat, Goldeneye. Fleming had just finished breakfast and had probably enjoyed his usual treat of fresh, sweet paw-paw with a slice of green lime, scrambled eggs, nearly black Jamaican marmalade, guava jelly, and Blue Mountain coffee. It was January 1952, and Fleming was forty-three and on the brink of marriage to Anne Rothermere. On the verge of middle age and at the anxious edge of marriage, it could be suggested that Fleming created an alternate bachelordom and perpetual youth in Bond.

But Bond was in the making long before that breakfast, and it was nowhere more obvious than in Fleming's eating history. When Fleming set up house at 22A Ebury Street, he founded his own private dining club, Le Cercle Gastronomique et des Jeux de Hasard, with old Etonian friends. Its purpose was the improvement of the palate, driven by Fleming's ideal of the perfect meal. Girlfriends were primed for an idyllic supper by Fleming and then would find, to their disappointment, that they'd be served up kedgeree by candlelight. Admittedly, Fleming, in a very Bondish manner, claimed that what he looked for in a woman was someone "double-jointed, and who knew when to keep quiet and make sauce Béarnaise."

In a way, Fleming's ideal woman came embodied in the fleshly proportions of the matronly Violet, his housekeeper at Goldeneye in Jamaica. Violet told Fleming's biographer, Pearson, "The Commander just like all things easy here. He not fussy. He just like Jamaica food. He just love shrimp and fish and oxtail and liver . . . fish soup and black crab soup and calah soup—that Jamaican dish we make him with spinach. The Commander like it very much. He no like make-up pudding. He like guava and stew tamborine and fish and lobster every day at lunch and stew goat in the evening. The fish he like real special is kingfish and butter fish and snapper fish and goat fish . . . Real Jamaica fish, goat fish. Not many English people like him. But the Commander real crazy about goat fish." In fact, the word *goat* appended to any dish seemed to do it for Fleming. A regular on the Goldeneye menu was goat curry, a scrumptious Jamaican stew that literally cooks in its own rich gravy. One wonders how that went down with British visitors.

Moving unruffled through the upper crust of transcontinental society, Fleming's food biography is packed with comic details, canasta games, and conch gumbo feasts with the likes of Noël Coward and Somerset Maugham, all served up in Jamaica with another of Fleming's creations—the lethal rum punch Poor Man's Thing.

Poor Man's Thing

INGREDIENTS

1 tbsp. butter
1 cup Muscovado sugar
Zest of 1 orange
Zest of 1 lemon
2 cups orange juice
1 bottle Three Daggers Rum

METHOD

Place a pan over medium heat. In it, melt a tablespoon of butter, and tip in a cup of dark, treacly Muscovado sugar. Stir. When the sugar melts, add the grated zest of one orange and one lemon. Stir well. Add 2 cups of fresh orange juice. Heat. Now pour in a bottle of cheap Three Daggers Rum (reserve a few tablespoons in case ignition needs some encouragement). Heat until very hot and set alight. Add those spare tablespoons if it's not playing along and try again. When the surface is being licked by blue flames, turn out all the lights and carry Poor Man's Thing in to your guests. Put *out* the flames before serving.

Coward claimed he made the sign of the cross before each mouthful of salt fish and stewed ackee fruit—"Ian," Coward pleaded, "it tastes like armpits!" Coward noted the irony that Fleming's dinner guests would sit bleakly toying with an octopus tentacle while reflecting on all those delicious meals Ian put into his novels. The disappointment was palpable. Having rented Goldeneye from Fleming in 1948, Coward renamed it "Golden Eye, Nose and Throat," claiming that Goldeneye boasted all the "discomforts of a hospital."

The Jamaica set were well connected to the royal family: Fleming advised Princess Margaret on what she should eat in 1955 Jamaica, making her stay all the jollier despite the fact that she was under orders not to dance with black Jamaicans. In fact, Noël Coward may well have regretted being so free with his criticisms of Fleming's food shortcomings. He himself panicked when the Queen Mum visited him for lunch in Jamaica in 1965—he primed her with several Bullshots before having the temerity to feed her curry—the more European fish mousse Coward had prepared for her earlier had developed the "texture of a collapsed Slazenger tennis ball." The curry was a great success, served out of steaming coconuts and topped off with a rum cream pie. With the Queen Mum's ability to knock back Bullshots, you can understand why Hitler had described her as the most dangerous woman in Europe.

There was a huge discrepancy between filmic versions of Fleming's novels and the real Bond we find in his prose. The real Bond never stops eating. Before James was going to do anything, he wanted to have a full tummy. Yes, he looked forward to his supper as much as sex.

In Fleming's first Bond novel, *Casino Royale*, Bond ponders the wiles of his archenemy, the flagellant Le Chiffre (purportedly based on another gourmand, Aleister Crowley), over breakfast—the first detailed meal Bond ever enjoyed. Bond puts away three eggs scrambled, bacon, a huge glass of cold orange juice, and a double-sized coffee—sugarless, of course. The size of portions isn't accidental. Fleming's eating pleasure was established through that sense of a little bit extra, and he was very specific in this. He liked to have double the amount of strong, dark coffee, that extra quarter pint of orange juice. A boiled egg at breakfast had to be brown shelled.

Bond only ever has one drink before dinner, but he says, "I do like that one to be very large and very strong and very cold and very well made. I hate small portions of anything, particularly when they taste bad." It is at this point in *Casino Royale* that he instructs the casino's bartender on how to make his "own invention"—a dry martini—to be served in a deep champagne goblet: "Just a moment. Three measures of Gordon's, one of vodka, half a measure of Kina Lillet. Shake it very well until it's ice cold, then add a large, thin slice of lemon-peel. Got it?"

Shortly afterward, Bond romances his latest love interest, Vesper Lynd, who is soon to be both shaken and stirred, by naming his vodka martini the Vesper. They dine together. Vesper and Bond both start with caviar, but they part company over the main course, Vesper opting for grilled veal with potatoes and finishing with raspberries and cream. Bond's charged masculinity demands no less than a steak with Béarnaise sauce and artichoke hearts. No wussy raspberries for him; he has avocado with a light salad dressing. Of course, Vesper is a double agent for the Russians and eventually kills herself after a Bridget-Jones-style minibreak in France with Bond (having nursed him back to health with stories of meals she has enjoyed during his convalescence), leaving Bond with his long-standing hatred of SMERSH. Despite the intimations of tragedy, Fleming can't resist mentioning that Madame la patronne prepared lobsters broiled with melted butter for the doomed couple.

Fleming himself was no stranger to espionage—he ate caviar, cream, and Russian pancakes on board the train to Moscow on a secret mission for the Foreign Office. Typically, he has left us with one key dining mystery that remains unsolved: Just what Georgetown fare did Fleming dine on with JFK when they planned how to humiliate Castro (or at least make his beard fall out with depilatory powder)? Does anybody know?

Goat Curry

A reliable, understanding local butcher can acquire goat meat for you—the surprise with which your request for goat meat is received in traditional butcheries makes the whole process a little embarrassing, like trying to order a Thai bride from the Jehovah's Witnesses. Be sure to order the meat a few days in advance. Oh, and ask the butcher to prepare the meat for you. You don't want to be left wrestling with a goat's leg in the suburban confines of your kitchen.

INGREDIENTS

MARINADE

3 lb. lean goat meat, cut into 2-inch cubes
Juice of 1 lime
6 garlic cloves, crushed
2 large onions, sliced
2 tsp. sea salt
2 tsp. crushed black pepper
2 tsp. fresh thyme leaves
2 tsp. Jamaican jerk seasoning
1 tbsp. curry powder
1 tsp. finely chopped Scotch bonnet pepper
2 large juicy tomatoes, chopped
3 to 4 tbsp. fresh, chopped cilantro

TO COOK . . .

4 oz. butter
4 tbsp. vegetable oil
1 tsp. brown sugar
6 scallions, finely sliced
3 potatoes, peeled and cubed

METHOD

Place the cubed goat in a large container; drizzle over the freshly squeezed lime juice. Add to the meat the crushed, sticky garlic, chopped cilantro, tomatoes, and sliced onions. Next add the curry powder, jerk seasoning, raw thyme, salt, black pepper, and Scotch bonnet pepper. Massage this marinade into the meat—but wear rubber gloves if you're afraid of the Scotch bonnet's short temper! Cover and refrigerate overnight.

The next day, remove the marinated goat from the fridge. Melt the butter and oil in a large pot, add the brown sugar, and stir until the sugar melts into the butter. Add the marinated goat and the sliced scallions. Stir. Next, place a lid on the pot, turn the heat down low, and allow the goat to simmer gently in its own juices for 2 hours. Check regularly to ensure that the curry is not drying out—generally, you won't have to add any water, as the curry produces its own rich gravy.

After 2 hours, add the diced potatoes and 2 tablespoons of water. Cover again and allow to simmer for about 25 minutes, until the potatoes have softened.

Serve with Jamaican coconut rice and beans—and a tumbler of Poor Man's Thing!

W. H. AUDEN

"Auden, I see, wants the Huns to win," noted one schoolmaster acidly as young W. H. Auden helped himself to yet another slice of margarine-coated bread. World War I raged, and rationing held Britain in its narrow, parsimonious grip. Hard times or not, Auden's appetite got the better of his war effort; he just couldn't resist that extra slice.

Nor did things change much as he grew older. An undergraduate at Oxford, Auden ate with gusto, shoveling large quantities of food into his mouth as if trying to beat a spectral clock, barely noticing what was on his fork. He could be a trying houseguest, rising bright-eyed at the crack of dawn, calling for endless cups of tea. One friend remarked that it was as if "his large, white, apparently bloodless body needed continual reinforcements of warmth." He might well turn on his hosts, demanding that they pay heed to his sudden food partialities and distinctions. When he stayed with Stephen Spender's family in 1925, a dishcover was raised at lunch and Auden peered at the contents of the dish before judgmentally grumbling, "*Boiled ham!*" He was even known to come close to tears if food disappointed him.

Auden managed not to cry at all about disagreeable food when traveling in China in 1937 with Christopher Isherwood. They had been commissioned by Faber & Faber to write a travel book about China, eventually to be titled *Journey to a War*. Faber left it up to them to determine their actual route. The way they chose across China was an interesting one, and they met up with staunch, freckled colonial types, one of whom looked at the route they had mapped, shook his head, and muttered, "Well, I wish you luck. But it's a hard road. A hard road," before adding, confidentially, "You may have to eat Chinese food."

Auden proved very adventurous, as if his conservatism was confined only to familiar English fare. Roast dog, snake wine, and ancient eggs were straightforward, ridiculous fun. Chinese food and its perceived eccentricity amused Isherwood and Auden to no end, appealing to their sense of the macabre. Wandering through Canton, Auden was aghast at the shiny, black beetles for sale to eat, while Isherwood stared in breathless horror at the vats of water squirming with swimming snakes. "I would go mad if I ate one of those," he whispered, at which point Auden made it his mission to see to it that Isherwood did just that.

Mischievously, the pair worked out their own secret game: to praise whichever dish they liked the least. "Delicious," Auden announced, sinking his teeth into what seemed to be a sponge bulging with glue; Isherwood's reply was to smile coquettishly as he chewed on an orange, flavored like bitter aloes, at the center of which nestled what appeared to be a large, muscular weevil.

When they were invited to lunch at the home of General Wu The-chen, the ex-mayor of Shanghai, now governor of Kwantung Province, Auden and Isherwood had rehearsed themselves in all the Chinese etiquette suitable for home visits, taken from a doubtful book called *The Chinese Bungalow*. They had secretly run through, and play-acted, the ritual for visiting someone's house—General Wu was supposed to say, "My poor house is honored." To which they were supposed to reply, "Our feet are quite unworthy to rest upon your honorable doorstep." Quick as lightning, the general was supposed to reply, "If my doorstep were gold, it would hardly be fit for your distinguished shoes."

Did it happen? Not at all, and before they had even time to visit the toilet for a quick consultation of *The Chinese Bungalow*, or look at anyone's shoes, eating events had moved on.

Auden found General Wu's lunch table to be barely a suggestion that one was to eat at all: chopsticks looked like paintbrushes; the miniature bowls of iridescent sauces resembled paint; and tea bowls, set out under their little hats of lids, might well have contained water in which to dip and clean brushes. Auden and Isherwood were further nonplussed by the fact that there seemed to be no recognizable European-style method or order to the meal. Where was the fish that should follow the shark's fin soup, which they found in flavor easily the equal of borscht or minestrone? There was no recognizable time limit to the meal. The end could not be foreseen, as dish after dish miraculously appeared, with what they termed "hors d'oeuvres" popping up all over the place. Anything that could be safely called a meat course vanished—chicken, lobster, rice, and fish could follow each other in dizzying succession. Most distressing of all, a guest might find that their favorite dish was served last, at the very point when he was too stuffed to manage another mouthful.

With each new dish, the general made obscure semaphoric movements with his chopsticks and then pounced on the dish. To add to the confusion, alcohol, closest in taste to Korn or Bols and made from maize and rose petals, was served in miniature metal teapots, or heated brown rice wine was followed by a chaser of wickedly pert rose petal gin.

Rose Petal Gin

INGREDIENTS

2 liters gin
2 pint glasses of rose petals
(make sure these are unsprayed)
½ lb. white sugar
1 tsp. rosewater (optional)
I sterilized demijohn

METHOD

Combine the gin, sugar, and rose petals in the demijohn. Seal. Leave for one week, gently shaking daily to help the sugar dissolve. At the end of seven days, drain the rose petals from the gin, taste, and add the rosewater if you want a more intense taste and aroma of roses. Serve in an iced glass with a thin, green slice of cucumber.

Auden and Isherwood always opted to eat with chopsticks, even though knives and forks were generally available. At one meal an English guest was showing one of them how to pick up a shrimp patty using chopsticks, only to succeed in catapulting the patty onto the carpet. Saving the guest's face, a very solicitous Mr. Tong cried out, "Ah, that shrimp must be alive!"

Even the Caucasian meals they had in China could be full of cross-purpose: at one point Auden and Isherwood lunched on meat loaf and salad with an American couple, Mr. and Mrs. White, and a Baptist minister. "I have a lot," confided the Baptist minister to Auden, "of bandits in my field." Auden commiserated: "How very unpleasant for you. Do they steal your vegetables?" "It's the mission field he means," explained Mr. White wearily.

As would be common nowadays, sometimes the very worst eating experiences to be had were when the British tried to cook Chinese food, or vice versa. When Auden and Isherwood landed up on the Su-chöw front—where they saw white horses painted green for military combat—transport problems meant that they were trapped in a prohibitively expensive hotel on the front. The restaurant offered its guests terrible hybrid food such a glutinous white chicken soup, in which could be found floating the wreckage of a ham. Other Frankenstein dishes advertised themselves on the menu as Lemen Pie, Hat Cake, Ham Egg and FF Potatoes, followed by horrid cocoa, served in coffee cups. They kept themselves numbed to such privations by draining the one bottle of whiskey behind the bar and Après Nous, an "unspeakable Shanghai sherry."

This hostelry proved good preparation for Journey's End, a remarkable, tumbledown, colonial offshoot run by a Mr. Charleton in the Kuling hills, a few miles from Kiukiang. They were drawn there by the unusual advertisement placed for Journey's End in the Hankow newspaper, which claimed that the hotel was "the Mount Lavinia of the Yangtse Valley. Grilled rainbow trout. Crab homegrown salads. Fresh prawn curries." It concluded with the peculiar offer: "Such days and nights in China's Switzerland are both fine things, little brother: Come and see for yourself." Auden's pulse quickened.

Imagine their joy when they turned up there and found that Journey's End was just as ridiculous as one could possibly hope. Mr. Charleton had trained squads of boys as staff, making them muster to do exercises, decked out in khaki shorts and white shirts. Daily, he issued different sock specifications: on some days the teams of boys were ordered to stretch their stockings up to their knees; on others, the stockings were to be rolled down to the ankle. "It depends," Mr. Charleton explained with all the largesse of an emperor, "on my mood." A stuffed dog, called Lady Loveable, graced the corner of the room—the mortal remains of Mr. Charleton's award-winning spaniel. One of Lady Loveable's glass eyes had popped out and vanished long ago; the other kept a fierce watch over the sitting room.

Isherwood and Auden carried Lady Loveable into supper as their dinner guest. Auden suggested the dog might visit his bedroom in the night, dragging her dried hindquarters behind her.

Later in life, the years Auden spent with his long-term love, Chester, were contented ones, foodwise. Their home at Kirchstetten was the first Auden had ever owned, and he shed tears of joy at having his first real home. He and Chester set out the kitchen, American style, with such newfangled modern conveniences as an infrared grill and a bread slicer that popped out suddenly from a drawer.

All the meals the two had were eaten in the largest room of the house: Auden had his seat reserved at the table, with a volume of the *Oxford English Dictionary* resting on the chair, on which he perched. Lunch was always preceded by a glass of vermouth or Campari, and, after the arrival of the roomy deep freezer in the kitchen, the martinis Auden enjoyed became more suave. Vodka replaced the gin as the main ingredient, and a pickled onion rolled at the base of the glass instead of an olive. No ice diluted the drink. Only two martinis were permitted before dinner: one at 6:30, the next at 7:00. Dinner arrived at 7:30 on the dot. This ritual was vigorously adhered to, but Chester and Auden were inventive with it in that the two predinner drinks became larger and larger. Purple, heady Valpolicella was served with dinner.

Calorie counting was banned, and Chester liked to use large quantities of heavy cream, butter, and eggs. The pair lingered over the dinner table; Chester might put on some music. Although his cookbook-crammed kitchen was a chaos of different meals, a kitchen constantly in transition, Chester always did the cooking and prepared wonderful meals. He cooked each chosen dish as if it were a beautiful, dedicatory object in its own right, forgetting completely about cooking anything to accompany it. Hence dinner might well be a single, unaccompanied, perfectly boned, spectacularly pressed duck. No bread. No dessert. No coffee. Just delicious duck.

Among the many gadgets in the kitchen, Chester picked up a sausage-making machine, which Auden welcomed, thinking it would be a money saver. The chicken and truffle sausages Chester produced for his first batch, though, immediately stretched Auden's sausage-making budget to the limit. The next batch was so enormous that Chester had to stay up until the early hours of the morning finishing the casings, assisted by their friend, Thekla.

Chester saw it as an obligation to try to make at least one of the recipes inside each of his eclectic jumble of cookbooks and greeted guests with announcements such as "Norwegian Fish Pie, never tried before," while Auden himself scooted about the dining table, closing the curtains and fiddling with the place settings.

There were special birthday treat dishes for Auden, too, as when they lived in Ischia and requested a leg of lamb to commemorate the day. No less than two small legs of lamb arrived, along with telegrams, one of which tickled Auden pink, coming as it did from Moscow and signed "Gay Burgess."

Indeed, it is near his home in Ischia that one can best picture Auden hungrily wandering home, where garlic, tomatoes, and onions hung braided from the door, his food shopping swinging in a string bag by his side and his dog, Mosè, at his heels.

Norwegian Fish Pie, Never Tried Before

INGREDIENTS

2 onions, finely chopped
1 lb. potatoes cut into fine chips
3 tbsp. butter
20 anchovy fillets
Freshly ground black pepper
½ pint double cream

METHOD

Preheat the oven to 150°C. Butter a pie dish. Using the remaining 2 tablespoons of the butter, gently sauté the onions until they are golden.

Place half of the finely chipped potatoes into the pie dish and sprinkle with the onions. Now make a layer of the anchovies and top this with the remaining potato. Pepper the top and dot with little blobs of butter.

Place the pie in the oven. After 10 minutes, pour half the cream over the potato dish and, 10 minutes later, pour over the remaining cream. Cook for a further 30 minutes.

Leg of Lamb

INGREDIENTS

5 lb. leg of lamb
4 quartered lemons
Zest of 1 lemon
4 garlic cloves, pulped
2 tbsp. Dijon mustard
4 tbsp. honey
1 tbsp. cumin
2 tbsp. fresh rosemary branch, chopped
Coarse sea salt
Freshly ground black pepper
1 glass white wine

METHOD

The night before you intend to cook the lamb, place it in a roasting tray, make small incisions all over the lamb's surface, and rub with the lemon zest, garlic, mustard, honey, cumin, and rosemary. Squash and squeeze the lemon quarters and place them alongside the lamb. Cover the whole with tinfoil and leave overnight.

The next day, heat the oven to 180°C. Sprinkle the lamb with sea salt flakes and black pepper and place in the oven for 10 minutes at 180°C. After 10 minutes, pour a glass of dry white wine over the lamb and turn down the oven to 160°C. Cook at this heat for 20 minutes per pound and 20 minutes over.

Remove from the oven, allow the lamb to sit for 15 minutes, and serve. Don't forget to toast Gay Burgess.

GEORGE ORWELL

Orwell's hop-picking diary from 1931 reveals what tramps could expect to find on their plates in the 1930s: he was sleeping rough in London with another man, eating with knives and forks stolen from Woolworths, and drinking condensed milk out of tins. Orwell fried his breakfast of bread on a tin lid, ate bacon sandwiches, supped on cold tea for his dinner, and roasted stolen apples on the fire. The real, professional hop pickers took pity on Orwell and his companion because they were tramps, rather than professionals, and so sent them leftover food—on one occasion a whole pig's head. I wonder how the Woolworth's cutlery coped with a skull.

Orwell's experiences of vagrancy made him much more intolerant of waste among the working classes when he had made the journey to Wigan in 1936 to collate material for *The Road to Wigan Pier.* He was astonished when he surveyed the kitchen contents at Mrs. H's lodging house (where he stayed): waste in the North was even more pronounced than waste in the South of England. He couldn't believe it. He listed that, lying like wreckage around the scullery, was a five-pound side of bacon, a dismally huge raw liver, enough raw shin beef to drape the legs of several cows, and a ruined castle of a meat pie with fallen walls of pastry. Like Russian dolls, there were the fragments of smaller fruit pies, equally as dragged about. Loaves upon loaves, numbering eighteen in total, lay about, along with about twenty eggs, small cakes, and warm butter, just turning rancid, all left uncovered, except the bread, on dirty, sticky shelves.

There were some horrors that not even the pig's head had prepared him for. He found the Lancashire method of eating tripe cold with vinegar truly horrible, and this wasn't helped by the fact that, after Mrs. H's house, Orwell went to lodge in a pie shop with a doubtful reputation—it was rumored the tripe was kept in cellars where the surfaces seemed to move with sheets of sooty black beetles. Under the breakfast table where the lodgers sat was an unemptied chamber pot, and the landlady used strips of newspaper to wipe food and spittle from her mouth, which she let drop onto the floor.

Finally, thankfully, Orwell stayed with a Mr. and Mrs. Searle in Sheffield. Orwell took a shine to Mrs. Searle—she was shrewd, a real bright spark, albeit illiterate. Orwell, despite the disapproval of the other lodgers, made a point of helping her with the washing up. In testimony to the goodness of her cooking, Orwell wrote down the recipe for her fruit loaf in his *Diaries*.

Mrs. Searle's Fruit Loaf

"Mrs. Searle's recipe for fruit loaf (very good with butter) which I will write down here before I lose it":

INGREDIENTS

1 lb. flour
1 egg
4 oz. treacle
4 oz. mixed fruit (or currants)
8 oz. sugar
6 oz. margarine or lard

METHOD

Cream the sugar and margarine, beat the egg and add it, add the treacle, mixed fruit and then the flour, put in greased tins and bake about ½ to ¾ hour in a moderate oven.

Also her "54321" recipe for sponge cake

INGREDIENTS

5 oz. flour
4 oz. sugar
3 oz. grease (butter best)
2 eggs
1 tsp. baking powder

METHOD

Mix as above and bake.

When not far afield investigating drudgery, Orwell's two main domestic passions were growing his own food—he also liked foraging and would stop to pick up and eat beechnuts—and tending to a small collection of goats and chickens; he had a rooster named Henry Ford. Bacon was in short supply, and he tried his hand at making "macon," essentially mutton cured to taste like bacon. He made his own apple wine and apple ginger, but he overdid the ginger. His apple jam was not a success, but he managed well enough with wild plum jam. At one point, in total, he managed to clock up twenty-five pounds of jam, including a blackberry jelly to be proud of.

Orwellian Blackberry Jelly

INGREDIENTS

5 lb. blackberries
2 lb. cooking apples
1 stick cinnamon
The rind of 1 orange
3 pints water
1 lb. sugar to each pint of juice
1 jelly bag

METHOD

Clean and cut up the apples—don't core them. Put them, with the blackberries, in a large preserving pan. Add the cinnamon stick and orange rind. Now pour the cold water over the berries, place the preserving pan over a medium heat, and cook the mixture until the blackberries are reduced to a sooty, purple pulp. Turn the pulp into a jelly bag, which must be hung securely over a large pan to drip overnight.

The next day, measure the rich blackberry juice into pints. Match this with the right amount of sugar. Now put the juice and the sugar into the preserving pan and cook on low heat, stirring as the sugar dissolves. Put a plate in the fridge to chill. When dissolved, turn the heat up to a fast boil and keep testing the juice on the very cold plate until it sets when tested—this means that when you drag the tip of your finger through the jelly, it doesn't pool together again, but maintains some degree of jellyishness! Finally, bottle in sterilized jars.

But it was really while living in Barnhill Cottage on the Scottish Island of Jura in 1946, in the company of his sister, Avril, and adopted son, Richard, that Orwell could be seen at his smallholding best. He was writing *1984*, and he was slowly succumbing to the tuberculosis that was to claim him. Self-sufficiency was crucial on Jura: Orwell couldn't nip across to the local shop; it was twenty-three miles away. Three times a week, however, a little mail boat, comically called "The Steamer," chugged up with food supplies—Avril, apparently, was very good at planning what provisions needed ordering from the steamer.

The waters around Jura were full of lobster and crab, brought into the harbor in the rimy creels of local fishermen; the creels looked almost as if they had bright headdresses on of greening hemp rope, cork floats, and buoys of inflated pig's or dog's bladders. Orwell had a fisherman friend named Ian who told him all sorts of engrossing creel lore, fascinating Orwell with the combination of terror and understanding that a lobster could feel. Having discovered itself caught in the creel, a lobster, Ian claimed, does not continue to eat the bait that lured it into its cage. It *knows* it has made a dreadful mistake. A chilling thought. Pollack, which the locals called "saithe," were plentiful, moving through the waters of the Minch in great, silver shoals. Orwell determined to find out from the locals how they dried them to preserve them over the winter, when fishing conditions were too harsh.

Orwell made good use of what the sea and land offered him to eat, killing and cooking all manner of creatures. After a brief, snarling struggle to get two lobsters into a pot, he boiled them, and their shells turned scarlet, as if in a final, furious protest against their fate. When a rabbit hopped into the garden, Orwell shot him (you can't imagine Beatrix Potter doing this) and decided to try cooking the rabbit with pickled onions.

When not writing about the Ministry of Truth, Orwell cured rabbit pelts and managed to make himself a tobacco pouch; when he records this, the reader's reaction can only be: OH, my God, Orwell, dying of tuberculosis, has been *smoking* all this time. Like a clever member of the Boy's Brigade, he whittled himself a mustard spoon out of a deer bone. His sister, Avril, meanwhile, collected dulse, edible seaweed, from the rocky shore and dried it. She wasn't sure quite how to cook it—my great grandfather used to wind it round a poker, roast it on a fire, and then thrust the poker into his beer. But Avril discovered one recipe that suggested she cook it in milk, the result of which they hoped might be a sort of blancmange: Orwell doesn't record how successful Avril's experiment was, but it doesn't appear in Room 101.

Jura Rabbit and Pickled Onions

INGREDIENTS

2 young rabbits, cleaned and jointed
2 tbsp. all-purpose flour, seasoned with sea salt and black pepper
4 oz. diced, unsmoked bacon
2 oz. butter
20 small pickling onions
½ pint jellied chicken stock
Sea salt
Freshly ground black pepper
¼ cup single cream

METHOD

Preheat the oven to 180°C. Roll the rabbit pieces in the seasoned flour. On the stove, melt the butter in a casserole dish. Add the diced bacon and the rabbit pieces, and brown both. Remove them from the casserole dish and brown the pickling onions. Now return the rabbit and bacon to the casserole. Add the jellied stock, season, and place the casserole in the oven. Cook for about an hour. Baste occasionally. The rabbit sauce should by the end be a rich reduction. Remove from the oven and add the cream. Now serve.

How to Cure Pollack (as discovered by Orwell)

First, gut the pollack and remove their heads. Pack them down between layers of rough sea salt, alternating each layer as fish-salt-fish-salt. Leave for several days. When the weather is dry and sunny, remove the fish from the salt and hang them in pairs. Knot string around their tails and tie them to your washing line or a line of rope. Leave them until they are thoroughly dry. After you have accomplished this, then you are free to hang them up indoors. All right, if the lounge doesn't work for you, try the potting shed. You will have a stock of pollack to last for several months.

In September 1946, Orwell repeated this procedure with the fat, sweet Jura mackerel and then smoked the mackerel over a wood fire for about twenty hours. He found them delicious.

AGATHA CHRISTIE

Agatha Christie's eating life began in Torquay, when, as the humbly named Agatha Miller, her early years were spent in the care of her warmhearted mother, her kind and slightly idle father, a precious budgie, a Yorkshire terrier named George Washington, and a stolid and skilled cook, Mrs. Rowe, who was the presiding spirit of the house. Agatha claimed Mrs. Rowe could never volunteer an idea for any dish except one. Asked, "What shall we have for pudding tonight?" she'd always reply, "What about a nice stone pudding, Ma'am?" as if it were revelatory.

Agatha's mother had her own ideas about food. "Always leave something on your plate for Lady Manners," she'd reprimand Agatha. More generously, she said Devonshire cream was much better for people than cod liver oil, and they spread the yellow cream on bread or ate it straight in spoonfuls. In adulthood, Agatha liked to drink a half-pint of cream as a treat.

In a gentle, bovine way, Mrs. Rowe was always eating something, rhythmically gnawing her way through scones and rock cakes. She immersed Christie's childhood in the warm, heavy scent of newly baked buns and currant, buttery rock cakes for elevenses. Mrs. Rowe's many visitors would drop by her kitchen in the morning in Torquay, just in time for a nice, warm rock cake. Young Agatha, meanwhile, was drawn down to Mrs. Rowe's kingdom by the floral sweetness of jam pastries that wended its way up from the kitchen.

One Idea Stone Pudding—you will need newspapers for this!!!

INGREDIENTS

2 cups double cream
¼ cup milk
1 vanilla pod
1 tbsp. caster sugar
A scant ½ oz. gelatin
¼ cup medium-dry sherry
Finely grated zest of 1 lemon
1 tbsp. apricot jam

METHOD

Heat the cream, milk, vanilla pod, sugar, and gelatin in a small saucepan, stirring constantly, until the gelatin has dissolved. Allow this to cool for 15 minutes—this gives the vanilla a chance to infuse. Remove the vanilla pod. Put a dollop of apricot jam on the base of a Pyrex dish, followed by the sherry and lemon zest. Assemble some newspaper on the floor and place the Pyrex bowl onto it. From as great a height as you can manage without causing personal disaster to yourself, pour the cream into the bowl. Put the stone pudding in the fridge overnight (Mrs. Rowe would have used her cold pantry) and serve the creamy gorgeousness that is this dish the next day.

Rock Cakes for a Young Criminologist

INGREDIENTS

8 oz. all-purpose flour
Pinch of sea salt
2 tsp. baking powder
6 oz. Demerara sugar
6 oz. butter, cubed
5 oz. dried fruit
½ tsp. grated nutmeg
1 tsp. vanilla extract
Zest of 1 lemon, finely grated
1 tsp. mixed spice
1 egg
1 tbsp. milk

METHOD

Line a baking tray with parchment and preheat the oven to 180°C. In a large mixing bowl, combine the flour, sugar, mixed spice, and baking powder. Rub the butter through the flour until it resembles fine breadcrumbs. Add the mixed fruit and combine. Whisk the egg and milk together. Add the lemon rind and vanilla extract. Combine the egg and flour mixtures together to form a fairly stiff dough; if it seems too dry, add a splash of milk. Shape the dough into rough little rocks (about the size of tangerines). Sprinkle more Demerara sugar on top of each and bake for 15 to 20 minutes, until they are a deep gold color.

Mrs. Rowe had her work cut out for her. For dinner, she might rustle up as many as five courses for seven or eight people. For Sunday lunch, Agatha's grandmother and various other aged relatives, numerous aunts and uncles, and probably more peckish passersby descended on the house. A vast, delicious joint of meat, of almost Neolithic proportions, was brought to the table, or there might be an allotment-sized beefsteak pie, to be followed by winsome cherry tart and thick cream. The dessert was served on special plates, each decorated with a different fruit—a fig, a gooseberry, or white currants—and placed in front of diners, with the decoration hidden by a delicate lace mat, and the family game, Sunday after Sunday, was to guess what fruit lay hidden beneath your mat.

Then everyone fell asleep, mown down by their sated appetites, drugged by a surfeit of cherries, until it was time for tea and Madeira cake. But lovely fragments of adult conversation floated through the gentle snoring. Agatha overheard her grandmother talking about Miss Grant, the sewing woman who came to their house: "Such a poor little creature, deformed, only one passage, like a fowl." Poor Miss Grant. Agatha's grandmother was also brilliantly innocent. Spying Agatha's sister's suitor, Ambrose, pick up some gravel from the drive that her sister had just strode across, her grandmother put this down to the deepest romantic motives. "I like Ambrose," she purred. "I saw Ambrose get up and follow [Madge], and he bent down and picked up a handful of gravel, where her feet had trodden, and put it in his pocket. Very pretty I thought it was, very pretty." They had barely the heart to tell her that Ambrose was passionate about geology. You can even see Miss Marple in Agatha's grandmother: she liked to say of shiftless types, "A downy fellow, that, I don't trust him."

Everything changed for Agatha at age eleven when her father died, leaving the family finances in tatters. And this change was particularly felt in the kitchen. Mrs. Rowe couldn't get used to cooking just for Agatha and her mother and only cooking miserable, small things like macaroni and cheese. "But I've ordered twelve fillets of sole," Mrs. Rowe would say, her voice trailing off as she looked down at her two remaining charges. Everything had to change, and Mrs. Rowe was sent off to feed a larger audience. She was never one for showing much emotion but, as she left Torquay to cook for Agatha's brother Monty's family in Cornwall, big tears rolled down her cheeks. She took her one trunk of possessions with her.

For Agatha, a hasty marriage to Archie Christie, whom she met at a dance, followed on the heels of the outbreak of World War I; he was stationed in France, and Agatha bunkered up with her mother in Torquay. Fortunately, Mrs. Rowe was no longer there to witness rationing, but their maid, Mary, was still around to complain about having to eat this terrible stuff called margarine and to wail at Mrs. Miller, "I'm sorry, Madam, but it's not right, the food we're given. We've had fish two days this week, and we've had insides of animals." Agatha's splendid grandmother moved in with them as well, and she spent the war years disapproving violently of tinned foods, suspecting them of harboring ptomaine poisoning.

Agatha got some work in a dispensary, learning to do things like make suppositories with cocoa butter, one of which she managed to drop and tread into the ground. She worked with a strange little pharmacist, whom she referred to obliquely as "Mr. P." Mr. P kept trying to stroke her gently and carried in his pocket a dark brown lump of curare—a poison. "Do you know why I carry it in my pocket?" he asked Christie. "It makes me feel powerful." A crime writer was born.

Finally, Christie moved into her first house with Archie at 5 Northwick Terrace, London, and decided it was time for her to learn how to be a cook in her own right. In their tiny kitchenette, Christie experimented with food. She'd been to cookery classes, but she also used National Soup Squares to open the meal. Archie liked to call this "sand and gravel soup." Lovingly, perhaps to make up for the soup, Christie made her own elaborate cheese soufflé, but this gave Archie acute dyspepsia, and she was surprised that he liked to eat pots of golden syrup or treacle when he was ill.

Following a gloomy pregnancy during which Archie nursed Agatha with "Benger's Food"—a vaguely pleasant wartime food supplement for invalids, it found its way into Red Cross food parcels in World War II—and tried to cheer her up by leaving a lobster on her pillow as a surprise, Agatha then started cooking with her daughter, Rosalind's, nanny, Site. Between the two of them they brought to the table a lively mix of dishes. Site made pickled herrings and jam tarts while Agatha rolled out cheese soufflés (again), Béarnaise sauce, and English syllabub. Meals were, to say the least, unusual.

Cheese Soufflé

INGREDIENTS

½ oz. soft butter
1 tbsp. finely grated Gruyère cheese
1 oz. all-purpose flour
1½ oz. butter
½ pint hot milk
Pinch of salt
Pinch of nutmeg
Freshly ground black pepper
4 egg yolks
6 egg whites
½ tsp. Dijon mustard
6 oz. finely grated Gruyère cheese
½ tsp. cream of tartar

METHOD

Preheat the oven to 200°C. Butter the inside of a 3-pint soufflé dish; sprinkle the tablespoon of Gruyère and shake the dish to distribute the Gruyère evenly.

Heat milk to just below boiling point. In a medium-sized saucepan, melt the butter. Add the flour and stir constantly for a minute or two—do not let the roux burn. Remove from the heat and add the hot milk. Stir until the roux is blended with the milk. Now return the pan to the heat and, stirring all the time, bring the sauce to boil. Allow it to simmer, then remove from the heat and beat in the egg yolks, very gradually and thoroughly. Salt and pepper to taste. Stir in the mustard. Let this sauce rest now.

Next, begin to whisk your egg whites with the nutmeg and the cream of tartar until they form turrets. Add a spoonful of aerated egg white to the yolk/milk sauce. Now add most of the Gruyère cheese—but reserve 1 tablespoon for the surface of the soufflé. Begin to fold in the remaining aerated egg, folding it in with a metal spoon. Fold—don't stir.

Pour the soufflé into the prepared dish, and sprinkle with the cheese. Put the soufflé in the center of the oven and immediately lower the temperature to 190°C. Bake for 25 to 30 minutes—make sure you tiptoe past the soufflé and never, ever, open the oven door until the time is up. It should be golden brown when it's ready. Serve immediately.

English Syllabub

INGREDIENTS

3 oz. caster sugar
2 lemons, rind and juice only
4 tbsp. sherry
2 tbsp. brandy
¾ pint of double cream
Pinch of ground cinnamon
¼ tsp. almond essence

METHOD

Combine the caster sugar, lemon zest and juice, sherry, brandy, cinnamon, and almond essence in a heatproof bowl. Make a bain-marie by placing the bowl over hot water, and warm gently until the sugar dissolves. Leave this to cool again. Whisk the double cream into a soft flummery of peaks; now fold the liquid into the cream. Spoon the syllabub into individual bowls and chill.

OSCAR WILDE

On Christmas Eve 1881, Oscar Wilde sailed from sooty Liverpool on board the vast Cunard liner *Arizona*, bound for New York. It was time for the young, optimistic, twenty-six-year-old Wilde to tour America, which he did with gusto. His lecture tour subject was aestheticism—in a word, beauty. His commitment to beauty was such that Wilde carted a fur-lined overcoat with him in America "to hide the ugliness of the sofas."

"Have you anything to declare?" asked the customs inspector.

"Nothing but my genius!" replied Wilde.

And it was in America that one of the great literary meetings of the nineteenth century happened: Wilde visited Walt Whitman at his home in Camden, New Jersey, on the Delaware River, at around two in the afternoon. According to a reporter from the *Philadelphia Press*, who interviewed Whitman the next day, Walt thought Oscar "a great big splendid boy," and they had got slightly tipsy on a "big glass of milk punch." They had sat in Whitman's den in Philadelphia; Wilde was in awe of Whitman, and he adored *Leaves of Grass*, which his mother had read to him in his boyhood. Among all else, Wilde must have admired Whitman's openness about his sexuality. Amazingly, Wilde was struck silent by the meeting, so moved was he by the presence of Walt.

Wilde begged to see Walt again, writing to him, "There is no one in this wide great world of America whom I love and honour so much." Consequently, there was a follow-up visit in May, after which, Wilde breathlessly told a friend, "The kiss of Walt Whitman is still on my lips."

Whitman-esque Milk Punch

INGREDIENTS

4 pints milk
½ pint milk
1 lemon
½ lb. sugar
2 eggs
1 pint rum
½ pint brandy
Freshly grated nutmeg

METHOD

Roughly grate the rind of the lemon. Whisk the two eggs and mix with a ½ pint of cold milk. Into a large, deep saucepan, pour in the four pints of cold milk, and add to this the lemon rind and gradually add the sugar. Bring this very gently to boil. Remove from the heat, strain to remove the lemon rind, and stir in the eggs and milk mixture.

Keep warm on a low heat. Do not let the milk boil. Gradually add a pint of rum and a ½ pint of brandy. Whisk the punch until it froths, dust with nutmeg, and serve it immediately in warmed glasses.

If only Wilde's life could have stayed that simple. Back in London, life got much more complicated. While smoking his opium-tinted cigarettes, Oscar could cause mayhem at the dinner tables of London. He loved to behave excessively, camping it up in the Café Royale. The Café was once described as a "hot-air cupboard"; its beveled mirrors and garlanded caryatids stared back at the café's inhabitants, drinking and playing dominoes. Anarchists, artists, exiles, and decadents ate there. D. H. Lawrence, true to form, had vomited at one of its tables; George Bernard Shaw had sipped Appolinaris there and settled down to concentrate on his macaroni; Aleister Crowley, Arthur Conan Doyle, Mark Twain, Rimbaud, Toulouse-Lautrec, and Edward VII had dined there since it first opened in 1865.

It was divided into a restaurant, domino room, and grill, and it was at a chipped but ornate marble table beside the grill that Wilde could be found most often. He acted like "a schoolboy in a tuck shop," said Arthur Ransome, "with an unexpected sovereign in his hand." According to Deghy and Waterhouse's account of Wilde in *Café Royale: Ninety Years of Bohemia*, Wilde considered each meal a beautiful, ritualized affair. He perused the menu lovingly, trying to choose between "suprème de volaille à la Patti (chicken supremes) or the caneton de Rouen à la presse (duckling), the sole Beaumanoir or the turbotin paysanne. . . . He discussed in inordinate detail the rival merits of the curiously-coloured Clicquot vin rosé, the St. Marceaux, or the Château le Tertre."

During rougher financial times in the past, Wilde might have joined his friend and neighbor on Tite Street, the hard-up artist James Whistler, for supper of a glass or two of cheap but tasty claret, a plain grill, or Whistler's favorite of poulet en casserole. When Whistler got married, the Café Royale provided the wedding fare, but the guests ate their banquet off the packing cases in Whistler's studio. But now that the royalty checks had rolled in, Wilde was determined to spend them as quickly as possible.

Poulet en Casserole (best eaten off a packing case)

INGREDIENTS

1 medium-sized chicken
2 oz. butter, softened
2 tsp. fresh thyme leaves
2 garlic cloves
1 oz. butter
4 oz. bacon, cut into lardons
2 oz. butter
15 small white onions, peeled
6 carrots, shaped into 2-inch bullets
15 2-inch potato bullets
½ pint chicken stock
½ pint dry white wine
Sea salt and freshly ground pepper
A bouquet garni of parsley and 2 bay leaves, tied together with string

Poulet en Casserole *(continued)*

METHOD

Preheat the oven to 180°C. In a mortar and pestle, crush the garlic and thyme in a little sea salt to release the aromatic oils of the thyme. Take your softened, creamed butter and combine it with the thyme and garlic. Now rub this aromatic butter inside the chicken. Truss the chicken and smear the remaining butter over its skin.

Melt a further ½ ounce of butter in an oval casserole dish (this must be large enough to hold the chicken and vegetables). Brown the bacon lardons in the butter. Now remove the golden, crisped lardons from the casserole and brown the chicken on all sides in the buttery bacon fat. Remove the casserole from the heat; put the chicken and the lardons to the side.

Now melt a further 2 tablespoons of butter in the casserole dish. Sauté the onions, carrots, and potatoes for 5 minutes, until they have a buttery sheen and a golden hue. Place the chicken and bacon back in the casserole. Tuck the bouquet garni in among the vegetables, salt, and pepper. Add the white wine and chicken stock. Seal the casserole tightly and cook for 1 hour and 15 minutes in the center of the oven.

Smiling through his long, yellow, camel-like teeth (according to one biographer, Wilde caught syphilis from a girl in Oxford and was put on a useless treatment whose only effect was to turn his teeth black), his cheeks rosy with broken veins and his bright, ironic gaze upon you, Wilde over lunch would not just offer you a cigarette but also choose it for you himself, in a kind and solicitous way. He might quaff some absinthe, but this was merely a pose; his preferred drink was a straight down the line whiskey and soda.

Throughout the early 1890s, Wilde and the twenty-two-year-old Lord Alfred Douglas, otherwise known as Bosie, were seen out and about in London restaurants. Wilde was clearly smitten with love; he wrote once to his friend Robert Ross from rooms in the Royal Palace Hotel, Kensington, "Bosie is quite like a narcissus—so white and gold. He lies like a hyacinth on the sofa, and I worship him." They were inseparable and lived, Wilde claimed, on "clear turtle soup," "luscious ortolans wrapped in their crinkled Sicilian vine-leaves," "amber-scented champagne," "pâtés procured directly from Strasburg," washed down with "special cuvées of Perrier-Jouet."

Then, in 1892, they made the two new acquaintances whose company was going to further damn Wilde at his trial in the eyes of the Victorian public: the brothers Bill and Charlie Parker, who had been living in flophouses. Both the Parkers could hardly read or write. Wilde took private rooms at Kettner's, and the group enjoyed a large meal, while Wilde rabbited on, as Charlie put it, about "poetry and art and the old Roman days." Candied cherries were passed from mouth to mouth, red and wet, until Wilde guffawed, putting his arm about Charlie, "This is the boy for me!"

"Love That Dare Not Speak Its Name" Candied Cherries

INGREDIENTS

½ lb. fresh sweet cherries
¾ cup water
½ cup sugar
1 tbsp. lemon juice
1 tbsp. kirsch

METHOD

Wash the cherries. Remove their stalks and pips. In a heavy-based saucepan, place all the ingredients, with the exclusion of the kirsch. Bring to boil and then turn down to a simmer. Stir frequently for 25 minutes, increasingly so as the sugar mixture reduces. Once the mixture has thickened to a syrup, add the tablespoon of kirsch and remove it from the heat. Cool the cherries on a nonstick surface. When cooled, share the cherries with your lover. If you don't have one, find one now. Wilde would approve.

Enter Bosie's father, John Sholto Douglas, the Marquess of Queensberry. Ginger-haired, full of swearing, stupid belligerence, and initiator of the Queensberry Rules of Boxing, Queensberry liked to settle difficulties with a dog whip. His wife had already divorced him on the grounds of cruelty and adultery. In the autumn of 1892 he came upon Wilde and Bosie at lunch in the Café Royal. At first, Queensberry sulked in a corner, and then was persuaded to join them by Bosie, only to find Wilde amusing and engaging. The fug of liqueurs and cigars worked, as did conversation about Christianity and Torquay. He wrote to Bosie that he wanted to "take back" any scurrilous things he had said about Wilde, but the Marquess was a changeable chap. The clubmen continued to gossip; Wilde and Bosie continued to be indiscreet.

He joined them again for lunch in the spring of 1894, but this time he refused to be wooed by Wilde's wit, watching the lovers suspiciously through narrowed eyes. Queensberry told Bosie, "With my own eyes I saw you both in the most loathsome and disgusting relationship, as expressed in your manner and expression. Never in my experience have I seen such a sight as that in your horrible features. No wonder people are talking as they are."

It was time to hound Wilde, he decided. Queensberry warned each of the headwaiters in the Café Royale that if he found Bosie and Wilde together, he would strike Wilde across the face with his cane and wreck the café into the bargain. Bent on mischief, Queensbury turned up on the opening night of *The Importance of Being Earnest* with a huge and repulsive bouquet of vegetables—though quite what the signification was is now lost. Relentless, he turned up unannounced at Wilde's house in Tite Street to tell him, "If I catch you and my son together in any public restaurant, I will thrash you."

Finally, at the Albemarle Club where Wilde dined, Queensberry left his calling card with Sidney Wright, the porter, on February 18, 1895, complete with his misspelling of the libellous word: "To Oscar Wilde, posing as a somdomite." Wilde felt he was left with no other choice but to defend his honor and sue for criminal libel. Queensberry had been stalking him, threatened his livelihood, and now insulted him publicly. The die was cast.

"All those dinners" in the Savoy, lunches in the Café Royale, suppers in private rooms at Kettner's, and aperitifs at Willis's were used against Wilde at his trial; it was suggested that they were means of wooing young men—the seductive prelude to an entirely different dessert. Why else, it was asked, would a man of Wilde's social position choose to socialize and eat with men of much lower class? Food and drink purchased Wilde the "gross indecency" he so craved. And, in a way, there was method to this madness: so unequal was Victorian London that many of these poorer young men may not have had a decent meal for quite some time. The jury shrank back into their seats when they heard of the candied cherries and Wilde feeding Charlie with a spoon, all signals of Wilde's moral delinquency. To the fin-de-siècle public, such feasts suggested that Wilde had other excessive appetites, and the trial judge had to mount a defense of the right of men to dine with men.

Sentenced to two years of hard labor for "homosexual practices," Wilde was carted off first to Pentonville Prison, then Wandsworth, and, from there, Reading Gaol. Wilde lost his appetite—indeed, the *Evening News* headline on the first night Wilde spent in Bow Street on April 6, 1895, was "HE CANNOT EAT." To Wilde, the frugal diet of gruel and punitive use of food withdrawal must have seemed like a trope of exile from his past life. The menu at Reading Gaol was without romance: Wilde supped on "skilly" in cell C.3.3., a thin oatmeal porridge, made with pale meat stock.

Released from prison in May 1897, Wilde still had some fire inside him—indeed, one could argue that this was Wilde at his best. Without drawing breath, he published in *The Daily Chronicle* a blistering attack on the barbarity of the British prison system. Fresh from prison—Wilde had only been out nine days but had already been spirited away from England to Dieppe—he wrote "The Case of Warder Martin." So, what had Warder Martin done? In an act of pity, he had handed some biscuits to an imprisoned, hungry child, thus transgressing prison rules. He was sacked outright. Enraged, Wilde wrote:

> The second thing from which a child suffers in prison is hunger. The food that is given to it consists of a piece of usually bad-baked prison bread and a tin of water for breakfast at half-past seven. At twelve o'clock it gets dinner, composed of a tin of coarse Indian meal stirabout (skilly), and at half-past five it gets a piece of dry bread and a tin of water for its supper. This diet in the case of a strong grown man is always productive of illness of some kind, chiefly of course diarrhoea, with its attendant weakness. . . . A child who has been crying all day long, and perhaps half the night, in a lonely dim-lit cell, and is preyed upon by terror, simply cannot eat food of this coarse, horrible kind. In the case of the little child to whom Warder Martin gave the biscuits, the child was crying with hunger on Tuesday morning, and utterly unable to eat the bread and water served to it for its breakfast. Martin went out after the breakfasts had been served and bought the few sweet biscuits for the child rather than see it starving. It was a beautiful action on his part, and was so recognised by the child, who, utterly unconscious of the regulations of the Prison Board, told one of the senior wardens how kind this junior warden had been to him. The result was, of course, a report and a dismissal.

Good for Wilde.

Wilde went on to drift between what friends he had left in Europe, a discredited and reduced figure. Allowed no contact with his sons after the death of Mrs. Wilde, he bumbled about the streets of Paris, being snubbed or welcomed by people, as was their wont. In an echo of his past, he sat drinking maraschinos or whiskey and soda; there was no need for the pretence of absinthe now, at a marble table in a corner of the Café de la Régence.

He was a ghost of Walt Whitman's boy who was intent on beauty and had insisted on calling white wine "yellow wine." He had probably forgotten his announcement that "if I were alone, marooned in a desert island and had my things with me, I should dress for dinner every evening." This was Wilde's desert island, and he had long since forgotten how to dress for dinner. Some cafés shooed him out.

Wilde was always being fished out of money difficulties, as he found it impossible to manage his finances. Bosie had inherited a very handsome sum after the death of his father, and when Wilde asked for a share, he accused him of "wheedling like an old whore": "I can't afford to spend anything except on myself," he told Wilde curtly. Perhaps he was more of his father's son than he had appeared. Wilde was to write to Bosie in *De Profundis*, "Out of the reckless dinners eaten with you nothing remains but the memory that too much was eaten and too much was drunk."

The kind owner of the Hotel d'Alsace on the Rue des Beaux-Arts, where Wilde died of cerebral meningitis at age forty-eight, helped Wilde by paying off the money he owed to another hotel. Life was all cutlets and boiled eggs, a far cry from the smoke and glory of the Café Royale.

SYLVIA PLATH

American poetess Sylvia Plath was both a poet and a sensualist when it came to food. Food could be taken as a metaphor for the lived moment and a throaty, tummy-rumbling, glorious experience. Sometimes Sylvia's food is resonant with sunlight, as when she was eighteen years old, working as a babysitter for Dr. and Mrs. Frederick Mayo's three children (Freddy, Pinny, and Joey) at 144 Beach Bluff Avenue in Swampscott, Massachusetts. It was an early taste of innocent independence: when the family was away on a cruise, Sylvia would swim in the blue tingle of the sea and sunbathe on the bleached rocks, licking the salt from her lips, and go home to eat fresh corn and lamb chops and steak followed by orbed iced peaches and vanilla ice cream, enjoying freedom from her job. Sylvia also watched the Mayos' marriage carefully and worried whether wifehood—which she summed up as "cooking scrambled eggs for a man"—would mean she would never write poetry.

Babysitting was fun and complicated, though; full of warm, babyish limbs, laughter, diapers, date nut bars, and applesauce made from bright, green apples. Little Joey Mayo was good at covering herself in beetroot juice and had a babyish passion for "budda," like melted gold on hot potato skins. This was an opportunity, Sylvia decided, to experiment with baking for the children—her very first Devil's Food Cake. The experiment, however, was complicated by Joey throwing Ivory Snow soap flakes on the kitchen floor, then racing through to the living room to cast tobacco and cigarettes over the Mayos' beautiful Oriental rug. Sylvia tidied up frantically, tucked Joey under one arm, and tried to assemble the many layers of Devil's Food Cake, but she couldn't quite keep hold of one particularly heavy rack and it crashed into the cooling cakes. Staring down at the bombed sponge, Sylvia realized she had not enough frosting for a coverup. She cut part of the cake into three slices, frosted these, and hid the derelict, chocolate flab that remained of her splendid cake idea in the back of the cupboard.

Perhaps being a daughter, rather than a wife, was a better deal altogether in 1952. When Sylvia broke her leg careening wildly down the ski slopes of Mount Pisgah in December of that year, she convalesced in bed at home on her mother Aurelia's soup thick with corn, or her tuna salad—one of Sylvia's favorites—packed with lush mayonnaise and sliced boiled egg, richly yoked. Aurelia delivered to Sylvia's bed cooling cups of milk, the "savory brown resilience" of a slice of ginger bread, and macaroni and cheese with lima beans on the side, followed by peach slices. As ever, when she describes food, Plath loves the implied luxury of listing food ingredients and savors the words *thyme*, *sherry*, *cream*, and *apricot*.

Sylvia really came alive, though, in October 1955, when on a Fulbright scholarship to study English at Newnham College in Cambridge she had her first taste of

British life. What could be better than rum and roast beef sandwiches in the Doves pub while watching swans at night floating in the black, sullen Thames? Or dark clover honey and scones in Granchester? But all of these snacks were a far cry from Newnham College fare; university dinners were slippery cabbage and blisteringly pink tongue, along with some water-logged turnip. Sylvia begged her mother to send her a parcel of food memories from America, and when some scrumptious hazelnut cookies arrived faithfully on the tenth of December, Sylvia ate her way through the lot. They tasted of home. But the dazzle of the present was too great to miss America for very long. She was delighted at the one-to-ten ratio of women to men on the Cambridge campus, and she couldn't wait to meet British men (and that was all in week one!). There were promises in the air of wonderful things to come. One exotic new friend was Mallory Wober, who could play the piano and had coal-black hair. Sylvia was briefly entranced by him; he had lived in Darjeeling for nine years and took her for a meal to the Taj Mahal Indian restaurant, where she tasted her very first lush mango and bindhi (okra) quaht; she cycled home on wheels of joy.

Sylvia manages to convey the charged excitement of being a young poet through the blur of sherries, too many downed; the purple, rich shock of late night wine; or spur-of-the-moment martinis. Like eating cheeses and salted nuts, alcohol was tinged with eroticism. Ill with a cold in early 1956, she made herself hot buttered rum with rum, cloves, lemons, and nuts. She enjoyed this so much she decided she had the makings of an alcoholic.

Hot Buttered Rum

INGREDIENTS

- 1 tsp. butter
- 2 tsp. dark brown sugar
- 2 cloves
- Pinch of cinnamon
- Pinch of nutmeg
- Juice of 2 freshly squeezed lemons
- ¼ pint hot water
- A generous measure of dark rum
- 1 tsp. toasted, sliced almonds

METHOD

Combine the butter, sugar, cloves, cinnamon, and nutmeg at the bottom of a heatproof glass. Now add the hot water; top this with the measure of dark rum. Stir. Finally, top with the toasted shards of almond.

The night she met Ted Hughes at a party in Cambridge, she felt brave on "red-gold" whiskey macs, surrounded by youths in turtle-necked sweaters and slinky, dark-lidded girls. The jazz music playing thrummed inside her; she tried to drink and missed her mouth, leaving her hands sticky with alcohol. She saw Hughes—she was intent on him—and started roaring poetry at him. He offered her brandy, and this time it made it to her mouth. Someone warned her that Hughes was the biggest seducer in Cambridge. He tried to kiss her; she bit him on the cheek. Their future was sealed. Sylvia wrote to her brother that Ted was very different from the adolescents in her past, the boys in Princeton who were "all bloodless like mushrooms inside."

Nothing could beat Ted Hughes; it was as if Sylvia had been struck by lightning. The lovers walked for miles through the Cambridge woods at night. Ted constantly wore an old corduroy jacket and turned up with poems and fresh trout in his pockets. Sylvia cooked on the small gas ring in her rooms, and they'd eat steak while Ted taught her how to cook herring roes and all about horoscopes. Ted was the first man she'd ever met who genuinely loved food. "He stalked in the door yesterday," she wrote home, "with a packet of little fresh shrimp and four fresh trout. I made a nectar of Shrimp Newburg with essence of butter, cream, sherry and cheeses; had it on rice with the trout. It took us three hours to peel all the little tiny shrimp, and Ted just lay groaning by the hearth after the meal, like a huge Goliath."

A Nectar of Shrimp Newburg

INGREDIENTS

- 1 lb. fresh, raw shrimp, peeled and deveined
- 2 tbsp. butter
- 1 onion, very finely chopped
- 3 tbsp. single cream
- 1 measure of sherry
- 2 tbsp. cream cheese
- Worcestershire sauce
- Tabasco sauce
- ½ cup fish stock
- Sea salt
- Freshly ground pepper
- 1 egg yolk
- 1 tbsp. finely grated Parmesan cheese

METHOD

In a frying pan, melt the 2 tablespoons of butter. Sauté the onion until it is soft and golden. Add the cream, sherry, cream cheese, Worcestershire sauce, Tabasco, black pepper, and fish stock. Stir to combine. Remove ½ cup of sauce from the pan and whisk into the egg yolk. Now return this to the pan, add the raw shrimp, and allow this to cook, stirring for 4 minutes. Top with Parmesan.

Serve with trout from Ted Hughes's pocket and rice.

Marrying Ted in London in June 1956, about four months after the whiskey macs entanglement, made all the difference to Plath's views on wifehood. Gone were her reservations about a drudge's life of cooking scrambled eggs. Sylvia expressed much of her joy in newly discovered married life through cooking, which she loved, spending hours poring over her "blessed Rombauer," whose *The Joy of Cooking* delighted Plath—she said she read it "like a rare novel," especially the vegetable section. The reverse of this was that Sylvia sometimes read about novelists' lives and read novels as if they were cookery books in themselves. Reading the diary of Virginia Woolf, she delighted in discovering that Woolf cooked haddock and sausage. Once, when rereading *Moby Dick*, Sylvia was compelled to make a vast pot of steaming, savory fish soup, with onions, chunks of fish and potato, hot bacon bits, and "buttery crackers floundering in it."

Their honeymoon took them to Benidorm, via Paris. At first, they thought they had landed lucky in their first accommodation, rooms at the Widow Mangada's house. The house was the color of milky coffee and lay close to the sea, with purple mountains in the distance. Two empty liter bottles at their doorstep were filled each morning with fresh goat's milk by the passing goatherd; Sylvia made herself café con leche and Ted a brandy milk to go with their breakfast of wild bananas and sugar. The widow herself was splendidly odd, with wings of blue eye shadow and her eyebrows drawn on, leaping blackly in opposite directions from the bridge of her nose to her temples. Things became increasingly rum, though. There seemed to be no water for drinking; the widow had a secret well in the kitchen. She expressed surprise that they'd arrived in Benidorm without their own cutlery, but then produced magnificent forks and knives. All cooking was to be done on an ancient gas burner, and there were several infantries of ants in the kitchen—which they had to share with some "piggy Spaniards." The Widow Mangada tutted at Sylvia's style of washing dishes and demonstrated that they should scour their dishes in greasy, cold water with handfuls of straw. When Sylvia was cooking a first meal of fried sardines and Ted's favored green beans, Widow Mangada threw a handful of white powder into the pan of water. Poison? Witchcraft? Plath wondered. Bicarbonate of soda, Ted replied.

Soon they moved on to better digs in a quieter area of Benidorm. A lovely place with a fig tree, they ate swollen figs from the tree, with the fig's leaves for plates. Ted walked out for fresh bread in the mornings, past the baskets of raw almonds, with their smoky, green taste. It was, for Hughes, a far cry from his upbringing in rural Yorkshire, with wiry old Mr. Hughes running his tobacconists and Mrs. Hughes pottering about in her tiny kitchen making pottages and meaty pies.

Sylvia and Ted loved exploring the fresh fish markets, looking wide-eyed at the stalls of lithe, huge tuna, gingery crabs, blue-black mussels, and pink shrimp. But they lacked the courage to buy the piles of slippery baby octopuses, their tentacles twined around each other like multiple, many-legged bald siblings, opting instead for fish steaks that Sylvia dipped in egg and lemon, then floured and fried until they were golden brown. They dined often on fish, but also rabbit from the market. In Plath's *Journals* we find she and Ted cooking this together. Into the larder went Hughes to fetch the ingredients, and then he lit a fire in the stout, black oven they used. The crumbling coals grew bright with the heat. Carrots, onions, and a battered tomato were cleaned and chopped. They heated a pot on the stove, and Sylvia fried plump strips of salt pork and browned rabbit meat dredged in flour. Sound delicious? Yes, until Sylvia mentions that she added two packets of condensed soup—one beef, the other chicken and vegetable. Fortunately, Ted stepped in and insisted they add a very large glass or two of red wine. Sylvia was not without qualms, though; the soup was necessary to the semicamping existence they had, but she worried that the chicken in canned soups was some form of "spiced catflesh" and wanted to make more and more of her own soup and dark bread.

Food and domesticity with Hughes went with wholeness and a life in poetry—a life of "Books & Babies & Beef Stew." Food was a vital, elemental part of their relationship. Sylvia imagined her ideal home as a place where geniuses would have good dinners and then drink gin in the kitchen. She wanted to keep chickens. And good food on the table signaled her love for Ted. Cooking was an entry point into her marriage, and her passport to domesticity might be Fannie Farmer or the Rombauers. Plus, she had good antecedents: Plath's grandmother, Aurelia Grünwald, being Austrian, made memorable sour cream sauce and delicious cream cheese apricot tarts, which Plath liked to conjure up. Then there was her mother's cooking. Plath wrote to her in September 1956, "I'd love you to give me recipes of our favorite things you make so well—corn and fish chowders, apple pie, apricot jam halfmoons etc.," and in an earlier letter signed off joyfully with "your caviar-ful daughter."

Life with Ted was heaven at first. There was always steaming, creamy, hot milk coffee in the morning, brought to her in bed by Hughes. Then on to the day and writing. Ted and Sylvia shared a large desk and sat at opposite sides, a pot of tea between them. "Restful cups of burning tea" helped them both to work. And among the poems and newspapers were her cookery books, read aloud from and left open. Comically, Sylvia and Ted supplemented their meager income by wildly entering every competition advertised on their groceries: Dole pineapple, Heinz, Libby's tomato juice, French's mustard, and even Slenderella. Days of hard work were followed by evenings of hard work, with both of them working in the library and coming home bright-cheeked to a vigorous, sensual meal of "seared steak, quenching chef salad, wine, luxurious lucent green figs in thick chilled cream." Once, ill with a cold, buried in a world of nose drops, Sylvia was nursed by Ted, who surprised her into loving thankfulness when he cooked a veal chop and brought it to her in bed, followed by bowls of iced pineapple and mugs of coffee. When she was "lit and glowing with love like a fire," she hid a chocolate rabbit and chocolate eggs in his slippers. A day or two later, Sylvia treated herself to a glass of iced white wine and a hash of tuna mayonnaise, onions, corn, and mashed potatoes; her real potato "high," though, came when she discovered how to make her special onion potatoes—essentially, creamy mashed potatoes mixed through with butter fried onions, or, as Sylvia so beautifully described them, "onions slippery glossed & bulbous popped & cracked from their rattle-paper skins."

Come January 1959, and Sylvia and Ted were working in America, with the famous poet Robert Lowell coming to dinner. What should she give the great American poet for dinner? Sylvia wondered, not realizing that she, too, would be a great American poet. Then the answer came, fairy-godmother bright: "My trusty angel-topped lemon meringue pie," with a wicked flutter of pure lemon and the perfect crust, fit for the mouths of poets.

"My Trusty Angel-Topped Lemon Meringue Pie" (good enough for Robert Lowell)

INGREDIENTS

FOR THE PASTRY . . .

4 oz. all-purpose flour
1 oz. butter
1 oz. lard
Finely grated zest of 1 lemon
Pinch of sea salt
Cold water (generally about 2 tbsp.)

FOR THE FILLING . . .

4 oz. butter
Juice of 4 lemons
Zest of 2 lemons
3 oz. caster sugar
Pinch of sea salt
3 eggs
3 egg yolks

FOR THE MERINGUE . . .

4 large egg whites, at room temperature
4½ oz. vanilla sugar

METHOD

Butter a deep, 8-inch pie dish. Preheat the oven to 190°C. Sieve the all-purpose flour into a bowl, and using a knife, combine the flour with the butter, lard, lemon zest, and sea salt. Add small amounts of cold water until you have a firm pastry consistency. Next, shape the pastry into a ball and wrap this in cling film. Let it chill in the fridge for about one hour. Flour a surface and your rolling pin. Now roll out the pastry into a circular shape to fit the bottom and sides of the pie dish. Using a fork, prick the base, taking care not to penetrate the pastry. Cover the pastry with greaseproof paper, and empty baking beans onto it. Bake blind for 10

"My Trusty Angel-Topped Lemon Meringue Pie" (*continued*)

minutes. Remove the baking beans and greaseproof paper and bake the pastry base for a further 15 minutes. When the pastry base is golden brown, remove from the oven and allow it to cool. Turn the oven down to 150°C.

Now for the delicious, zesty, lemon custard filling. Begin by warming the butter, lemon zest, lemon juice, sugar, and salt in a saucepan. Meanwhile, in a Pyrex bowl, cream together the eggs and egg yolks. Once the buttery lemon mixture has melted, add a little to the creamed eggs, whisking all the time. Now transfer the egg mixture into the saucepan and, whisking constantly, warm this until it thickens into a lemony custard—but don't boil or lemony scrambled eggs will be the result. Pour this lemon custard over the pastry case. Put this in the fridge to cool completely.

After 30 minutes, turn your attention to the meringue. Put the egg whites in a large, very clean bowl and, using an electric whisk, whisk them until they begin to form gentle peaks. Add the vanilla caster sugar, a third at a time. Whisk until the meringue forms glossy, snowy peaks with an ivory sheen. Next, pour the raw meringue over the lemon custard; have fun making angel shapes of meringue, but make sure you cover the edges of the dish with meringue, as it seals in the filling. Bake in the oven for about 30 minutes, until the meringue has taken on some caramel tones.

Serve hot or cold, and with a dollop of lush cream.

5

Finally, the Nuts

Will it be love at first bite with Casanova? Or will you try the dark repasts of Sybil Leek, the world's most famous witch? Who can predict what's on Nostradamus's table? Would you sip a Kubla Khan cocktail with occultist Aleister Crowley?

CASANOVA

It wasn't all oysters . . .

Eighteenth-century Venetian lothario Casanova was, in his time, a prison escapee, necromancer (a ghoulish cure for nosebleeds steered him in this direction), violinist, freemason, lottery director, adventurer, spy, law student in Padua, and a preacher—but not all at once. One fact, however, remains constant: Casanova was constantly having little suppers before sex and pistol duels: pork chops and polenta with a flask of Orvieto on the side; a soupçon of cheese; and topping up his love engine on cocoa at bedtime, with little sleep to be had. Even when, in 1755, Casanova was bundled into Piombi prison for spying (from which he subsequently escaped with a monk!), things brightened up when he discovered he could buy his own food, and he held intimate suppers with fellow prisoners for which he'd rustle up a little macaroni and cheese.

Spy's Macaroni and Cheese

INGREDIENTS

½ lb. macaroni
4 tbsp. Parmesan cheese
2 eggs
1 tsp. Dijon mustard
Sea salt
Freshly ground black pepper

METHOD

Bring a three-quarters-full, deep pan of water to boil. Empty the macaroni into the water, stir, and cook for about 10 minutes until it is al dente. Drain the macaroni and add the eggs, mustard, 4 tablespoons of Parmesan, and a pinch of sea salt and black pepper. Mix all together thoroughly. Then serve.

If you were an innocent with good bosoms, preferably from a religious order of some sort, and with a liking for shellfish, chances are Casanova might have deflowered you (and your twin if you had one). Casanova's amuse-bouche for love was to teach his date how to eat oysters: as soon as oyster-eating lessons were offered, like it or not, you'd know you were in with a chance. Oysters were involved in the seduction of more nuns than you've had hot dinners, including a nun known obliquely as Sister M**M**. And lots of punch drinking. Unfortunately, he hasn't left us a killing recipe for this, but he does strongly advise in favor of oysters in his *Memoirs*: "Voluptuous reader, try it, and tell me whether it is not the nectar of the gods!"

So, voluptuous reader, tonight's the night!

Oysters

INGREDIENTS

12 oysters

METHOD

Scrub and shuck the oysters, reserving their briny juices. Serve them open and trembling with sweetness on the half-shell on a bed of white ice. Drizzle the oyster juices back onto the half shell.

Now to look for some twins.

Fixing his eyes on *their* bosoms, Casanova was particularly turned on by some special twins—two nuns in training, of course—Armellina and Emilia, who are forever famous in aphrodisiacal mythology for a fishy version of "Pass the Ice

Cube." The twins, although supposedly utterly naïve about where this game could lead, were quick learners—though Casanova had to scold greedy Armellina for swallowing the oyster liquid before passing it to him. Raise a rampart on your tongue, he explained. And just in case the lesson hadn't been learned properly, Casanova came up with the bright idea that the twins insert their tongues in each other's mouths so that those tricky oysters didn't slip away—the *full* length of the tongue is required, he instructed . . . and then, of course, an oyster Emilia was passing to Casanova dropped between her breasts. It was his to claim, he insisted . . . and then darn if the same thing didn't next happen with Armellina, but the oyster slipped even further down!

Casanova's visit to England in June 1763 was remarkable mostly for making our hedonist more intensely miserable than he had ever been before. Did the British have fewer twins? They certainly had fewer nuns since the Reformation. Was this why Casanova was depressed? Nope, it was mostly down to (a) the English and (b) English cooking. England, Casanova found, was completely different from the rest of Europe: even the water of the Thames tasted murkily different. Lemonade in London was distinctive (not in a good way) and British beer was rotten—and in their brutal cookery the English were unattractively different, too. Casanova didn't come to this conclusion lightly; like an investigating detective, he dined in every type of tavern, high and low, to understand the English "flavour." As he couldn't speak a word of English, Casanova was left in a silent pantomime with many of them. Even when he met George III, the king spoke so quietly that Casanova, hearing nothing, had to just nod politely and bow. To top it all, the English were a bit snobbish, he concluded, considering themselves a cut above the rest of Europe, and yet their manners stank, as when he had oysters and champagne with the son of the Duke of Bedford and he asked Casanova to cough up the cash for the second bottle! Other aristocrats were more to Casanova's taste, like Lord Pembroke, who would shave three times a day to spare his lovers the touch of his beard. In short, Casanova concluded irritably, "The stranger who sets his foot on English soil has need of a good deal of patience."

Sitting before plates of roast beef in London, swimming in watery grease, left Casanova with little appetite. He lamented the absence of international food as if he were counting former lovers on his fingers: Neapolitan macaroni and rice—oh, he would have given *anything* for Spanish olla podrida; the meat of the fat, white codfish of Newfoundland; the enigmatic glory of roasted, dark game, with its deep, complex flavors; the peppery intensity of moist blue cheese and its damp aroma, which gave him the same sentimental, passionate arousal he experienced from the odor of women. Hmm . . .

Thank God for the personal chef Casanova installed in his private apartments in Pall Mall, who, beyond English dishes, had a strong repertoire of French fricandeaus, ragoûts, cutlets, and French soup—"one of the principal glories of France."

The English fell foul when it came to soup, too, and mocked Casanova when he asked for it. "Are you ill?" one maidservant asked. "Soup is only fit for invalids." Pah! The English even fed the meat they used for soup stock to their dogs—something Casanova found amazing, given that the English, he scoffed, were wildly, boringly carnivorous (although he had to concede their salt beef was excellent). As bad, in his opinion, were English girls. When he went to look for one in a tavern in London, the first loomed over him like Hercules, and he turned down eleven more such murky-complexioned Anglo-Saxon hulks. Indeed, the British managed to impose on Casanova the longest spell of celibacy he'd ever endured—a full six weeks.

Spanish Olla Podrida

INGREDIENTS

½ lb. dark purple beans, preferably alubias de Ibeas
1 lb. oxtail
1 pig's ear
2 pigs' tails
1 small smoked ham hock
½ lb. jamón Serrano, diced
1 leek, coarsely chopped
1 onion, sliced
3 carrots, halved
1 head garlic, unpeeled, cut at either end
2 bay leaves
2 sprigs fresh thyme, crumbled
½ lb. chicken, a mixture of legs and thighs
1 chorizo sausage
1 morcilla
2 tomatoes, peeled, seeded, and halved
3 medium-sized potatoes, halved
¼ Savoy cabbage, roughly chopped
¼ lb. green beans, halved
1½ tsp. smoked sweet paprika
Pinch of saffron threads
1 tsp. cumin seeds, crushed
1 tsp. black peppercorns
2 tbsp. finely chopped parsley
Olive oil

METHOD

Overnight, soak the dark beans in water. Put the pig's ear, tail, and smoked ham into water—this will remove any excess salt. The next day, drain and wash the soaked meats. Don't drain the beans; instead, put the beans and their soaking juices into a large, deep pan. Now add the oxtail, pig's ear, tail, ham hock, jamón Serrano, leek, onion, carrots, garlic head, bay leaves, and thyme. Top up with enough cold water to cover the stew by about two inches. Bring this slowly to boil, skimming off any impurities. Allow this to simmer gently for an hour.

Using a mortar and pestle, grind the saffron, smoked paprika, cumin, and peppercorns with a very small pinch of sea salt. Add one of the tomatoes and form a paste.

After an hour, add the chicken, chorizo, morcilla, tomatoes, potatoes, cabbage, and green beans. Now add the aromatic spice and tomato mixture.

Continue to simmer the olla podrida for two hours. Remove the chorizo and morcilla from the stew, and chop these sausages roughly. Return to the olla podrida and serve the stew in bowls and garnish with freshly chopped parsley and a drizzle of olive oil.

SYBIL LEEK

If you are looking for twentieth-century witches, it doesn't get better than Sybil Leek. The Witchcraft Law was only repealed in 1951, and so Sybil Leek had to be fairly circumspect about her activities, or as circumspect as a person regularly seen in cloaks while spooking about perfectly respectable small English villages with a large, shaggy black bird on her shoulder could be. It didn't take long until she was discovered by TV and embraced by the press, who, of course, loved Sybil Leek and her pet jackdaw, Mr. Hotfoot Jackson. It was as if someone had shaken them out of the pages of a children's fable. She had her own quiet part to play in history, too: purportedly, Sybil was recruited by the British government in World War I to provide phony horoscopes for those key Nazi figures who believed in such things. Rumor has it that Sybil wrote the astrological chart for Rudolph Hess that convinced him it was an excellent idea to fly to Britain.

And from where did this knowledge of horoscopes spring? In terms of witch pedigree, Sybil was top notch, claiming descent from the Pendle witches. She wasn't just any old witch. Her grandmother, also a witch, taught little Sybil astrological symbols through baking pies and tarts with astrological symbols decorating them. She taught Sybil some tough lessons, too, in the cutthroat world of animal sacrifice. When Sybil caught diphtheria, Granny Leek came to tuck her in, with Sybil's pet owl on her arm. "If you had to choose between your pet owl and yourself, what would you choose?" Sybil couldn't come up with an answer. Granny Leek pronounced, "The owl will die." Sybil was never to see her owl again but come morning her throat felt much, much better—a sobering thought (particularly for the owl).

Nor was the Leek household any old backwoods—no, no, it was abuzz with alternative, free thinkers. H. G. Wells used to come calling for tea and cakes, and master wizard Aleister Crowley would pop by to be scolded by Granny Leek about his diet. Sybil's school didn't know what to make of her when she declared that she knew a lot about herbs; the headmistress drew the line at that, stating firmly, "Here we call the study of plants botany, it is regarded as a subsidiary subject." But things were going to get even stranger: Sybil spooked her playmates by calling birds to her. It didn't go down well in the playground or the staff room. Even worse, one day Sybil was called to the headmaster's office, who asked why she had been marked present in two subject classes at the same time. Of course, it was blindingly obvious that the spirit of Sybil could just roam about popping into geography and materializing in French. From Sybil: "I tried to explain that it was only a simple matter of astral projection, but it did not help at all." Unfortunately, Sybil must have been projecting herself elsewhere in domestic science classes and got a really bad grade. What was Granny Leek's solution? Rolling up her sleeves, she commanded Sybil, "You'd better get used to some cookery. Get that cauldron cleaned out and look lively. You've wasted enough time at that girl's school."

Before she went on to trick the Third Reich, run an antique shop, and enjoy celebrity status in America, Sybil attended a sort of witches' "finishing school" with the gypsies in the New Forest, whom she joined with only one English pound tucked into her shoe—where else would a witch keep her money? She learned to tickle her own trout and saw the secret glade for ponies in the New Forest where they go to die (apparently ponies, like witches, know the time of their death). Fitting in was easy; she'd already been living in a cottage nearby, was known to the gypsies as "The Lady," and would often be surprised by finding a gift of a trout on her doorstep, wrapped in dock leaves or ferns, or they would leave her bundles of eyebright for making eyewash or juniper berries to aromatize gin. Those are just the sort of neighbors anyone wants. Sybil loved eating with the gypsies—it was a mistake, she insisted, to imagine they had to stick to a dull diet of hedgehog wrapped in clay and baked; there were rabbits and hares to be snared or flushed out by the greyhounds. The gypsies loved poached pheasant; she watched, enchanted, as they lured pheasants from the trees, using one slow-burning piece of gorse, the scented smoke of which would drug the pheasants, which fell from their high perches.

Rabbit stew was cooked in enormous iron cauldrons and shared very democratically by all who sat around the crackling gorse-wood fires—it was the food most often eaten by the witch and the gypsies. Someone, Sybil was sure, could have made a fortune if the rabbit stew was sold in a restaurant, with its piquant, rare smoky taste and many green herbs. Every rabbit stew was unrepeatable, its vegetables "borrowed" from nearby farmers' fields, changing seasonally. I doubt it was much comfort to farmers at the time, but the gypsies always reburied the vegetable parings in the field. This made Sybil curious, too, and she asked, "What do you do that for?"

"So that he has a good crop, of course," was the reply.

Sybil tried to get the gypsies to switch to coffee, but they remained unshakeable in their loyalty to ground dandelion root or their own black tea, "brewed in a can on a wood fire, so strongly that the stirring stick would stand up in it. Well laced with wild honey . . . it was drunk very hot and in winter would send a warm glow through the body more quickly than alcohol. In the summer it produced a sweat which I was assured was beneficial by ridding the system of poisons."

The gypsies taught the Lady an arsenal of extra information about the "herbs" she so loved as a child: dandelion not only works as a diuretic but also is good for "female organs" and anemia and the liver and the pancreas. Raspberry leaves are good for puberty, and large, coarse dandelion leaves work as a pregnancy test—place a few spots of urine on one of these leaves, and if red blisters form, a woman is pregnant. For rheumatism, rub bruised nettle on your skin—nettle will also, when steeped in water, provide pain relief for neuralgia; foxgloves, they knew, were for the heart; and lightly stewed chickweed works as a blood purifier. Broom flowers could help high blood pressure; sphagnum moss would staunch wounds and should be used in childbirth. And finally, always rinse your hair with a little of your own urine if you want to avoid baldness.

You'll note Sybil had a very good head of hair.

Rabbit and Pheasant Stew

Ideally, there would be a cauldron and a gorse fire, and you would have drugged the pheasants.

INGREDIENTS

4 tbsp. all-purpose flour
Black pepper
Sea salt
2 lb. rabbit, roughly chopped (preparing the meat is called "drawing it")
1 pheasant, quartered
3 tbsp. dripping—gypsies *never* use oil
A kettleful of hot water
3 onions, chopped
4 celery stalks, cut into 1-inch pieces
Thyme, rosemary, parsley, lovage, bay leaves, wild garlic, bay, sage
8 juniper berries, slightly crushed
3 potatoes, halved
1 swede, chopped
4 carrots, chopped
Whichever other vegetables are in the field
1 lb. various wild mushrooms

METHOD

Blend the all-purpose flour with the sea salt and black pepper. Coat the meat in the flour. In a deep, heavy pan, melt the dripping, and brown the rabbit meat in batches if necessary. Now add the onions, celery, and herbs. Cover the meat and vegetables with water. Bring to boil. Now reduce the heat; cover and simmer about 1½ hours. Next, add the root vegetables (potatoes, swede, and carrots) and wild mushrooms and cook for another hour.

This is best served with campfire bread. Don't forget to return your parings.

Campfire Bread

INGREDIENTS

8 cups flour
2 tbsp. baking powder
2 tsp. sea salt
4 tbsp. butter, roughly chopped
1 tsp. dripping
1 cup milk

METHOD

In a bowl, mix together the flour, sea salt, and baking powder. Now run the butter, sea salt, dripping, and baking powder into the flour to form a crumbly, yellow mixture. Gradually add the milk, working it in with your hands until dough is formed; add a little more milk if necessary. To cook this bread, you can do one of two things: If you are indeed at a campfire, then shape the dough into a long sausage and wind it around a sturdy stick and suspend the branch over whichever section of the fire is low; the bread will be ready when it is golden brown. If, however, you are cooking on a stove, then the bread should be shaped into a circle and cooked on a lightly buttered or larded griddle for about 7 minutes on each side.

And finally, if you've ever wondered how it's done . . .

Hotchi-Witchi

A hedgehog is, apparently, not difficult to lay your hands on, depending on where you look. They are very heavy breathers, and their regular runs can be found this way. They are known in Romany as boorsron or hotchi-witchi.

A wooden skewer is used to open up the stomach of the hedgehog, and it is cleaned. Next, the hedgehog is singed until their fan of spines is burned off. After this, the hedgehog is scalded in a basin of boiling water. Now it is skinned, washed down in salt water, and roasted on a stick. Easy?

NOSTRADAMUS

Spooky Nostradamus was a really nice guy. In fact, during his work as a doctor in plague-ridden sixteenth-century France, good old Nostradamus came up with some very sound ideas to help treat the victims of the plague. Ironically enough, they were based on sound common sense and were in opposition to all the mumbo-jumbo put about by quacks. For a start, Nostradamus chose to strip off the weird David Bowie outfit favored by many plague doctors. There was no way he was going to wear a sponge strapped to his nose, garlic on his tongue, shoes with cymbals, a gaudy, powder-streaked blouse that had been steeped in "magical juices," a waxed tunic of racy red leather (a waterproof for fouled air), and, to top it all, a headdress with spectacles or inset stone eyes and a long birdlike beak/nose containing sweet "medicines" to cleanse the air. No way!

Some 40 percent of Europe's population was wiped out by this particular pandemic. Sensibly, Nostradamus espoused a treatment program, the central tenets of which were the isolation of the infected victim, burning the fusty old straw mattress they had been lying and dying on, and supplying clean and fresh air and fresh water for both apothecary and patient. In other words, Nostradamus had the novel idea that hygiene might be important in the prevention of disease and epidemic.

And if he called on you, Nostradamus would not bleed you with leeches, which is a good thing, as they weren't *quite* sure how much blood we humans had and, a century later, thought a blood transfusion of sheep's blood might just do the trick. However, Nostradamus might be inclined to give you a sip of his purging rosewater. How sweet—and it did have high concentrations of vitamin C. It is also rather hard work to make; Nostradamus blithely recommends that one "take 900 or almost 1,000 of the most beautiful flesh-coloured roses," pick off their leaves, clean the buds, and then rub the buds between both hands. Phew!

Yes, when he wasn't forecasting September 11, the sinking of the *Titanic* (I wonder if he got the menu right), or the teeth-chattering prospect of Hitler, Nostradamus liked to cook up medicines, and especially preserves and jellies. The *Elixirs* of Nostradamus make interesting reading. Undoubtedly, his advice about makeup was a bit slapdash in its reliance on mercury and Venetian white lead. His recommended method for getting rid of spots and dreaded red moles was a tad partisan in expecting his reader to burrow about the garden searching for squirting cucumber roots or to have a seemingly endless supply of personal spittle. However, he does do an exciting line on jellies, jams, and preserves. Nostradamus preserved lemons, pumpkins—"which cool internal fevers and have a very pleasant taste"—bitter oranges, muscadel pears, maraschino cherries, and walnuts. The recipe for the boiled wine he used in which to preserve the walnuts was taken from the ancient Roman recipe for *defrutum*. He was sure green ginger was good for chilly stomachs or women with "abdominal frigidity" (!?!), though preserved, welted thistle roots could do the same job and were much sweeter.

Nostradamus proudly treated the papal legate at Avignon, Cardinal de Clarmont, to a jar of his quince jelly—even King Henri II of France got a spoonful. It was expensive to make, though, Nostradamus warned his reader, and might be best kept for when one is called upon to cook for princes and kings. However, Nostradamus wasn't a snob, and I believe that the true generosity of Nostradamus is nowhere more apparent than in his advice in *The Elixirs of Nostradamus* on "How to Make Marzipan."

Nostradamus's Marzipan

INGREDIENTS

- 1 lb. sweet, peeled almonds
- ½ lb. Madeira sugar
- A little rosewater
- Thin biscuits or wafers
- A feather

METHOD

Pound the sweet almonds with a mortar and pestle with the Madeira sugar. Now add a little rosewater to moisten the marzipan. Next, roll the mixture into small cakes and put these on top of thin biscuits or wafers. Bake them in the oven at 170°C for 10 minutes. Take them out, and, using the feather, dust them with a little sugar and put them back in the oven for another 10 minutes. Once they are baked they will have a "delicate and excellent taste."

And he adds, humbly, "These small cakes were called marzipan by Hermolad Barbarus; they may be used as medicine but are very nice to eat at any time. It may well be that some people will mock me for describing such a simple thing, which any apothecary can make. You should know, however, that I do this much more on behalf of the ordinary man and ordinary woman, who are very pleased to learn new things. . . . Take note, however, that if you want to make a delightful, fresh and delectable little cake, bake it when the almonds are still fresh and have only recently been picked from the trees."

Although Nostradamus's provident gift for soothsaying attracted the attention of Catherine de' Medici, some sceptics couldn't resist testing the futurologist's powers. One Seigneur de Florinville rubbed his hands with glee when he thought he'd worked out a wily trick. De Florinville asked Nostradamus to supper and, as they were strolling to his house through his farmlands, they passed some pigs. De Florinville asked Nostradamus if they were going to eat a black pig or a white one.

"Well," said Nostradamus, "we'll be eating the black pig because the white one will be killed by a wolf." Ho, ho, ho, thought de Florinville, and immediately told his cook to kill and cook the white pig.

There they were, later that evening, sitting over a nice plate of pig. Unable to resist a fleeting, triumphant smirk, de Florinville said that clearly the white pig had escaped the jaws of Mr. Wolf, as they were about to eat it. "Nope, this is the black pig," insisted Nostradamus. De Florinville called for his cook. It turned out that the white pig *had* been killed for their supper *but* a servant's young pet wolf had stolen it from the spit. So guess what happened to the black pig?

One can only wonder how Seigneur de Florinville coped with his pork scratchings after that.

ALEISTER CROWLEY

If you were enjoying a soupçon of Sole à la Meunierre in the Café Royale at the tail end of the nineteenth century, you might well have spotted the wizard Aleister Crowley. He might be dressed as a Highland chieftain (one pseudonym of his being the Laird of Boleskin, after the Loch Ness home he bought), or he would have donned an Afro-style black wig and eyeliner. His shoes had huge, silver buckles. If his pagan practices weren't weird enough, Crowley also looked refreshingly odd, having perfected a pop-eyed stare. And he may have needed the Afro wig: publisher Sylvia Beach noted that the "self-mummified" Crowley had a "clay-coloured head," while Maurice Richardson likened Crowley's face to a sizeable penis.

Crowley created an emporium of marvelous other selves and names to posture with. He adopted a high-pitched, cockneyfied voice. He was variously called Le Comte de Fenix, Count Vladimir Svareff, and Prince Chioa Khan. They must have come to him in a heroin-induced dream.

Laboring under the conviction that he was possessed of a magical cloak that rendered him invisible, Crowley delighted in walking slowly past smart sets in the café, a cone-shaped, star-spangled hat perched on his head. Polite groups of the British public would look straight ahead, frozen, as the grave, portly figure drifted past them, like an enormous elephant smuggling itself out of the Café Royale. Of course, being British, they politely averted their gaze and desperately tried not to stare at him or make eye contact with a lunatic, so Crowley was convinced his invisibility cloak had worked!

Once his cloak came off and he'd caught your eye, in typical "bounder" fashion, Crowley might try to sell you some "Elixir of Life" cakes, which he pushed as magic cakes but, unbeknownst to many, had some ingredients that were, in part, derived from the sacred form of Crowley himself—his semen. Or he'd happily get you to subscribe to a course of "Amrita," costing only twenty-five guineas a week and guaranteeing sexual reawakening.

Crowley's self-referential religion of "Crowleyanity," the Cult of Thelema, cooked up in the African desert, didn't do much to dent the popular appeal of Christianity. One could count on Darwinism to do that. Thelema was Crowley's religion to rival the Golden Dawn movement after a nasty falling out with W. B. Yeats. Aleister briefly flirted with the Golden Dawn but disgraced himself by trying to hire some louts to rough up or polish off Yeats (though Yeats also put curses on Crowley).

There is something monstrously comic about Crowley's version of the occult. If he invited you back after the Café Royale for a tipple at his flat in Chancery Lane, you might well be dazzled by the huge mirrors Crowley used to repel spells. This, then, might send you crashing into the arms of the human skeleton as you skidded on a mess of dead sparrows and blood Crowley had been "feeding" the skeleton. Hopefully, he wouldn't have asked you to participate in "sex magick." Feared by some as demonic, Crowley seems disarmingly childlike; for instance, he used novel methods of avoiding the dentist. When an appointment was due to be made, he would throw his *I Ching* sticks in the air and, lo, they always commanded him not to go.

Crowley must have been a nightmare tenant for any unsuspecting landlord. Alan Burnett-Rae was just such a one, driven to despair trying to hunt down rent-dodging Crowley for disturbance of the peace. Eventually, he managed to fob Crowley off on some other poor fool:

> He moved in that day. I was out of town for a while after this and it was on my return that the steward reported to me that the new tenant was making rather a nuisance of himself by burning powerful incense. This was beyond a doubt; I could perceive it myself. Further, he was most exacting in his demands. The Belgian steward's son Adolphe . . . was constantly being sent on errands to purchase strange foods and drinks. Pigs' trotters, I remember, were one of Crowley's favourite dishes, usually ordered at impossible hours.

All of this just confirms what a Plymouth Brethren upbringing can do to you—or perhaps it is the effect Leamington Spa has on an impressionable child? When the Brethren came calling at the Crowley family home in Leamington, naughty boy Aleister put a dose of castor oil in the tea urn, refused to eat his jam (it was too messy), and proved to be such a blight on the lives of his respectable parents that his own mother first coined the adage "The Beast" for him. It was no small relief to her when underwear-refuser young Crowley set off for Cambridge University. But isn't it ironic that all of Crowley's early excesses were financed by his Plymouth Brethren fortune?

In his post-Cambridge years, Aleister was drawn to odd people and rigorous pastimes. Rock climbing was his chosen sport, and one he enjoyed in the company of Oscar Eckenstein, inventor of the crampon and an engineer so picky that he would send back a meal if it had the "wrong" number of potatoes. In preparation for a climbing trip to the Himalayas, Aleister and Oscar set off to ascend the 4,356-meter-high Dent Blanche, a pyramidal mountain in Switzerland playfully nicknamed "la monstrueuse coquette" by Guy de Maupassant. But bad weather got the better of them. Living in a small camp in freezing conditions did nothing to deter Aleister. Famed for his peppery fare, Aleister invented "Glacier Curry," which required a mouthful of snow after each spoonful. Crowley recalled in his *Confessions*:

> It was very amusing to see these strong men, inured to every danger and hardship, dash out of the tent after one mouthful and wallow in the snow, snapping at it like mad dogs. They admitted, however, that it was very good as curry and I should endeavour to introduce it into London restaurants if there were only a glacier. Perhaps, some day, after a heavy snowfall . . .

Crowley had an unending fondness for eccentric curry parties, the timing of which was designed to coincide with the anniversary of his death—like Sybil Leek and the New Forest ponies, any self-respecting occultist would know the day in advance. In old age, Crowley's favorite snack was sardines sprinkled with curry powder.

Crowley didn't always take so well to the rigors of foreign travel and food. Although he adored the cooking of the French-Spanish Quarter in New Orleans, he found Mexico disappointing: he noted glumly as he and Oscar Eckenstein traveled through the interior by orange pony that "nobody bothers about eating." The same could be said of drinking—Mexicans seemed content to pour only agaurdiente or mescal down their throats and not give a damn about "fine vintages." Oscar was a martyr to diarrhea (I wonder what that did for his numerical fetishism), and the two of them had to confine themselves to a diet of champagne and Danish butter! When they came across the uneaten corpse of a Mexican, Crowley attributed its state of preservation to the chilies in the Mexican diet. In later years, when camping with the Bedouin in the desert in order to learn their arcane skills, Crowley steeled himself for adventure by tucking into "potted pheasant and garibaldi biscuits at not infrequent intervals." Crowley conceded an innate fussiness about food: "I must have been nearly forty before I would touch salad. It seems absurd. I was very fond of lobster mayonnaise; but lobster salad, never! I dislike the combination of consonants. The word suggests something indefinite."

Great fun was to be had at Crowley's Loch Ness abode, Boleskin. He set up his own still, supplied his guests with freshly caught salmon, and he hunted deer and rabbit with his dog, Lady Etheldreda. An impish and gregarious host, with a good line in practical jokes, Crowley urged one visitor to hunt haggis by following its "scream-whistle," and trembling highland tradesmen left their deliveries at the gate of the "Great Beast's" house and slipped away in fear. When he was over sixty, "the wickedest man on earth" threw rip-roaring, scandalous dinner parties. With typical Crowley-esque humor, "the Beast" would drink from a bottle labeled *Poison*. In Crowley's *Diary of a Drug Fiend* he claimed to have invented a cocktail of gin and vermouth sportingly called Kubla Khan No. 2, and another fiery little number in which equal parts of kirsch, absinthe, and cognac were combined with a slight sidekick of a dash of Tabasco and ether. This would then be shaken with ice. If you survived this baptism of kirsch, then gooseberry-eyed Crowley would rustle up his infamous curries.

Glacier Curry

INGREDIENTS

12 whole quails, skinned and cleaned inside and out
2 medium onions, roughly chopped
3 medium tomatoes, roughly chopped
12 red chilies
2 tbsp. pureed ginger
1½ tbsp. garlic, pulped
1½ tbsp. ground cumin
1 tbsp. ground cilantro
½ tsp. turmeric
Juice of 2 limes
Sea salt
1 tsp. brown sugar
3 tbsp. rapeseed oil or ghee
2 cups water

TEMPERING

½ tsp. whole cumin seed
6 green cardamoms
½ tsp. black mustard seeds
1 tsp. sesame seeds
6 dried bird's-eye chilies

GARNISH

3 tbsp. crisply fried juliennes of ginger
3 tbsp. crisply fried, thinly sliced onions
2 juliennes of fresh green chilies (raw)
½ tsp. garam masala

METHOD

Grind the onions in a food mixer and put aside. Grind the tomatoes and chilies together and put aside.

Use a large pan (big enough to take 12 quails side by side with room to stir). Heat the pan, and then pour in the oil (ghee). When the oil starts to crackle, brown the quails all over, three at a time, and put aside.

Now put all the tempering ingredients into the pan and fry for about 2 minutes or until the mustard seed starts to dance. Then pour in the ground onions and a tablespoon of sea salt and fry well, stirring occasionally to prevent sticking. When the onions are a light golden color, add the turmeric, ginger, and garlic and fry for another 2 minutes. Now squeeze in the juice of 2 limes and cook for another 2 minutes. You should have a nice, homogenous, thick sauce at this stage. Now add the tomatoes and chilies and mix well. Cook covered until the oil separates from the sauce, about 10 minutes on gentle flame. Now add all the remaining spices, sugar, and a cup of water and mix well. Add the quails and another cup of water. Cover and simmer until the quails are tender (about 15 minutes). If the curry starts to dry out, add some more water. You will be left with plenty of rich, thick, smooth gravy. Check salt and add more if necessary.

When the quails are nice and tender—the meat should flake off in your fingers—sprinkle the garnish evenly on top. Provide cooling snow in bowls for your guests.

Kubla Khan No. 2

INGREDIENTS

Gin
Dry vermouth
Grand Marnier
Orange bitters
A strip of orange zest

METHOD

Put a handful of crushed ice in a cocktail shaker; add one measure of gin, one measure of dry vermouth, Grand Marnier, and a dash of orange bitters. Rub the edge of the glass with the strip of orange zest. Now pour Kubla Khan No. 2 into the glass and pop in the orange zest.

The Beast (we'll agree to leave out the ether for now)

INGREDIENTS

Kirsch
Absinthe
Cognac
Tabasco

METHOD

Put one ice cube in a cocktail shaker and mix half a measure of kirsch, half a measure of absinthe, and half a measure of cognac. Pour into a chilled glass and drizzle with a dash of Tabasco. Knock it back in one go.

As if he hadn't endured enough as Crowley's landlord, Alan Burnett-Rae in *Aleister Crowley: A Memoir of 666* gives a nervous account of eating curry with Crowley:

> I was invited to have one of these, prepared by himself, one day just before the war. At the first mouthful I thought I had burned my tongue with caustic acid and reached for the water and thereafter took water with every successive spoonful. Crowley, however, shovelled an enormous plateful away with record speed, fortifying it as he went with chillies and other spices, the sweat pouring down his face, as if he were in a Turkish bath.

Aleister chatted away all through the meal, suggesting with great largesse that Burnett-Rae visit India and similar lands, motivated as much as anything because a point of hospitality there was to have your testicles lifted by a maiden and fanned from below. "You could enjoy all these things," he cheerily suggested, "to say nothing of the delights of opium, hashish and heroin." Alan Burnett-Rae sat with his legs very tightly crossed.

Perhaps the best firsthand account we get of dinner with "The Great Beast" comes from writer Maurice Richardson, author of such texts as *The Fascination of Reptiles*, who had lunch with Crowley in his Belgravia flat in 1939. Richardson had first come into contact with Crowley when Crowley sent him a letter of complaint about a book review (on writing paper embossed with penises, written no doubt in ink from Crowley's "Baphomet"-inscribed fountain pen), and the two had arranged to have lunch at Crowley's home. Richardson was considerably amused by Crowley's devilish reputation. Lunch lasted four hours. Crowley, a figure "blurred by fat," was dressed in green plus-fours and a tartan bow tie.

It took several vodkas before Crowley and Richardson settled down to lunch, served by Crowley's housekeeper, a brusque Scotswoman referred to as "Kathy." Crowley boomed a pagan incantation over the table—"Do what thou wilt shall be the whole of the law"—only to be hurried along by Kathy saying, "Hurry up, Aleister, the potatoes will be burnt." A dreamy lobster bisque was served up, and Crowley pointed out a sliver of lobster protruding from the soup. Gazing hauntingly in Richardson's eyes, he said slowly, "Looks like a devil roasting in hell, does it not, Mr. Richardson?" Bottles of chilled Chianti floated past the table, a roast duck was eaten, followed by brie and Jamaica Blue Mountain coffee, accompanied by Cyprus brandy "that would take the shell off an egg" and heady black Mexican cigars. The conversation drifted along and out of Richardson's memory. Eventually, Richardson was led to apologize for the book review. Quick as a wink, crafty Crowley asked Richardson to write a short note to that effect. Fortunately, Richardson found it impossible to hold a pen and thus may have avoided being sued for libel. Who knows?

Devils in Hell Bisque de Homard

INGREDIENTS

2 small lobsters
1 tbsp. olive oil
3 tbsp. butter
3 shallots, peeled and finely chopped
1 clove garlic, minced
1 carrot, peeled and finely chopped
1 celery stalk, finely chopped
1 bay leaf
1 dessert spoon of chopped, fresh French tarragon
1 bouquet garni
3 tbsp. cognac
1 can chopped plum tomatoes
200 ml. dry white wine
2 liters fish stock
Pinch grated nutmeg
Pinch cayenne pepper
Juice of ¼ lemon
100 ml. double cream

Devils in Hell Bisque de Homard (*continued*)

TO SERVE . . .

4 tbsp. cream
1 tbsp. finely chopped chives

METHOD

Place the lobsters in the fridge for 2 hours, as this will lull them to sleep. Make sure the rubber bands are still on the lobsters' claws. To kill them, stab them through the cross marking between their eyes in the center of their heads. Now split the lobsters down the middle and remove the sack in the head and the internal tract. Separate the claws from the body and crack with a rolling pin.

Get a large, deep, and heavy-bottomed pan. Melt the 3 tablespoons of butter; add the tablespoon of olive oil to stop the butter from burning; then add the shallots, garlic, carrot, celery, and bay leaf to the butter. Sauté over a medium heat for 4 minutes. Do not allow them to color. Now add the lobster and cook for a further 5 minutes. Add the cognac to the pan and turn up the heat: the soup base should be simmering. Take out a section of cooked lobster tail and slip the meat from its shell; this will garnish the soup and allow you to say—slowly and with a penetrating stare—to your companion, "Looks like a devil roasting in hell, does it not?"

Return the tail shell to the pan and pour in the plum tomatoes, tarragon, bouquet garni, white wine, and fish stock. Bring to boil, then cut down to a simmer and allow to cook for 15 minutes.

After this time, fish the lobster out of the pan and clean all the lobster meat from it. Remove both the bouquet garni and the bay leaf. Return the lobster meat to the soup. In a bender, puree the rough soup until it is smooth. Now strain all of this through a fine mesh sieve and return to the pan.

Heat the soup again and add the cayenne, lemon juice, nutmeg, sea salt, and black pepper. Add the double cream. Cook for a further 10 minutes.

To serve, drizzle each serving with cream, scatter chives over, and place a piece of the lobster tail in each bowl.

However, such shenanigans didn't prevent Crowley and Richardson from enjoying several follow-up meals together. Over lunch at one of these, Crowley introduced Richardson to his friend, Gerald Hamilton, who had shared digs with Crowley in Berlin. Brilliantly, both Hamilton and Crowley had been paid by British intelligence to spy on each other in Berlin. Richardson caught sight of Hamilton wildly shaking his head at him when Crowley, thinking Richardson was drunk enough, again tried to cajole him to write a note of apology for the book review.

A truce had been called by the time they met up for what would appear to be their final lunch together at L'Escargot in Soho. No notepaper appeared. Instead, odorous Crowley came bustling in in duke's attire "preceded by an overpowering smell as of an old-fashioned operating theatre." When questioned by a gasping Richardson, Crowley roundly claimed that this was the scent of his "daily eye-opener, half a pint of ether." Crowley rolled up the sleeves of his swallowtail coat and proceeded to tuck into three dozen snails and a wild duck pie, all washed down with a bottle of burgundy and eye-watering brandy. Crowley sat in a haze of smoke from his beloved black Mexican cigars, enigmatic, preposterous . . .

Satanic.

Wild Duck Pie

INGREDIENTS

- 4 wild ducks—they are much smaller than farmed duck
- 8 rashers bacon
- 1 small glass port
- Sea salt
- Freshly ground black pepper
- 5 shallots, minced
- 1 tbsp. brandy
- 2 tbsp. olive oil
- 1 tbsp. mushroom ketchup
- 7 oz. fresh chestnuts
- 2 apples, peeled and quartered
- 7 oz. wild mushrooms
- 1 tsp. fresh thyme leaves
- 4–5 sage leaves, shredded
- Pinch ground allspice
- ½ pint game stock, made with the giblets and bones of the duck
- Puff pastry

FOR THE GAME STOCK . . .

- 2 tbsp. olive oil
- Duck carcasses
- 1 brown onion, skin on
- 1 carrot
- 1 stick celery
- Boiling water
- 1 bay leaf
- Small bunch parsley
- 4 branches thyme
- Handful of black peppercorns
- A big pinch of sea salt

ROUGH PUFF PASTRY

- 9 oz. all-purpose flour
- 9 oz. butter
- 1 tsp. sea salt
- 150 ml. water
- 1 beaten egg

METHOD

Wash, clean, and dry the ducks and wrap them in bacon, allowing two rashers per bird. Preheat the oven to 170°C and place the ducks on a baking tray. Cook for 35 minutes, and then remove from the oven. Strip off the bacon, pour the glass of port wine over the birds, and return to the oven for 5 minutes. Remove and allow to cool.

Wild Duck Pie *(continued)*

Once the ducks are cool enough to handle, strip all the meat from them, reserving their carcasses to make stock. Keep the meat in the fridge until it is time to assemble your pie.

Now make the stock. In a large, deep, heavy-bottomed pan, heat the olive oil until it is smoking. Add the duck giblets and carcasses and the onion, skin on. Close with a lid and keep at a searingly hot temperature while browning the giblets and carcasses. Hold the lid tight and shake the pan to move the contents. Now add the other ingredients and follow this with the boiling water up to the top of the pan—the hot fat will erupt and then die down immediately. Continue to simmer for 1 hour. Strain the stock, removing the bones and vegetables. If you have more stock than the ½ pint needed, then cook down the strained stock.

While the stock is simmering, make the puff pastry. Sift the flour and sea salt into a large bowl. Cut the butter roughly into smallish chunks, and rub these through your flour. You need to do this roughly so that chunks of butter are still visible. Now make a well in the mixture, stir in the egg, and add about 100 milliliters of the water, adding more water if necessary, to make a rough dough. Wrap this in cling film and put the pastry in the fridge to rest for 25 minutes.

Flour the board you intend to work the pastry on. Gently shape the pastry into a rectangle. Begin to roll, working in one direction until it is three times wider. Don't lose the clear, straight lines of the rectangle. The butter should be streaking its way through the pastry. Take the bottom third of the pastry and fold it up to the center. Then take the top third and fold it down over that. Turn the dough by a quarter and repeat as before, rolling out in one direction until the rectangle is three times wider, and so on. Once you have completed the folding this second time around, cover with cling film again and let it rest and cool in the fridge again for 20 minutes before rolling to form the piecrust.

Preheat the oven to 230°C. Warm the olive oil in a deep frying pan and sauté the shallots and mushrooms for 10 minutes. After 5 minutes add the cooked chestnuts, allspice, sage leaves, and thyme. Add 1 tablespoon brandy and 1 tablespoon mushroom ketchup. Add the stock and bring to boil.

Now you can begin to assemble your pie. In a pie dish, place shallots, mushrooms, and chestnuts mixture. Arrange the duck on top with the quartered apples. Roll out the pastry lid and cover the pie dish with this crust. Brush with a beaten egg.

Bake in the oven at 200°C for 20 minutes.

Bibliography

Ades, Dawn. *Dalí*. London: Thames and Hudson, 1995.

Alcantara, Isabel, and Sandra Egnolff. *Frida Kahlo and Diego Rivera*. Munich/London: Prestel, 2011.

Aldridge, John. *Satisfaction: The Story of Mick Jagger*. London/New York: Proteus Books, 1984.

Amateau, Albert. "Julio Zito of Former Zito & Sons Bakery Dead at 83." *The Villager* 77, no. 47 (April 23–29, 2008).

Amburn, Ellis. *Elizabeth Taylor: The Obsessions, Passions and Courage of a Hollywood Legend.* London: Robson, 2000.

Andersen, Christopher. *Michael Jackson: Unauthorized.* London: Michael Joseph, 1994.

Ansen, Alan. *The Table Talk of W. H. Auden*. London: Faber, 1991.

Armstrong, Louis. *Louis Armstrong, in His Own Words: Selected Writings*. Edited by Thomas Brothers. Oxford: Oxford University Press, 1999.

Auden, W. H. *W. H. Auden*. London: Faber, 2005.

Auden, W. H., and Christopher Isherwood. *Journey to a War*. London: Faber and Faber, 1973.

Bacall, Lauren. *By Myself.* Secaucus, NJ: Citadel Press, 1986.

Bacall, Lauren. *By Myself and Then Some*. London: Headline, 2005.

Bacall, Lauren. *Now*. London: Century, 1994.

Barbour, Alan. *Humphrey Bogart*. London: W. H. Allen, 1974.

Barr, Charles. *Laurel and Hardy*. London: Studio Vista, 1967.

Baxter, John. *Woody Allen: A Biography.* London: HarperCollins, 1999.

Beaton, Cecil. *Beaton in the Sixties: The Cecil Beaton Diaries as They Were Written*. London: Weidenfeld and Nicolson, 2003.

Beaton, Cecil. *The Unexpurgated Beaton: The Cecil Beaton Diaries as He Wrote Them*. London: Weidenfeld and Nicolson, 2002.

Benchley, Nathaniel. *Humphrey Bogart*. London: Hutchinson, 1975.

Benson, Ross. *Paul McCartney: Behind the Myth*. London: Gollancz, 1992.

Berman, Ronald. *Fitzgerald, Hemingway and the Twenties*. Tuscaloosa/London: University of Alabama Press, 2001.

Bergreen, Laurence. *Louis Armstrong: An Extravagant Life*. London: HarperCollins, 1977.

Billeter, Erica. *The World of Frida Kahlo: The Blue House*. Seattle: University of Washington Press, 1993.

Bockris, Victor. *Keith Richards: The Unauthorised Biography*. London: Hutchinson, 1992.

Boeser, Knut, Guy Slatter, and Carola Friedrichs-Friedlander. *The Elixirs of Nostradamus: Nostradamus' Original Recipes for Elixirs, Scented Water, Beauty Potions, and Sweetmeats*. London: Bloomsbury, 1995.

Bogart, Stephen Humphrey, and Gary Provost. *Bogart: In Search of My Father*. London: Sidgwick and Jackson, 1995.

Bowker, Gordon. *George Orwell*. London: Little, Brown, 2003.

Boyd, Pattie. *Wonderful Today: The Autobiography*. London: Headline Review, 2007.

Bragg, Melvyn. *Rich: The Life of Richard Burton*. London: Hodder and Stoughton, 1988.

Bray, Christopher. *Michael Caine: A Class Act*. London, Faber and Faber, 2006.

Breslin, James. *Mark Rothko: A Biography*. Chicago/London: University of Chicago Press, 1993.

Bret, David. *Elizabeth Taylor: The Lady, the Lover, the Legend: 1932–2011*. Edinburgh: Mainstream, 2011.

Bret, David. *Marlene Dietrich, My Friend: An Intimate Biography*. London: Robson, 2000.

Brian, Denis. *The Faces of Hemingway: Intimate Portraits of Ernest Hemingway by Those Who Knew Him*. London: Grafton Books, 1988.

Bruccoli, Matthew. *Fitzgerald and Hemingway: A Dangerous Friendship*. London: André Deutsch, 2003.

Bruccoli, Matthew. *The Romantic Egoists: F. Scott and Zelda Fitzgerald*. New York: Scribner, 1974.

Bryce, Ivar. *You Only Live Once: Memories of Ian Fleming*. London: Weidenfeld and Nicolson, 1984.

Bryer, Jackson. *Dear Scott, Dearest Zelda: The Love Letters of F. Scott and Zelda Fitzgerald.* London: Bloomsbury, 2002.

Buddicom, Jacintha. *Eric and Us: A Remembrance of George Orwell.* London: Frewin, 1974.

Burgess, Anthony. *Ernest Hemingway.* London: Thames and Hudson, 1999.

Burnett-Rae, Alan. *Aleister Crowley: A Memoir of 666.* Edited by Victor Hall. London: Victim Press, 1971.

Burton, Richard. *The Richard Burton Diaries.* New Haven, CT: Yale University Press, 2013.

Buttitta, Tony. *The Lost Summer: A Personal Memoir of F. Scott Fitzgerald.* Dunton Green: Sceptre, 1988.

Caine, Michael. *What's It All About?* London: Arrow, 2010.

Calhoun, Randall. *Dorothy Parker: A Bio-Bibliography.* Westport, CT: Greenwood Press, 1993.

Callaghan, Morley. *That Summer in Paris: Memoirs of Tangled Friendships with Hemingway, Fitzgerald, and Some Others.* London: MacGibbon and Kee, 1963.

Capel, Susan. *Nostradamus: His Life and Predictions.* London: Studio Editions, 1995.

Cargill, Morris. *Ian Fleming Introduces Jamaica.* London: Deutsch, 1965.

Carpenter, Humphrey. *The Inklings: C. S. Lewis, J. R. R. Tolkien, Charles Williams and Their Friends.* London: HarperCollins, 2006.

Carpenter, Humphrey. *W. H. Auden: A Biography.* Oxford: Oxford University Press, 1992.

Carpozi, George. *The John Wayne Story.* London: R. Hale, 1974.

Carroll, Tim. *Woody and His Women.* London: Little, Brown, 1993.

Casanova, Giacomo. *Casanova in London.* London: Mayflower Books, 1969.

Casanova, Giacomo. *History of My Life.* London: Longmans, 1967.

Casanova, Giacomo. *The Memoirs of Casanova.* New York: Bantam Books, 1957.

Castle, Charles. *Joan Crawford: The Raging Star.* London: New English Library, 1977.

Caws, Mary Ann. *Dora Maar—with and without Picasso: A Biography.* London: Thames and Hudson, 2000.

Chandler, Charlotte. *It's Only a Movie: Alfred Hitchcock: A Personal Biography.* London: Simon & Schuster, 2005.

Chandler, Charlotte. *Marlene: A Personal Biography.* London: J. R. Books, 2011.

Charone, Barbara. *Keith Richards.* London: Futura, 1979.

Christie, Agatha. *An Autobiography.* London: HarperCollins, 1993.

Churchwell, Sarah. *The Many Lives of Marilyn Monroe.* London: Granta, 2005.

Clark, Thekla. *Wystan and Chester: A Personal Memoir of W. H. Auden and Chester Kallman*. London: Faber, 1995.

Clayson, Alan. *Keith Richards*. London: Sanctuary, 2004.

Clayson, Alan. *Mick Jagger: The Unauthorised Biography*. London: Sanctuary, 2005.

Clayson, Alan. *The Quiet One: A Life of George Harrison*. London: Sanctuary, 1996.

Clayson, Alan. *Ringo Starr: A Life*. London: Sanctuary, 2005.

Coe, Jonathan. *Humphrey Bogart: Take It and Like It*. London: Bloomsbury, 1991.

Como, James. *C. S. Lewis at the Breakfast Table, and Other Reminiscences*. London: Collins, 1980.

Coward, Noël. *Autobiography*. London: Methuen, 1987.

Crawford, Christina. *Mommie Dearest*. London: Mayflower, 1980.

Crawford, Joan. *My Way of Life*. London: W. H. Allen, 1972.

Crawford, Joan. *A Portrait of Joan: The Autobiography of Joan Crawford*. London: F. Muller, 1963.

Cray, Ed. *Ramblin' Man: The Life and Times of Woody Guthrie*. London: W. W. Norton, 2006.

Crick, Bernard. *George Orwell: A Life*. Penguin: Harmondsworth, 1982.

Croft-Cooke, Rupert. *Bosie: The Story of Lord Alfred Douglas, His Friends and Enemies*. London: W. H. Allen, 1963.

Croft-Cooke, Rupert. *The Unrecorded Life of Oscar Wilde*. London: W. H. Allen, 1972.

Crowley, Aleister. *The Confessions of Aleister Crowley: An Autohagiography*. Edited by John Symonds and Kenneth Grant. London: Jonathan Cape, 1969.

Crowley, Aleister. *Diary of a Drug Fiend*. London: Sphere, 1972.

Crowley, Aleister. *The Magical Record of the Beast 666: The Diaries of Aleister Crowley, 1914–1920*. Edited by John Symonds and Kenneth Grant. London: Duckworth, 1972.

Dalí, Salvador. *Dalí*. New York: Abradale Press/H. N. Abrams, 1986.

Dalí, Salvador. *The Secret Life of Salvador Dalí*. London: Vision Press, 1976.

Dalí, Salvador. *The Unspeakable Confessions of Salvador Dalí*. London: Quartet Books, 1977.

Davenport-Hines, R. P. T. *Auden*. London: Heinemann, 1995.

Davidson, Emily, and Robert Santelli. *Hard Travelin': The Life and Legacy of Woody Guthrie*. Hanover: Wesleyan University Press, 1999.

DeCurtis, Anthony. "Memoirs of a Girl from the East Country (O.K., Queens)." *New York Times*, May 11, 2008. http://www.nytimes.com/2008/05/11/arts/music/11decu.html?pagewanted=all&_r=0.

Deghy, Guy, and Keith Waterhouse. *Café Royal: Ninety Years of Bohemia*. London: Hutchinson, 1955.

de Monfreid, Daniel. *Gauguin's Letters from the South Seas*. New York: Dover, 1992.

Dietrich, Marlene. *My Life*. London: Pan, 1991.

Donaldson, Maureen. *An Affair to Remember: My Life with Cary Grant*. London: Macdonald, 1989.

Donaldson, Scott. *Fitzgerald and Hemingway: Works and Days*. New York/Chichester: Columbia University Press, 2009.

Donaldson, Scott. *Fool for Love: F. Scott Fitzgerald*. New York: Congdon and Weed, 1983.

Dos Passos, John. *The Best Times: An Informal Memoir*. London: Deutsch, 1968.

Dos Passos, John. *Fourteenth Chronicle: Letters and Diaries of John Dos Passos*. London: Deutsch, 1974.

Douglas, Alfred Bruce. *The Autobiography of Lord Alfred Douglas*. London: Martin Secker, 1931.

Dowswell, Paul. *Paul McCartney*. Oxford: Heinemann Library, 2001.

Dylan, Bob. *Chronicles*, Vol. 1. London: Simon & Schuster, 2004.

Etherington-Smith, Meredith. *Dalí: A Biography*. London: Sinclair-Stevenson, 1992.

Eyles, Allen. *John Wayne*. London: A. S. Barnes, 1972.

Eyman, Scott. *John Wayne: The Life and Legend*. New York: Simon & Schuster, 2014.

Faithfull, Marianne, and David Dalton. *Faithfull*. London: Penguin, 1995.

Faithfull, Marianne, and David Dalton. *Marianne Faithfull: Memories, Dreams and Reflections*. London: Harper Perennial, 2008.

Farnan, Dorothy. *Auden in Love*. London: Faber, 1985.

Ferguson, Alastair, and Alf Bicknell. *Ticket to Ride*. London: Glitter Books, 1999.

Fields, Danny. *Linda McCartney*. London: Little, Brown, 2000.

Finler, Joel. *Alfred Hitchcock: The Hollywood Years*. London: Batsford, 1992.

Fitzgerald, F. Scott, Matthew Bruccoli, Margaret Duggan, and Susan Walker. *The Correspondence of F. Scott Fitzgerald*. New York: Random House, 1980.

Fleming, Ian. *Casino Royale*. London: Viking, 2002.

Fleming, Ian. *Thrilling Cities*. London: Vintage Books, 2013.

Freedland, Michael. *Michael Caine*. London: Orion Media, 1999.

Frewin, Leslie. *Blond Venus: A Life of Marlene Dietrich*. London: MacGibbon and Kee, 1955.

Fyvel, Tosco R. *George Orwell: A Personal Memoir*. London: Weidenfeld and Nicolson, 1982.

Gallagher, Elaine. *Candidly Caine.* London: Pan, 1991.

Gambaccini, Paul. *Paul McCartney: In His Own Words.* London: Omnibus Press, 1976.

Garner, Ava. *Ava: My Story*. London: Bantam Press, 1990.

Gauguin, Paul. *The Intimate Journals of Paul Gauguin.* London: KPI, 1985.

Gauguin, Paul. *Noa Noa: The Tahitian Journal.* New York: Dover, 1985.

Gauguin, Pola. *My Father, Paul Gauguin.* London: Cassell, 1937.

Gayford, Martin. *The Yellow House: Van Gogh, Gauguin, and Nine Turbulent Weeks in Arles*. London: Penguin, 2006.

Giuliano, Geoffrey. *Blackbird: The Unauthorised Biography of Paul McCartney.* London: Pan, 1992.

Giuliano, Geoffrey. *Dark Horse: The Secret Life of George Harrison.* London: Pan, 1991.

Gold, Todd. *Michael Jackson: The Man in the Mirror.* London: Pan, 1992.

Graham, Sheilah. *The Real F. Scott Fitzgerald Thirty-Five Years Later.* New York: Grosset and Dunlap, 1976.

Grant, Kenneth. *Remembering Aleister Crowley.* London: Skoob, 1991.

Grayson, Dave, Donald Shepherd, and Robert Slatzer. *Duke: The Life and Times of John Wayne.* London: Sphere, 1985.

Greene, Joshua. *Here Comes the Sun: The Spiritual and Musical Journey of George Harrison.* London: Bantam, 2006.

Grissom, C. Edgar. *Ernest Hemingway: A Descriptive Bibliography.* New Castle, DE: Oak Knoll Press, 2011.

Gross, Miriam. *The World of George Orwell.* London: Weidenfeld and Nicolson, 1971.

Grunwald, Henry. *Salinger: A Critical and Personal Portrait.* London: Peter Owen, 1964.

Guiles, Fred Lawrence. *Joan Crawford: The Last Word.* London: Pavilion, 1995.

Guiles, Fred Lawrence. *Norma Jean: The Life of Marilyn Monroe.* London: Mayflower, 1971.

Guthrie, Mary-Jo. *Woody's Road: Woody Guthrie's Letters Home, Drawings, Photos and Other Unburied Treasures.* Boulder, CO: Paradigm, 2012.

Guthrie, Woody. *Bound for Glory.* London: Penguin, 2004.

Guthrie, Woody. *Pastures of Plenty: A Self-Portrait.* New York: HarperCollins, 1992.

Haeffner, Nicholas. *Alfred Hitchcock.* Harlow: Pearson Longman, 2005.

Hajdu, David. *Positively 4th Street: The Life and Times of Joan Baez, Bob Dylan, Mimi Baez Fariña and Richard Fariña.* London: Bloomsbury, 2001.

Hall, William. *Sir Michael Caine: The Biography.* London: John Blake, 2007.

Hamilton, Alan. *Paul McCartney.* London: Hamish Hamilton, 1983.

Hamilton, Ian. *In Search of J. D. Salinger*. London: Heinemann, 1988.

Harris, Frank. *My Life and Loves*. Paris: Obelisk Press, 1960.

Harris, Frank. *Oscar Wilde: His Life and Confessions.* New York City: Frank Harris, 1918.

Harrison, Olivia. *George Harrison: Living in the Material World.* New York/London: Abrams, 2011.

Hemingway, Ernest. *A Moveable Feast*. London: Vintage, 2000.

Hemingway, Ernest, and Carlos Baker. *Ernest Hemingway, Selected Letters, 1917–1961*. New York/London: Scribner Classics, 2003.

Hemingway, Ernest, A. E. Hotchner, and Albert J. DeFazio. *Dear Papa, Dear Hotch: The Correspondence of Ernest Hemingway and A. E. Hotchner*. Columbia: University of Missouri Press, 2005.

Hemingway, Ernest, and Sandra Spanier. *The Letters of Ernest Hemingway*. Cambridge: Cambridge University Press, 2011.

Herrera, Hayden. *Frida: A Biography of Frida Kahlo*. London: Bloomsbury, 2003.

Heylin, Clinton. *Bob Dylan: Behind the Shades Revisited.* London: Faber and Faber, 2011.

Heymann, David. *Liz: An Intimate Biography of Elizabeth Taylor*. London: Heinemann, 1995.

Higham, Charles. *Marlene: The Life of Marlene Dietrich*. London: Mayflower, 1978.

Hitchcock O'Connell, Pat, and Laurent Bouzereau. *Alma Hitchcock: The Woman behind the Man.* New York: Penguin, 2003.

Hodkinson, Mark. *Marianne Faithfull: As Tears Go By*. London: Omnibus, 1991.

Hogue, John. *Nostradamus: Life and Myth: The First Complete Biography of the World's Most Famous and Controversial Prophet*. London: Element, 2003.

Hoog, Michel. *Paul Gauguin: Life and Work*. London: Thames and Hudson, 1987.

Hyde, H. Montgomery. *Lord Alfred Douglas: A Biography*. London: Methuen, 1984.

Hyde, H. Montgomery. *Oscar Wilde*. London: Mandarin, 1990.

Hyde, H. Montgomery. *The Trials of Oscar Wilde*. New York: Dover, 1973.

Hymans, Joe. *Bogie: The Biography of Humphrey Bogart*. London: W. H. Allen, 1971.

Jackson, Laura. *Heart of Stone: The Unauthorized Life of Mick Jagger*. London: Blake, 1998.

Jackson, Michael. *Moonwalk*. London: Heinemann, 1988.

Jagger, Mick. *Mick Jagger in His Own Words.* New York: Delilah/Putnam Book, 1982.

Jenkins, David. *Richard Burton: A Brother Remembered.* London: Arrow Books, 1994.

Julian, Philippe. *Oscar Wilde*. London/New York: Granada.

Kahlo, Frida. *The Diary of Frida Kahlo: An Intimate Self-Portrait*. Edited by Sarah Lowe. London: Bloomsbury, 1995.

Kashner, Sam, and Nancy Schoenberger. *Furious Love: Elizabeth Taylor, Richard Burton, and the Marriage of the Century*. London: JR, 2011.

Keats, John. *You Might as Well Live: The Life and Times of Dorothy Parker*. New York: Simon & Schuster, 1970.

Kelley, Kitty. *Elizabeth Taylor: The Last Star*. Dunton Green: Coronet, 1982.

Kelley, Kitty. *His Way: The Unauthorized Biography of Frank Sinatra*. London: Bantam Press, 1986.

Kennedy, Gerald, and Jackson Bryer. *French Connections: Hemingway and Fitzgerald Abroad*. Basingstoke: Macmillan, 1998.

Klein, Joe. *Woody Guthrie: A Life*. London: Faber, 1981.

Kobal, John. *Marlene Dietrich*. London: Studio Vista, 1968.

Laporte, Geneviève. *Sunshine at Midnight: Memories of Picasso and Cocteau*. London: Weidenfeld and Nicolson, 1975.

Latham, Aaron. *Crazy Sundays: F. Scott Fitzgerald in Hollywood*. London: Secker and Warburg, 1972.

Leaming, Barbara. *Marilyn Monroe*. London: Weidenfeld and Nicolson, 1998.

Lear, Amanda. *My Life with Dali*. London: Virgin Books, 1985.

Leek, Sybil. *Diary of a Witch*. New York: New American Library, 1968.

Leek, Sybil. *Mr. Hotfoot Jackson*. London: Muller, 1965.

Lemesurier, Peter. *The Unknown Nostradamus: The Essential Biography for His 500th Birthday*. Alresford: O Books, 2003.

Lennon, Cynthia. *John*. London: Hodder and Stoughton, 2005.

Lennon, Cynthia. *A Twist of Lennon*. London: Star Books, 1978.

Le Vot, André. *F. Scott Fitzgerald: A Biography*. Garden City, NY: Doubleday, 1983.

Levy, Alan. *The Elizabeth Taylor Story*. New York: Hillman Books, 1961.

Lewis, C. S. *All My Road before Me: The Diary of C. S. Lewis, 1922–1927*. London: HarperCollins, 1991.

Lewis, Lloyd, and Justin Smith. *Oscar Wilde Discovers America*. New York: Harcourt, Brace, 1936.

Lord, James. *Picasso and Dora: A Memoir*. London: Weidenfeld & Nicolson, 1993.

Louvish, Simon. *Stan and Ollie, the Roots of Comedy: The Double Life of Laurel and Hardy*. London: Faber and Faber, 2001.

Lycett, Andrew. *Ian Fleming*. London: Weidenfeld and Nicolson, 1995.

Mangum, Bryant. *F. Scott Fitzgerald in Context*. Cambridge: Cambridge University Press, 2013.

Mann, William. *How to Be a Movie Star: Elizabeth Taylor in Hollywood.* London: Faber, 2009.

Marley, Rita. *No Woman No Cry: My Life with Bob Marley*. London: Pan, 2005.

Marnham, Patrick. *Dreaming with His Eyes Open: A Life of Diego Rivera.* London: Bloomsbury, 1998.

Maynard, Joyce. *Looking Back: A Chronicle of Growing Up Old in the Sixties*. London: Joseph, 1975.

McCabe, John. *Babe: The Life of Oliver Hardy*. London: Robson, 2004.

McCabe, John. *The Comedy World of Stan Laurel*. London: Robson, 2004.

McCann, Graham. *Marilyn Monroe*. Cambridge: Polity, 1988.

McCann, Ian. *Bob Marley: In His Own Words*. London: Omnibus, 1993.

McCarthy, Albert J. *Louis Armstrong*. London: Cassell, 1960.

McCartney, Linda. *Sixties: Portrait of an Era*. London: Pyramid, 1992.

McCormick, Donald. *17F: The Life of Ian Fleming*. London: Peter Owen, 1993.

McGilligan, Patrick. *Alfred Hitchcock: A Life in Darkness and Light*. Chichester: Wiley, 2003.

McGrath, Tom. *Laurel and Hardy*. Edinburgh: Capercaillie Books, 2005.

Mellow, James. *Invented Lives: F. Scott and Zelda Fitzgerald.* Boston: Houghton Mifflin, 1984.

Meyers, Jeffrey. *Bogart: A Life in Hollywood.* London: André Deutsch, 1997.

Meyers, Jeffrey. *The Genius and the Goddess: Arthur Miller and Marilyn Monroe*. London: Hutchinson, 2009.

Michaels, Ross. *George Harrison: Yesterday and Today*. London: Omnibus, 1982.

Milford, Nancy. *Zelda Fitzgerald: A Biography*. London: Bodley Head, 1970.

Milkowski, Bill. *Keith Richards: A Rock 'n' Roll Life*. Newton Abbot: David and Charles, 2012.

Miles, Barry. *Paul McCartney: Many Years from Now*. London: Vintage, 1998.

Miller, Linda. *Letters from the Lost Generation: Gerald and Sara Murphy and Friends*. New Brunswick, NJ/London: Rutgers University Press, 1991.

Mogg, Ken. *The Alfred Hitchcock Story*. London: Titan, 2008.

Monroe, Marilyn. *Marilyn on Marilyn*. London: Comet Books, 1983.

Monroe, Marilyn. *My Story*. London: W. H. Allen, 1975.

Moor, Jonathan. *Diane Keaton: The Story of the Real Annie Hall.* Bath: Chivers Press, 1991.

Morgan, Janet. *Agatha Christie: A Biography*. London: HarperCollins, 1997.

Morgan, Michelle. *Marilyn Monroe*. London: Robinson, 2012.

Morley, Sheridan. *Marlene Dietrich.* London: Elm Tree Books, 1976.

Moses, Kate. "Baking with Sylvia." *The Guardian*, February 14, 2003. http://www.theguardian.com/books/2003/feb/15/fiction.sylviaplath.

Munn, Michael. *Richard Burton: Prince of Players*. London: JR, 2009.

Murry, Douglas. *Bosie: A Biography of Lord Alfred Douglas*. London: Hodder and Stoughton, 2000.

Norman, Philip. *Mick Jagger*. London: HarperCollins, 2012.

Olivier, Fernande. *Picasso and His Friends*. London: Heinemann, 1964.

Orwell, George. *Diaries*. London: Harvell Secker, 2009.

Orwell, George. *Down and Out in London and Paris*. London: Secker and Warburg, 1997.

Orwell, George. *George Orwell: Essays*. London: Penguin Books, 2014.

Orwell, George. *Hop-Picking: George Orwell in Kent*. Wateringbury, Kent: Bridge Books, 1970.

Orwell, George. *A Life in Letters*. London: Penguin Books, 2011.

Orwell, George. *The Road to Wigan Pier*. London: Secker and Warburg, 1986.

Osborne, Charles. *W. H. Auden: The Life of a Poet*. London: Papermac, 1982.

Pang, May. *Loving John*. London: Corgi, 1983.

Pearson, John. *The Life of Ian Fleming*. London: Aurum, 2003.

Pepitone, Lena. *Marilyn Monroe Confidential: An Intimate Personal Account*. London: Sidgwick and Jackson, 1979.

Philips, Gene. *Alfred Hitchcock*. London: Columbus, 1984.

Pinfold, Mike. *Louis Armstrong: His Life and Times*. London: Omnibus, 1988.

Plath, Sylvia. "Kitchen of the Fig Tree." *Christian Science Monitor*, May 5, 1959.

Plath, Sylvia. *Letters Home*. Edited by Aurelia S. Plath. London: Faber and Faber, 1975.

Prigozy, Ruth. *F. Scott Fitzgerald*. London: Penguin, 2001.

Ransome, Arthur. *The Autobiography of Arthur Ransome*. London: Jonathan Cape, 1976.

Ransome, Arthur. *Signalling from Mars: The Letters of Arthur Ransome*. London: Pimlico, 1998.

Rawlings, Terry. *Rock on Wood: Ronnie Wood—the Origin of a Rock and Roll Face*. London: Boxtree, 1999.

Renoir, Jean. *Renoir, My Father*. Paris: Hachette, 1962.

Richards, Keith. *Keith Richards: In His Own Words*. London: Omnibus, 1994.

Richards, Keith. *Life*. London: Orion, 2010.

Richards, Vernon, Colin Ward, and Nicolas Walter. *George Orwell at Home (and among the Anarchists): Essays and Photographs*. London: Freedom Press, 1998.

Ring, Frances Kroll. *Against the Current: As I Remember F. Scott Fitzgerald*. San Francisco: D. S. Ellis, 1985.

Riva, Maria. *Marlene Dietrich By Her Daughter*. Dunton Green: Coronet, 1994.

Rivera, Diego. *My Art, My Life: An Autobiography*. New York: Dover, 1991.

Rivera, Guadalupe, and Marie-Pierre Colle. *Frida's Fiestas: Recipes and Reminiscences of Life with Frida Kahlo*. London: Pavilion, 1994.

Rombauer, Irma S., and Marion Rombauer Becker. *The Joy of Cooking*. London: J. M. Dent, 1963.

Rothko, Mark. *Mark Rothko*. London: Thames and Hudson, 2000.

Rotolo, Suze. *A Freewheelin' Time: A Memoir of Greenwich Village in the Sixties*. London: Aurum Press, 2008.

Rowse, A. L. *The Poet Auden: A Personal Memoir*. London: Methuen, 1987.

Salewicz, Chris. *Bob Marley: The Untold Story*. London: HarperCollins, 2010.

Sandford, Christopher. *Keith Richards: Satisfaction*. London: Headline, 2003.

Sandford, Christopher. *Mick Jagger: Primitive Cool*. London: Victor Gollancz, 1993.

Scaduto, Anthony. *Bob Dylan*. London: Helter Skelter, 2001.

Scaduto, Anthony. *Mick Jagger*. London: W. H. Allen, 1974.

Sellers, Robert. *Hellraisers: The Life and Inebriated Times of Richard Burton, Richard Harris, Peter O'Toole and Oliver Reed*. New York: Thomas Dunne Books, 2009.

Shapiro, Marc. *All Things Must Pass: The Life of George Harrison*. London: Virgin, 2002.

Shipton, Vicky. *Bob Marley*. London: Scholastic, 2013.

Sinatra, Barbara. *Lady Blue Eyes: My Life with Frank Sinatra*. London: Hutchinson, 2011.

Slawenski, Kenneth. *J. D. Salinger: A Life Raised High*. Hebden Bridge: Pomona, 2010.

Smith, Susan. *Elizabeth Taylor*. Basingstoke: Palgrave Macmillan, 2012.

Sniff, Fannie, ed. *Famous Stars Favorite Foods*. Hollywood: Fannie Sniff, 1938.

Sounes, Howard. *Fab: An Intimate Life of Paul McCartney*. London: HarperCollins, 2010.

Sperber, A. M., and Eric Lax. *Bogart*. London: Weidenfeld and Nicolson, 1997.

Spoto, Donald. *Dietrich*. London: Bantam, 1992.

Spoto, Donald. *Elizabeth Taylor*. London: Warner Books, 1996.

Spoto, Donald. *The Life of Alfred Hitchcock: The Dark Side of Genius*. London: Collins, 1983.

Spoto, Donald. *Possessed: The Life of Joan Crawford*. London: Arrow, 2012.

Steckles, Garry. *Bob Marley*. Oxford: Macmillan, 2008.

Steinbeck, John. *The Log from the Sea of Cortez*. London: Penguin, 1995.

Steinbeck, John. *Steinbeck: A Life in Letters*. Edited by Elaine Steinbeck and Robert Wallsten. London: Heinemann, 1975.

Steinbeck, John. *Travels with Charley: In Search of America*. London: Penguin, 2000.

Stenning, H. J., and Maurice Malingue. *Paul Gauguin: Letters to His Wife and Friends*. London: Saturn Press, 1948.

Summers, Anthony. *Goddess: The Secret Lives of Marilyn Monroe*. London: V. Gollancz, 1985.

Symonds, John. *The Great Beast: The Life of Aleister Crowley*. London/New York: Rider, 1951.

Taraborrelli, Randy. *Michael Jackson: The Magic and the Madness*. London: Sidgwick and Jackson, 2003.

Taraborrelli, Randy. *The Secret Life of Marilyn Monroe*. London: Pan, 2010.

Taylor, Kendall. *Sometimes Madness Is Wisdom: Zelda and Scott Fitzgerald; a Marriage*. London: Robson, 2002.

Thompson, Laura. *Agatha Christie: An English Mystery*. London: Headline Review, 2007.

Thomson, Belinda. *Gauguin by Himself*. Boston/London: Little, Brown, 1998.

Thurlow, Clifford. *The Sex Life of Salvador Dalí: The Memoirs of Carlos Lozano*. Bromsgrove: Tethered Camel, 2004.

Toklas, Alice B. *The Alice B. Toklas Cookbook*. London: Folio Society, 1993.

Tomkies, Mike. *The Big Man: The John Wayne Story*. London: Barker, 1971.

Tomkins, Calvin. *Living Well Is the Best Revenge: The Life of Gerald and Sara Murphy*. New York: Viking Press, 1971.

Vaill, Amanda. *Everybody Was So Young: Gerald and Sara Murphy; a Lost Generation Love Story*. London: Little, Brown, 1998.

Van Gogh, Vincent. *Vincent by Himself*. Edited by Bruce Bernard. London: Time Warner, 2004.

Van Gogh, Vincent, Ronald de Leeuw, and Arnold Pomerans. *The Letters of Vincent van Gogh*. London: Penguin Books, 1997.

Van Ronk, Dave. *The Mayor of MacDougal Street*: *A Memoir*. Cambridge, MA: Da Capo Press, 2005.

Vollard, Ambroise. *Renoir: An Intimate Record*. London: Constable, 1990.

Warhol, Andy. *The Andy Warhol Diaries*. London: Penguin, 2010.

Waterbury, Ruth. *Elizabeth Taylor: Her Life, Her Loves, Her Future*. London: Hale, 1964.

Waugh, Evelyn. *The Diaries of Evelyn Waugh*. London: Phoenix, 2009.

Waugh, Evelyn. *The Letters of Evelyn Waugh*. London: Phoenix, 1995.

Waugh, Evelyn. *Mr. Wu and Mrs. Stitch: The Letters of Evelyn Waugh and Diana Cooper*. London: Hodder and Stoughton, 1991.

Wayne, Aissa. *John Wayne, My Father*. London: Hale, 1992.

Wayne, Jane Ellen. *Ava's Men: The Private Life of Ava Gardner*. Oxford: Clio Press, 1990.

Wayne, Jane Ellen. *Marilyn's Men: The Private Life of Marilyn Monroe*. London: Robson, 1992.

Wayne, Pilar. *John Wayne: My Life with the Duke*. Dunton Green: New English Library, 1987.

Welch, Chris. *Paul McCartney: The Definitive Biography*. London/New York: Proteus Books, 1984.

White, Barbara Ehrlich. *Renoir: His Life, Art and Letters*. New York: Abrams, 1984.

White, Timothy. *Catch a Fire: The Life of Bob Marley*. London: Omnibus, 2006.

Wilde, Oscar. *The Annotated Oscar Wilde*. Edited by H. Montgomery Hyde. London: Orbis, 1982.

Wilde, Oscar. *De Profundis*. Mineola, NY: Dover, 1996.

Wilde, Oscar. *Selected Letters of Oscar Wilde*. Edited by Rupert Hart-Davis. Oxford: Oxford University Press, 1979.

Wolfe, Bertram. *Diego Rivera: His Life and Times*. London: R. Hale, 1939.

Wolfe, Donald. *The Assassination of Marilyn Monroe*. London: Little, Brown, 1998.

Wood, Ean. *Dietrich: A Biography*. London: Sanctuary, 2002.

Wood, Ron. *Ronnie*. London: Pan, 2008.

Wydra, Thilo. *Alfred Hitchcock*. Berlin: Suhrkamp, 2010.

Wyman, Bill. *Stone Alone: The Story of a Rock 'n' Roll Band*. London: Penguin, 1991.

Wyman, Bill. *Rolling with the Stones*. London: Dorling Kindersley, 2002.

Index

About the Author

Like most of us, **Fiona Ross** leads a double existence: in her "normal" life as a writer of fiction in Bishop's Stortford, United Kingdom, Fiona keeps company with two bossy chickens and her dog, Parsnip. She spends a lot of time fishing chickens out of her bathtub and Parsnip out of the chicken run. In between, she stares into space a lot, looking for inspiration for her stories. Meanwhile, her glamorous and exciting double works as a gastro-detective whose headquarters is the famous Bodleian Library in Oxford; she spends her time there pondering which sandwich filling she would prefer for lunch when she is not hot on the trail of a famous gastronome.

The *Dining with Destiny* series is the result of just such weighty thoughts—oh, and a short-term memory problem, which means that Fiona can *never* recall anything important like the date of a war or how to hoover, but she can *always* be counted upon to remember how much jam Marx liked on his tarts. Time will tell which is the more important.